P9-DTM-630

Trace: Prairie Writers on Writing

TRACE:

PRAIRIE WRITERS ON WRITING

Birk Sproxton, editor

TURNSTONE PRESS

copyright © 1986 The Authors

Turnstone Press
607-99 King Street
Winnipeg, Manitoba
Canada

Typeset by b/w type service ltd. and printed by Hignell Printing Ltd. for Turnstone Press.

Printed in Canada.

Cover design: Steven Rosenberg

Canadian Cataloguing in Publication Data
Main entry under title:
Trace
    ISBN 0-88801-102-4
    1. Canadian literature (English)—Prairie Provinces—History and criticism—Addresses, essays, lectures.* 2. Canadian literature (English) —20th century—History and criticism—Addresses, essays, lectures.* I. Sproxton, Birk.
PS8131.P7T73 1986   C810'.9'9712   C86-091208-6
PR9198.2.P7T73 1986

Turnstone Press gratefully acknowledges the following for funding assistance in the publication of this book:
Alberta Foundation for the Literary Arts
Canada Council
Canadian Studies Bureau of the Association of Canadian Community
    Colleges, through a contribution from the Secretary of State,
    Government of Canada
Manitoba Arts Council
Saskatchewan Arts Board

Reprinted February 1988 with the assistance of:
Alberta Foundation for the Literary Arts
Manitoba Arts Council
Saskatchewan Arts Board

Thanks go first to the authors of this collection for their cooperation, patience and enthusiasm. Jacques LaPointe, Lila Stonehewer and the Canadian Studies people of the A.C.C.C. gave support to this project from the very early stages. Red Deer College granted a sabbatical leave during which time much of the research was completed. Renate Scheelar provided able assistance during the final stages of preparation. Thanks again to the Turnstone bunch.

AUGUSTANA LIBRARY
UNIVERSITY OF ALBERTA

CONTENTS

Part Three

PREFACE

Trace began in the frustration that goes with not being able to find a book. I wanted a book that included statements on writing by major writers from the prairies, a book that I could use as a student and teacher of reading and writing. The book didn't exist, but some of the pieces did, though they were scattered about in various places. The book I wanted would bring into one volume essays essential for an understanding of what has happened in the last twenty years in prairie writing; it would also describe contexts of contemporary prairie writing; it would serve as an invitation to the rich body of writing from the prairies. What I wanted changed and grew even as the book evolved from desire to proposal, from application to research to writing, dozens of letters. I began to want a map, a directory, a telephone book, an encyclopedia, audio tapes, videos, a shelf of books, a library, a computer network, the writers in person in the flesh, reading and writing.

Another voice said to make the book manageable, a compact handful, a few pages to suggest many more, a book that people would carry and read, rather than lift to build graceful and curving muscles. The book you now hold in your hands is the issue of these competing voices. It has gaps for you to fill in; and what is here is a beginning, again, a gathering of points for departure.

Part I includes statements by writers who have helped us read and write the prairie west: Margaret Laurence, Robert Kroetsch, Henry Kreisel, Dorothy Livesay, Miriam Waddington, Rudy Wiebe, and Eli Mandel offer a rich and exciting symposium. Such classic pieces as "The Prairie : A State of Mind," Laurence and Kroetsch in conversation, "Writing West: The Road to Wood Mountain," are brought together here for the first time in a single volume. To these are added articles or statements from diverse sources by novelists Wiebe and Laurence, poets Waddington and Livesay. In having their say, these writers look both ways in time, articulating a past and exploring a future, making it happen now. Though each can be taken as separate and distinct, I find a special pleasure in hearing these statements talk back and forth with each other and with those pieces gathered in Part II.

Twenty-four writers contribute statements to make up Part II; most were written specifically for this volume. Contributors were invited to choose a form they thought appropriate, to make personal statements about writing, to focus on questions of poetics or matters of technique, how the writing gets written, to say what needs to be said, above all to be lively. In some cases I suggested subjects for exploration, or posed questions for consideration. I invited rants, manifestoes, arguments, a breaking down/up of party lines, a tracing of lines of descent and dissent. The diverse voices of Part II cleave to and depart from the writers of Part I, and from each other, even as they are having their say. *Trace* becomes a book of generation (gender, genre, generativity), arguing about and through modernism and postmodernism, a collision of languages, gathering points, places of departure.

Trace concludes with biographical and bibliographical notes and with a list of titles for further reading. *Trace* aims in these three parts to stimulate arguments about writing, to challenge writers to throw over the traces and make reading and writing new.

Birk Sproxton, May, 1986.

ACKNOWLEDGEMENTS AND PERMISSIONS

David Arnason

"Story Forming," David Arnason interviewed by Robert Enright, first appeared in *Arts Manitoba*, vol. 4 no. 2 (Spring 1980), 8-10. Copyright David Arnason. Reprinted by permission.

Pamela Banting

"There's a Trick with a Mirror I'm Learning to Do" was delivered in slightly different form at "Starwords: A Writer's Guide to the Galaxy," Manitoba Writers' Guild conference, October 3-5, 1985. Copyright Pamela Banting, 1986.

Douglas Barbour

"Open/Entrance: Raw Notes Towards Poetics" is an elaboration of an earlier piece, "An Engagement with Words," part of which appeared in *Quarry* 32 (Autumn 1983), 65-67. Copyright Douglas Barbour.

Dennis Cooley

"Some Principles of Line Breaks" is an excerpt from "Breaking and Entering: Some Thoughts on Line Breaks," which is forthcoming in *Open Letter*.

Lorna Crozier

An earlier version of "Searching for the Poem" appeared in *Waves*, vol. 14 no. 1/2 (Fall 1985), 81-83. Copyright Lorna Crozier, 1986. Reprinted by permission.

Henry Kreisel

"The Prairie: A State of Mind" first appeared in *Transactions of the Royal Society of Canada* vol. 6 series 4 (June 1968), 171-180. Copyright Henry Kreisel. Reprinted by permission.

Robert Kroetsch
"A Conversation with Margaret Laurence," from *Creation*, ed. Robert Kroetsch (New Press, 1970). Copyright Robert Kroetsch. Reprinted by permission.

Margaret Laurence
"The Artist Then, Now and Always" is extracted from "My Final Hour," *Canadian Literature* no. 100 (Spring 1984), 187-197. Copyright Margaret Laurence. Reprinted by permission.

Dorothy Livesay
"A Putting Down of Roots," first appeared in *CV/II* no. 1 (Spring 1975), 2. Copyright Dorothy Livesay. Reprinted by permission.

The excerpt from "Roots" is reprinted from *Collected Poems: Two Seasons* by permission of the author. Copyright Dorothy Livesay 1986.

Eli Mandel
"Writing West: On the Road to Wood Mountain" from *Out of Place* by Eli Mandel is reprinted by permission of Press Porcépic Limited, Victoria and Toronto.

Birk Sproxton
An earlier version of "What the World was Saying when I Made It" was presented to "High Rise/Horizon," a conference of the arts, NeWest Institute for Western Canadian Studies, Strawberry Creek, August 3, 1985. Copyright Birk Sproxton, 1986.

Anne Szumigalski
"Our Sullen Art" is reprinted from *Doctrine of Signatures*, Fifth House, 1983, copyright Anne Szumigalski. Reprinted by permission. The lines from "The Question" are reprinted from *Instar*, Red Deer College Press, 1985, copyright Anne Szumigalski. Reprinted by permission.

Wayne Tefs

"Current Prairie Fiction: Openings/Beginnings" first appeared
in *Border Crossings*, Vol. 5, No. 1 (Winter 1985) 55-56. Copyright Wayne Tefs 1985. Reprinted by permission.

Miriam Waddington

"The Golden Eye" and "Aspects of Owls" first appeared in *The
Structurist* no. 23-24 (1983-84), 18-20 under the title "Poetry
and Nature." Copyright Miriam Waddington 1984. Reprinted
by permission.

"Poetry as Communication" was delivered to the Canadian Communications Association annual meeting in Halifax, May 24,
1981. Copyright Miriam Waddington.

Rudy Wiebe

"The Blindman River Contradictions" first appeared in *The
Camrose Review* #5 (Fall 1984), 40-44. Reprinted by permission.

Part One

Part One

The Prairie: A State of Mind

Henry Kreisel

Soon after I first arrived in Alberta, now over twenty years ago, there appeared in the *Edmonton Journal* a letter in which the writer, replying to some article which had appeared some time earlier, asserted with passionate conviction that the earth was flat. Now in itself that would have been quite unremarkable, the expression merely of some cranky and eccentric old man. Normally, then, one would not have been likely to pay very much attention to such a letter, and one would have passed it over with an amused smile. Nothing pleases us more than to be able to feel superior to pre-scientific man, secure behind the fortress of our knowledge. I am no different in this respect from most other people. But there was something in the tone of that letter that would not allow me that kind of response. Far from feeling superior, I felt awed. Even as I write these lines, the emotion evoked in me by that letter that appeared in a newspaper more than twenty years ago comes back to me, tangible and palpable.

The tone of the letter was imperious. Surveying his vast domains, a giant with feet firmly rooted in the earth, a lord of the land asserted what his eyes saw, what his heart felt, and what his mind perceived. I cut the letter out and for some time carried it about with me in my wallet. I don't really know why I did that. I do know that in my travels round the prairie in those early years of my life in the Canadian west I looked at the great landscape through the eyes of that unknown man. At last I threw the clipping away, but the imagined figure of that giant remained to haunt my mind.

Years later I finally came to terms with that vision in a story that I called "The Broken Globe." This story deals with the clash between a father and his young son. The son, who is eventually to become a scientist, comes home from school one day and tells his father that the earth moves. The father, a Ukrainian settler, secure in something very like a mediaeval faith, asserts passionately that it does not and that his son is being tempted and corrupted by the devil. The story is told by a narrator, an academic who goes to visit the father, now an old man, to bring him greetings from his estranged scientist-son. At the end of the story, after the narrator has heard from the father about the conflict that alienated him from his son, the narrator rises to leave:

> Together we walked out of the house. When I was about to get into my car, he touched me lightly on the arm. I turned. His eyes surveyed the vast expanse of sky and land, stretching far into the distance, reddish clouds in the sky and blue shadows on the land. With a gesture of great dignity and power he lifted his arm and stood pointing into the distance, at the flat land and the low-hanging sky.
>
> 'Look,' he said, very slowly and very quietly, 'she is flat and she stands still.'
>
> It was impossible not to feel a kind of admiration for the old man. There was something heroic about him. I held out my hand and he took it. He looked at me steadily, then averted his eyes and said, 'Send greetings to my son.' I drove off quickly, but had to stop again in order to open the wooden gate. I looked back at the house, and saw him still standing there, still looking

at his beloved land, a lonely, towering figure framed against the
darkening evening sky.[1]

You will have noted that the images I used to describe my
imagined man seem extravagant—"a lord of the land," "a giant."
These were in fact the images that came to me and I should myself
have regarded them as purely subjective, if I had not afterwards in
my reading encountered similar images in the work of other writers
who write about the appearance of men on the prairie at certain
times. Thus in Martha Ostenso's *Wild Geese* a young school teacher
sees "against the strange pearly distance...the giant figure of a man
beside his horse," and when he comes closer she recognizes Fusi
Aronson, "the great Icelander....He was grand in his demeanor, and
somehow lonely, as a solitary oak on the prairie." (31)[2] On the very
first page of *Settlers of the Marsh*, Philip Grove, describing two men
"fighting their way through the gathering dusk," calls one of them,
Lars Nelson, "a giant, of three years' standing in the country." (11)[3]
And in his autobiography, *In Search of Myself*, Grove, recalling the
origin of *Fruits of the Earth* and his first encounter with the figure
who was to become Abe Spalding, describes the arresting and startling
sight of a man ploughing land generally thought to be unfit for farming. "Outlined as he was against a tilted and spoked sunset in the
western sky," he writes, "he looked like a giant. Never before had I
seen, between farm and town, a human being in all my drives." Grove
goes on to tell how he stopped his horses and learned that this man
had only that very afternoon arrived from Ontario, after a train
journey of two thousand miles, had at once filed a claim for a homestead of a hundred and sixty acres, had unloaded his horses from the
freight-car, and was now ploughing his first field. And when Grove
expresses his surprise at the speed with which this newcomer set to
work, the man replies, "Nothing else to do." (259)[4]

I set the image of the giant in the landscape over against the
more familiar one of man pitted against a vast and frequently hostile
natural environment that tends to dwarf him, at the mercy of what

Grove calls, in *Settlers of the Marsh*, "a dumb shifting of forces." (152) Man, the giant-conqueror, and man, the insignificant dwarf always threatened by defeat, form the two polarities of the state of mind produced by the sheer physical fact of the prairie.

There are moments when the two images coalesce. So the observant Mrs. Bentley, whose diary forms the substance of Sinclair Ross' novel *As for Me and My House*, records the response of a prairie congregation during the bleak and drought-haunted 1930s:

> The last hymn was staidly orthodox, but through it there seemed to mount something primitive, something that was less a response to Philip's sermon and scripture reading than to the grim futility of their own lives. Five years in succession now they've been blown out, dried out, hailed out; and it was as if in the face of so blind and uncaring a universe they were trying to assert themselves, to insist upon their own meaning and importance. (19)[5]

All discussion of the literature produced in the Canadian west must of necessity begin with the impact of the landscape upon the mind. "Only a great artist," records Mrs. Bentley, "could ever paint the prairie, the vacancy and stillness of it, the bare essentials of a landscape, sky and earth." (59) W. O. Mitchell, in the opening sentences of *Who Has Seen the Wind*, speaks of the "least common denominator of nature, the skeleton requirements simply, of land and sky." (3)[6] He goes on to describe the impact of the landscape on Brian O'Connal, a four-year-old boy, living in a little prairie town and venturing for the first time to the edge of town:

> He looked up to find that the street had stopped. Ahead lay the sudden emptiness of the prairie. For the first time in his four years of life he was alone on the prairie.
>
> He had seen it often, from the veranda of his uncle's farmhouse, or at the end of a long street, but till now he had never heard it. The hum of telephone wires along the road, the ring of hidden crickets, the stitching sound of grasshoppers, the

sudden relief of a meadow lark's song, were deliciously strange to him....

A gopher squeaked questioningly as Brian sat down upon a rock warm to the back of his thigh....The gopher squeaked again, and he saw it a few yards away, sitting up and watching him from its pulpit hole. A suave-winged hawk chose that moment to slip its shadow over the face of the prairie.

And all about him was the wind now, a pervasive sighing through great emptiness, unhampered by the buildings of the town, warm and living against his face and in his hair. (11)

Only one other kind of landscape gives us the same skeleton requirements, the same vacancy and stillness, the same movement of wind through space—and that is the sea. So when Mrs. Bentley records in her diary that "there's a high, rocking wind that rattles the windows and creaks the walls. It's strong and steady like a great tide after the winter pouring north again, and I have a queer, helpless sense of being lost miles out in the middle of it," (35) she might well be tossing in heavy seas, protected only by a small and fragile little bark. In Grove's *Over Prairie Trails*, that remarkable book of impressionistic essays describing seven trips that Grove made in 1917 and 1918 between Gladstone and Falmouth near the western shore of Lake Manitoba, the prairie as sea becomes one of the controlling patterns shaping the imagination of the observer. On one of these trips—in the dead of winter—Grove prepares his horse-drawn cutter as if it were a boat being readied for a fairly long and possibly dangerous journey:

Not a bolt but I tested it with a wrench; and before the stores were closed, I bought myself enough canned goods to feed me for a week should through any untoward accident the need arise. I always carried a little alcohol stove, and with my tarpaulin I could convert my cutter within three minutes into a windproof tent. Cramped quarters, to be sure, but better than being given over to the wind at thirty below. (60—61)[7]

Soon the cutter, the horses, and the man meet the first test—very like a Conradian crew coming to grips with a storm at sea. A mountainous snowdrift bars the way. The horses, Dan and Peter, who become wonderful characters in their own right, panic. They plunge wildly, rear on their hind legs, pull apart, try to turn and retrace their steps. "And meanwhile the cutter went sharply up at first, as if on the vast crest of a wave, then toppled over into a hole made by Dan, and altogether behaved like a boat tossed on a stormy sea. Then order returned into the chaos....I spoke to the horses in a soft, quiet, purring voice; and at last I pulled in." (69)

He becomes aware of the sun, cold and high in the sky, a relentless inexorable force, and suddenly two Greek words come into his mind: Homer's *pontos atrygetos*—the barren sea. A half hour later he understands why:

> This was indeed like nothing so much as like being out in rough waters and in a troubled sea, with nothing to brace the storm with but a wind-tossed nutshell of a one-man sailing craft....When the snow reached its extreme in depth, it gave you the feeling which a drowning man may have when fighting his desperate fight with the salty waves. But more impressive than that was the frequent outer resemblance. The waves of the ocean rise up and reach out and batter against the rocks and battlements of the shore, retreating again and ever returning to the assault....And if such a high crest wave had suddenly been frozen into solidity, its outline would have mimicked to perfection many a one of the snow shapes that I saw around. (77)

And when, at the end of another journey, the narrator reaches home, he is like a sailor reaching harbour after a long voyage:

> ...there was the signal put out for me. A lamp in one of the windows of the school....And in the most friendly and welcoming way it looked with its single eye across at the nocturnal guest.

> I could not see the cottage, but I knew that my little girl lay
> sleeping in her cosy bed, and that a young woman was sitting
> there in the dark, her face glued to the window-pane, to be ready
> with a lantern which burned in the kitchen whenever I might
> pull up between school and house. And there, no doubt, she had
> been sitting for a long while already; and there she was destined
> to sit during the winter that came, on Friday nights—full often
> for many and many an hour—full often until midnight—and
> sometimes longer. (18)

The prairie, like the sea, thus often produces an extraordinary
sensation of confinement within a vast and seemingly unlimited
space. The isolated farm-houses, the towns and settlements, even
the great cities that eventually sprang up on the prairies, become
islands in that land-sea, areas of relatively safe refuge from the great
and lonely spaces. In *Wild Geese* Martha Ostenso describes a moment
when the sensation of safety and of abandonment are felt to be evenly
balanced:

> Fine whips of rain lashed about the little house, and the wind
> whistled in the birch trees outside, bleak as a lost bird. These
> sounds defined the feelings of enclosed warmth and safety....
> But they did also the opposed thing. They stirred the fear of
> loneliness, the ancient dread of abandonment in the wilderness
> in the profounder natures of these two who found shelter here.
> For an imponderable moment they sought beyond each other's
> eyes, sought for understanding, for communion under the vast
> terrestrial influence that bound them, an inevitable part and
> form of the earth, inseparable one from the other. (64)

At the same time the knowledge of the vast space outside brings
to the surface anxieties that have their roots elsewhere and thus
sharpens and crystallizes a state of mind. In *As for Me and My House*
Mrs. Bentley uses the prairie constantly as a mirror of her own
fears, frustrations, and helplessness:

> It's an immense night out there, wheeling and windy. The lights
> on the street and in the houses are helpless against the black
> wetness, little unilluminating glints that might be painted on it.
> The town seems huddled together, cowering on a high, tiny perch,
> afraid to move lest it topple into the wind. Close to the parsonage
> is the church, black even against the darkness, towering ominously
> up through the night and merging with it. There's a soft steady
> swish of rain on the roof, and a gurgle of eave troughs running
> over. Above, in the high cold night, the wind goes swinging past,
> indifferent, liplessly mournful. It frightens me, makes me feel
> lost, dropped on this little perch of town and abandoned. I wish
> Philip would waken. (5)

That, however, is not the only, perhaps not even the most significant response to the challenge of lonely and forbidden spaces. It is easy to see Mrs. Bentley's reaction as prototypical of the state of mind induced by the prairie, but it would not be altogether accurate. It is one kind of response, but set over against it there is the response typified in Grove's *Settlers of the Marsh* by Neils Lindstedt, who, like a Canadian adventurer, a Lord Jim or a Stein, is driven to follow a dream. It expresses itself in "a longing to leave and go to the very margin of civilization, there to clear a new place; and when it is cleared and people began to settle about it, to move on once more, again to the very edge of pioneerdom, to start it all over anew.... That way his enormous strength would still have a meaning." (80)

To conquer a piece of the continent, to put one's imprint upon virgin land, to say, "Here I am, for that I came," is as much a way of defining oneself, of proving one's existence, as is Descartes' *Cogito, ergo sum.* That is surely why that man whom Grove saw ploughing a field barely two hours after his arrival was driven to do it. He had to prove to himself that he was in some way master of his destiny, that he was fully alive, and that his strength had meaning. When he told Grove that he was doing what he was doing because there was nothing else to do, he was telling him the simple truth, but leaving a more complex truth unspoken, and probably even unperceived.

The conquest of territory is by definition a violent process. In the Canadian west, as elsewhere on this continent, it involved the displacement of the indigenous population by often scandalous means, and then the taming of the land itself. The displacement, the conquest, of the Indians, and later the rising of the Métis under Louis Riel, are events significantly absent from the literature I am discussing. Occasionally Riel breaks into the consciousness of one or another of the characters, usually an old man or an old woman remembering troubled times; occasionally the figure of an Indian appears briefly, but is soon gone. No doubt that is how things appeared to the European settlers on the prairie; no doubt our writers did not really make themselves too familiar with the indigenous people of the prairie, seeing them either as noble savages or not seeing them at all, but it is likely that a conscious or subconscious process of suppression is also at work here.

The conquest of the land itself is by contrast a dominant theme, and the price paid for the conquest by the conqueror is clearly and memorably established. The attempt to conquer the land is a huge gamble. Many lose, and there are everywhere mute emblems testifying to defeat. "Once I passed the skeleton of a stable," Grove records in *Over Prairie Trails*, "the remnant of the buildings put up by a pioneer settler who had to give in after having wasted effort and substance and worn his knuckles to the bone. The wilderness uses human material up." (11) But into the attempted conquest, whether ultimately successful or not, men pour an awesome, concentrated passion. The breaking of the land becomes a kind of rape, a passionate seduction. The earth is at once a willing and unwilling mistress, accepting and rejecting her seducer, the cause of his frustration and fulfillment, and either way the shaper and controller of his mind, exacting servitude.

The most powerful statement of that condition in the literature of the Canadian west is, I think, to be found in Martha Ostenso's *Wild Geese*, the story of Caleb Gare, a tyrannical man who, himself enslaved to the land, in turn enslaves his whole family to serve his own obsession. Characteristically, Ostenso sees him as a gigantic figure. "His tremendous shoulders and massive head, which loomed forward from the rest of his body like a rough projection of rock from the edge of a cliff," she writes, "gave him a towering appearance." (13) He is conceived in a way which makes it difficult to speak of him in conventional terms of human virtue or human vice, for he is conceived as "a spiritual counterpart of the land, as harsh, as demanding, as tyrannical as the very soil from which he drew his existence." (33) He can only define himself in terms of the land, and paradoxically it is the land and not his children that bears testimony to his potency and manhood. As he supervises his sons and daughters, grown up, but still only extensions of himself, working in the fields, he is gratified by the knowledge that what they are producing is the product of *his* land, the result of *his* industry, "as undeniably his as his right hand, testifying to the outer world that Caleb Gare was a successful owner and user of the soil." (171) At night he frequently goes out with a lantern swinging low along the earth. No one knows where he goes or why he goes, and no one dares to ask him, but his daughter Judith once remarks scornfully "that it was to assure himself that his land was still there." (18) Only the land can ultimately give him the assurance that he is still alive: "Before him glimmered the silver grey sheet of the flax—rich, beautiful, strong. All unto itself, complete, demanding everything, and in turn yielding everything—growth of the earth, the only thing on the earth worthy of respect, of homage." (126-7)

Being so possessed by the prairie, his mind and body as it were an extension of it, he cannot give himself to anyone else. Since he is incapable of loving another human being, he can receive no love in return. He marries his wife knowing that she has had a child born out of wedlock because this gives him the power of blackmail over her and, in a stern and puritan society, chains her forever to him and to his land. He knows that she once gave herself to another man in a way in which she can never give herself to him, but he cannot see that he chose her because he wanted someone who could not demand from him a love he is incapable of giving. Having committed his mind and his body to the land, greedily acquiring more and more, he can only use other human beings as instruments to help feed an appetite that can never be satisfied. His human feelings must therefore be suppressed, and the passion of his blood must remain forever frustrated, sublimated in his passion for the acquisition of more and more land. Man, the would-be conqueror, is thus also man, the supreme egoist, subordinating everything to the flow of a powerful ambition. "Caleb Gare—he does not feel," says Fusi Aronson, the Icelander. "I shall kill him one day. But even that he will not feel." (31)

He does feel for his land. But the land is a fickle mistress, and he must live in perpetual fear, for he can never be sure that this mistress will remain faithful. She may, and indeed she does, with hail and fire destroy in minutes all that he has laboured to build.

Caleb Gare's obsession may be extreme, and yet a measure of egocentricity, though more often found in less virulent form, is perhaps necessary if the huge task of taming a continent is to be successfully accomplished. At the same time the necessity of survival dictates cooperative undertakings. So it is not surprising that the prairie has produced the most right-wing as well as the most left-wing provincial governments in Canada. But whether conservative or radical, these governments have always been puritan in outlook, a true reflection of their constituencies.

The prairie settlements, insecure islands in that vast land-sea, have been austere, intensely puritan societies. Not that puritanism in Canada is confined to the prairie, of course, but on the prairie it has been more solidly entrenched than even in rural Ontario, and can be observed in something very like a distilled form.

It can be argued that in order to tame the land and begin the building, however tentatively, of something approaching a civilization, the men and women who settled on the prairie had to tame themselves, had to curb their passions and contain them within a tight neo-Calvinist framework. But it is not surprising that there should be sudden eruptions and that the passions, long suppressed, should burst violently into the open and threaten the framework that was meant to contain them. In the literature with which I am dealing this violence often takes the form of melodrama, and though this sudden eruption of violence sometimes seems contrived for the sake of a novel's plot, it is also clearly inherent in the life the novelists observed. It is natural that novelists should exploit the tensions which invariably arise when a rigid moral code attempts to set strict limits on the instinctual life, if not indeed to suppress it altogether. Thus illicit love affairs, conducted furtively, without much joy, quickly begun and quickly ended, and sometimes complicated by the birth of illegitimate children, can be used as a perhaps obvious but nevertheless effective centre for a novel's structure, as for example in Stead's *Grain*, in Ostenso's *Wild Geese*, in Laurence's *A Jest of God*, in Ross' *As for Me and My House*.

It is because *As for Me and My House* contains the most uncompromising rendering of the puritan state of mind produced on the prairie that the novel has been accorded a central place in prairie literature. In the figure of Philip Bentley, a Presbyterian minister and artist *manqué*, we have—at least as he emerges from the diary of his wife—an embodiment of the puritan temperament, the product of his environment and much more a part of it than he would ever admit, angry not really because the communities in which he serves are puritan, but because they are not puritan enough, because they expect him to purvey a genteel kind of piety that will serve as a respectable front to hide a shallow morality. But his own emotions remain frozen within the puritan framework from which he cannot free his spirit. So he draws more and more into himself, becomes aloof and unknowable, not in the end so different from Caleb Gare, though in temperament and sensibility they seem at first glance to move in totally different worlds. Philip's wife is certain that "there's some twisted, stumbling power locked up within him, so blind and helpless still it can't find outlet, so clenched with urgency it can't release itself." (80) His drawing and painting reflect an inner paralysis. He draws endless prairie scenes that mirror his own frustration—

the false fronts on the stores, doors and windows that are crooked and pinched, a little schoolhouse standing lonely and defiant in a landscape that is like a desert, "almost a lunar desert, with queer, fantastic pits and drifts of sand encroaching right to the doorstep." (80) Philip Bentley's emotional paralysis affects of course his relationship with his wife. Thus she describes in her diary how he lies beside her, his muscles rigid, and she presses closer to him, pretending to stir in her sleep, "but when I put my hand on his arm there was a sharp little contraction against my touch, and after a minute I shifted again, and went back to my own pillow." (116)

Only once does the twisted power that's locked up within him find some kind of outlet — and then disastrously, when he seduces the young girl Judith who has come to help in the house during his wife's illness.

Prairie puritanism is one result of the conquest of the land, part of the price exacted for the conquest. Like the theme of the conquest of the land, the theme of the imprisoned spirit dominates serious prairie writing, and is connected with it. We find this theme developed not only in Ross' novel, where it is seen at its bleakest and most uncompromising, not only in Grove's and Ostenso's work, but also in more recent novels, such as Margaret Laurence's two novels, *The Stone Angel* and *A Jest of God*, and in George Ryga's *Ballad of a Stone Picker*, and, surprisingly perhaps, in W. O. Mitchell's *Who Has Seen the Wind*, which is conceived as a celebration and lyrical evocation of a prairie childhood. Brian O'Connal is initiated into the mysteries of God and nature, of life and death, but he is also brought face to face with the strange figure of the young Ben, a curious amalgam of noble savage and Wordsworthian child of nature. Again and again he appears, seemingly out of nowhere, soundlessly, the embodiment of a kind of free prairie spirit. His hair is "bleached as the dead prairie grass itself," (12) his trousers are always torn, he never wears shoes. He has "about as much moral conscience as the prairie wind that lifted over the edge of the prairie world to sing mortality to every living thing." (31) He does not play with other children, takes no part in organized school games. Though he can run "with the swiftness of a prairie chicken," and jump like an antelope, he refuses to have anything to do with athletic competitions. School itself is "an intolerable incarceration for him, made bearable only by flights of freedom which totaled up to almost the same number as the days he attended." (147) The solid burghers of the town, strait-laced and proper, try desperately to tame him, for his wild spirit represents a danger to them. But they cannot control him any more than they can control the wind. Brian O'Connal is drawn to the young Ben, and though they rarely speak to each other, there grows up between them a strong bond, what Mitchell calls "an extrasensory brotherhood." (89) The young Ben is Brian's double, the free spirit Brian would like to be, but dare not be. For Brian, one feels, will ultimately conform to the demands of his society and he will subdue the young Ben within himself.

Most of the works that I have dealt with were conceived and written more than a quarter of a century ago. There have been great social and industrial changes on the prairie since then, and the tempo of these changes has been rapidly accelerating in the past ten years or so. Yet it is surprising that such novels as Adele Wiseman's *The Sacrifice* and John Marlyn's *Under the Ribs of Death*, published in the 1950s, and Margaret Laurence's *The Stone Angel* and *A Jest of God* and George Ryga's *Ballad of a Stone Picker*, published in the 1960s, should still adhere to the general pattern of the earlier works. The Winnipeg of Wiseman and Marlyn is the city of the 1920s and 1930s, a city of newly arrived immigrants, and the small towns of the Laurence and Ryga novels are clearly the small towns Ross and Ostenso knew.

For though much has changed in the west, much also still remains unchanged. Prairie puritanism is now somewhat beleaguered and shows signs of crumbling, but it remains a potent force still, and the vast land itself has not yet been finally subdued and altered. On a hot summer day it does not take long before, having left the paved streets of the great cities where hundreds of thousands of people now live, one can still see, outlined against the sky, the lonely, giant-appearing figures of men like Caleb Gare or the Ukrainian farmer in my story. And on a winter day one can turn off the great super-highways that now cross the prairies and drive along narrow, snow-covered roads, and there it still lies, the great, vast land-sea, and it is not difficult to imagine Philip Grove in his fragile cutter, speaking softly to Dan and Peter, his gentle, faithful horses, and preparing them to hurl themselves once more against that barren sea, those drifts of snow.

(1968)

---

1. Henry Kreisel, "The Broken Globe," in *The Best American Short Stories 1966*, edited by Martha Foley and David Burnett (Boston: Houghton Miffin Co., 1966), 165. [Reprinted in *Another Country*, NeWest, 1985.]

2. Martha Ostenso, *Wild Geese* (originally published 1925). References in parentheses are to the New Canadian Library edition (Toronto: McClelland, 1961).

3. Frederick Philip Grove, *Settlers of the Marsh*. References in parentheses are to the first edition (Toronto: Ryerson, 1925).

4. Frederick Philip Grove, *In Search of Myself*. References in parentheses are to the first edition (Toronto: Macmillan, 1946).

5. Sinclair Ross, *As for Me and My House* (originally published 1947). References in parentheses are to the New Canadian Library edition (Toronto: McClelland, 1957).

6. W. O. Mitchell, *Who Has Seen the Wind* (originally published 1947). References in parentheses are to a new edition (Toronto: Macmillan, 1960).

7. Frederick Philip Grove, *Over Prairie Trails* (originally published 1922). References in parentheses are to the New Canadian Library edition (Toronto: McClelland, 1957).

A Conversation with
Margaret Laurence

Robert Kroetsch

ML: How important in your own work has your personal background in Canada been? Both in the stories of this collection and throughout your novels there is an enormous sense of geographical background. The treatment seems to be strictly realistic in your first book, *But We Are Exiles*, progressing through *The Words of My Roaring* and into *The Studhorse Man*, where there is almost a mythic treatment of that same background.

RK: You and I, because we are western Canadians, are involved in making a new literature out of a new experience. As I explore that experience, trying to make both inward and outward connections, I see new possibilities for the storyteller. In the process I have become somewhat impatient with certain traditional kinds of realism, because I think there is a more profound kind available to us.

ML: In a story like "That Yellow Prairie Sky," for example, which I think was early, you give a strictly realistic representation of the prairie background. But there is also the problem of coming to terms with that background. This story was part of your split desire to go or to stay, which is a very western thing, it seems to me.

RK: Exactly. I remember working on "Prairie Sky"—and it was my first published full-length story. I had come back from Labrador. I was living in Montreal. I sat down to write about my adventures in the north, but instead I found myself writing about my memories of the west. And at that time I thought I was working with the problem of language—how to record a spoken language in Canada. But as I look back on the story now—remembering the remembering—I see I was wrestling with that western problem that goes back to the homesteaders: do I stay or do I leave? And I resolved it dramatically by having two brothers, one who stayed and one who went east.

ML: This relates to a great many westerners' feelings, including my own. As you know, for years I wrote nothing about Canada. I wrote about Africa, because we were living there, and then I came back. As it happened, this coincided with a physical return to Canada, but it need not have done: in some ways I had to come back spiritually and write about my own roots. Whether or not I ever lived in the prairies again was really unimportant in a sense. There is a kind of spiritual return. I don't know whether it is a kind of totally Canadian experience. I know it is very western.

RK: Yes, as a matter of fact, I see it so much in your novels—that sense of roots and yet at the same time that sense of motion. You are always going somewhere else from where you begin.

ML: People always want to get out, and yet profoundly want to return. It almost seems that people have to go away and go through the process of learning about the rest of the world, and then they have to return. But whether or not they return in the flesh is not important. It is a return in a spiritual way.

RK: Yes. We both did it physically. Maybe that was our western literal-mindedness at work. You went and had your Africa for those years. As I read your criticism and your novels, I see how that has had a tremendous influence on your insights into Canada. I went north — No, I think the United States was my Africa — my departure —

ML: And then the return is not necessarily in the physical sense, but it really is a coming back in the mind, a coming to some kind of terms with your roots and your ancestors and, if you like, with your gods.

RK: Exactly. That is why I like your Africa stuff; you have to recognize it is your gods you are coming to terms with. I think the complexity of the problem is summed up in your image of the stone angel …stone and angel. They suggest all the oppositions we are caught up in, and that of roots and motion is only one. It isn't always a pleasant thing.

ML: I think this comes out very much — your sense of pain — in your novel *The Studhorse Man*, because this seems to me to be in essence a kind of rediscovery or retelling, with a peculiar anguish and an ironic tone, of the whole myth of the golden west.

RK: The tall-tale tradition is there, but more fundamentally it is just what you've said.

ML: It is the quest, really. It is the quest for the promised land, I suppose. And Hazard's purpose in life is the blue stallion. What he is really looking for, I suppose, is a kind of Valhalla.

RK: The goal is destroying him even as he achieves it. And the narrator is being taken over by someone else's dream —

ML: He makes of the thing a myth and yet Hazard comes across enormously clearly as a man, an individual, and this is the important thing about archetypes — they have to come across in the writing as individual people.

RK: I couldn't agree more. For me as a boy out west, the visit of the studhorse man was a big event. Jessie Graham or Jim Dietrich leading a stallion in the lane. But even to children, it was a kind of mythological moment.

ML: Let's talk about that for a bit, the point of realism, the point of background from which a novel like *The Studhorse Man* came.

RK: My father had a big farm, so he had a lot of horses when I was a boy. But we were moving from a horse economy to a mechanical world. Incidentally, it bothered my father — he likes horses and didn't especially like machines, so I was super-aware of this transition.... Every spring this man showed up with his stallion, and it was a kind of mystery. As little children, we were told not to watch. Then, of course, we had to peek — from behind a corral. And then one day I was invited to join the men — and that kind of initiation.... Westerners tend to see my fiction very much in local colour terms, which irks me once in a while. Yet the number of people who have had parallel experiences is remarkable.

ML: I'm sure. And were you really surprised? Were you surprised when people said to you, "Well that is just the way it was when I was a kid"? This surprised me with *The Stone Angel*, because I wrote about Hagar as one individual old woman, who certainly came out of my own background. But I was astonished when a number of other Canadians wrote to me or said to me that this was their grandmother.

And I didn't know that it was going to turn out to be everybody's grandmother.

RK: This is one of the paradoxes of writing — you have to believe that by being very subjective, you become representative in a sense. As you say, when you are talking about your own grandmother, you turn out to be talking about somebody else's grandmother. But you don't begin by talking about his grandmother.

ML: No. And you don't begin by talking about the grandmother figure or even the figure of the studhorse man; you don't begin by talking about a mythical figure. You begin by talking about an individual who, quite without your knowledge, has a wider application. I think if you start from the abstract and the theoretical, you fail.

RK: I quite agree. We have both portrayed an undertaker in a novel, and I suspect that somebody might generalize and say it is curious that in western Canadian writing you have the undertaker figure as a kind of archetype. Which, come to think of it, *is* curious. But in fact I borrowed heavily from so-called "real life" — and I suspect that you knew very intimately the world you were writing about.

ML: Yes I did. My grandfather was an undertaker at one time, and so was one of my uncles. But this was just a childhood thing that remains in the memory and we use it in different ways.

RK: But even I would have to ask about the name of your undertaker. You know, "Hector Jonas" starts to look awfully mythological.

ML: Quite accidental, that was. And what about the name of the studhorse man, "Hazard Lepage"? It could be interpreted in many ways too. You know "Hazard" seems such a great name for him.

RK: The day I hit on that, I felt good. And "Lepage" was a loner French-Canadian in our community who always fascinated me. As I used his name, just as a "working name" at first, I slowly came to realize it had perfect overtones for this character. Then the names started to connect up with the sexual dimensions of the book, with a wonderful amorality, with the trickster figure as the penis or whatever....But I started from a very literal force.

ML: That's right. I remember a remark of Norman Mailer that impressed me. He said that the truth is in the detail. And the truth *is* in the detail, and this is why the mythical quality in your last two novels comes across so well, because the characters stand up so well on their own as real people—like the figure of Johnnie Backstrom. I think personally he is one of the most alive figures in Canadian writing. He absolutely delighted me—this man—because he is both larger than life and yet he is very much an individual alive human being.

RK: I am very much attracted to that point where words, where things or people, start to undergo a metamorphosis. But you have to work from your observed literal world. You can't go through after putting in the symbols.

ML: You can't even think of them as symbols at the time. You can't think—now this river is going to be the river of life. It is useless unless it is a real river with real water. It has to be that first. If it has echoes in the mind, then that is fine.

RK: As in *A Jest of God*, when the character comes to River Street, one is tempted, at least I am tempted, to think about the implications of that name—

ML: The fantastic thing is, it hadn't occurred to me until this very moment when you mention it. And yet there obviously are echoes in the mind when you are doing the writing. You sense the symbols. If they are organic symbols, if they grow there, if they belong there, you sense them. But it is something you don't analyse at the time. People point out certain things in your work and say, "Well you know this particular bit of symbolism works extremely well," and you say, "Good Lord, I didn't know it was there!" But in a way, you half-knew it was.

RK: I fall back on paradox again—you've got to be absolutely self-conscious, self-aware; and yet you are absolutely at the mercy of the muse. I guess I believe in the muse, if you press me.

ML: Well, I think everybody does in that sense, in whatever way they express it. I think upon it as something mysterious.

RK: Yes—magic. I have to believe in magic. But I also believe in rewriting and rewriting. Reconceiving.

ML: Characters sometimes take off and appear to be acting quite under their own motivations, which in fact they are. That is what I think of as a kind of direct connection with the characters. You don't have any control really over what happens to them. Did you find this happening?

RK: Yes, I think that when we say a character takes over—it is really a kind of metamorphosis. The whole structure is starting to become inevitable in a way we don't quite understand, at least at the moment. I think we are both much interested in the structure of the novel. Your kind of economy, for instance, isn't arrived at by accident, I'm sure.

ML: No. That is true, it's something you think about consciously beforehand, at least I do, quite a lot. But when I am writing, I don't think about it consciously; it sort of happens, but at a sub-conscious level the formal structure takes shape, and is there. But it isn't something that you consciously impose upon the writing.

RK: Even if you have a controlling idea, you are always being surprised into new dimensions.

ML: Don't you think that when you are surprised like this, very often the writing is the best, because by this time you are not a puppet master? I feel that very strongly about my characters....In a profound sense you are not manipulating them. They are free—it isn't that you set them free—they *are* free.

RK: When you bring a group of characters together—and in your novels you offer a pretty large cast—do you start to think in terms of balances and so on? Consider the two sisters in *A Jest of God*—did you think of them as counterpointing each other?

ML: Well, I don't think I really was that conscious, until—really until *A Jest of God* was nearly finished, and Stacey had been in my mind for just as long as Rachel—perhaps this is a counterpart of the thing you did with "That Yellow Prairie Sky," where one, in a sense, divides oneself.

RK: I was asking a leading question, because I think you are right and we are involved in this as Canadian writers: the *doppelgänger* thing. You meet yourself in another form; Canadians now are undergoing this exciting and painful experience of meeting themselves. We used to have to read everybody else's literature. All of a sudden, here are books about us!...Well, maybe it's more comfortable to read about other people. Reading about us is like writing about us: you discover our own complexity, our own contradictions.

ML: A great deal of your experience and your attitudes to life and your perceptions of life are in—say, characters like Hazard Lepage and Johnnie Backstrom. *The Words of My Roaring* is set in the Depression, as most of *The Studhorse Man* takes place at the end of the war. But the idiom of both those novels is a very contemporary one. It has taken quite a few years for Canadian writing to change in this way—the idiom of the narration is the idiom of ordinary speech, and this is something that comes out very clearly to me in your writing, and one of the things I like best about it.

RK: You don't have to use the contemporary scene to write a contemporary novel. Consider Twain or Hawthorne. I've tried to use the experience of the recent past to talk about the present.

ML: It seems to me in your writing you've got a sense of continuity —particularly in the two prairie novels—a sense of history. You are not writing an historical novel in any sense of the word, but what you are doing is seeing that the past in a sense is always the present and the present is always the future—

RK: That's it. Yes. I'm trying very much to work with that idea. I've heard Jim Bacque say that the loss of a generation in the First World War created a vacuum in Canadian life. And I notice now in looking back that a couple of my characters lost a father in a war. But the vacuum idea is wrong. The experience of an absence is an experience. The continuity, if we must call it that, is not of the usual sort. I'm writing a group of three novels that interrelate— *The Studhorse Man* is the second. But I'm not interested in the old-fashioned chronological trilogy. The language itself is more important to me.

ML: I wonder if we can talk a little about—a word that I hate—style. It seems like such a pretentious word to me. I really prefer the words *form* and *voice* in the novel. One thing about your style is that it is very contemporary—a profound sense of irony and a kind of self-mocking humour....

RK: Yes—I like *tone*—tone is something that intrigues me. There is the little echo, when someone is speaking. And I am fascinated by the Canadian need to be morally superior and to put oneself down at the same time.

ML: A great deal of your writing is extremely humorous, but you know it is a strange kind of humour, because it is the humour of irony and echoes, and in the end *The Studhorse Man* is a profoundly sad novel.

RK: Maybe that's in the nature of the prairie experience. Or in the nature of comedy itself. When the problem is survival....

ML: Oh, comedy now is extremely serious. It is almost the only way in which you can be serious enough.

RK: Tragedy looks a bit pretentious now. At least to laugh is...absurd? A ferocious hope, maybe. Like the opening chapter of *The Words*. It goes back to what we were trying to say about genuine experience. You know — as a young man who wanted to be a writer, I embraced the experience cult. Go out and get Experience. It was always a noun, not a verb. I went up north. The Mackenzie River is a fascinating, strange, beautiful, ugly world. I wrote *But We Are Exiles* from that freshly acquired Experience. But now I see that I was unaware of being the outsider....taking notes....

ML: You were in a sense, even though you were involved with the experience, cared about it, and all the rest of it — just as I did in Africa — in some way you were a tourist. You could quit. You could get out. But with your own experience, your own background, your own roots — you have to come to terms.

RK: Exactly. It is the material you are caught in that you are going to write about. The notes are already there, stored in your head, in your nerve ends. But discovering them is a long process.

ML: A great many people write very autobiographical first novels. Well, your writing didn't begin in that way and neither did mine. I don't know whether one can really make any generalizations about this in terms of western Canada. I think that a great many people who grew up, as we both did, in the prairies, could hardly wait to get out. And it took a long time to see the value of that experience or to see it in some kind of perspective.

RK : We didn't have the advantage that a young writer might have in an older area where there is a literature about his experience. I remember reading voraciously as a boy, and the fictional boys I read about were always doing things I couldn't begin to do, because we didn't have the big oak trees or whatever. And that sense of alienation made me feel that first I had to go see—I didn't really believe you could construct a world without huge wheatfields.

ML : But this was one thing about growing up either on a farm or in a small town, in the prairies anyway. It was both a stultifying experience and a very warm protective one, too, because this was a place where no child could get lost: everybody knew who you were and who you belonged to. It was like a tribe, a clan, and I am sure this was your experience, too. And as you said, the books that you read were not related to your experience. I remember—I must have been in my late teens, I suppose—when I read Sinclair Ross' novel, *As for Me and My House*, which was about a minister in a small prairie town; it hit me with tremendous force, because I realized for the first time that people could really write about my background.

RK : I remember the excitement of finding a W.O. Mitchell story in *Maclean's*.

ML : You know, I read Kipling, and what the hell did Kipling have to do with where I was living? And that isn't to say that we shouldn't read widely, but it is a good thing to be able to read, as a child, something that belongs to you, belongs to your people. And you and I might have sort of subconsciously had a compulsion to set down our own background.

RK: I've suspected that often. We want to hear our story.

ML: It's a strange thing, because Mordecai Richler has said almost exactly the same thing about his feeling about the Montreal in which he grew up, and, of course, he is one of our generation too. And he said once in an article about St. Urbain in Montreal, "This was my period and my time and my place and I have set myself to get it exactly right."

RK: In a sense, we haven't got an identity until somebody tells our story. The fiction makes us real.

ML: You know, years ago I translated, with the help of some Somali friends, of course, some Somali poetry, and this was the first Somali poetry that had ever been translated from that part of Africa into English. Then various other people did other things. And years later, I met again the Somali chap with whom I'd worked on this poetry, and he said, "You know, a strange thing happened. That was the first little book and then others came out and so on. And my people had had this vast body of oral poetry, but until the book came out we never really knew that we had a literature."

RK: You helped them discover — invent — themselves.

ML: Fiction relates to life in a very real way.

RK: How do we fit our time and our place? To answer is a simple necessity.

(1970)

A Putting Down of Roots

Dorothy Livesay

Against what have been called "the rampages of optionalism" in our schools and colleges, against alienation and violence in our society and on the screen, in mass paperbacks, one positive force has held firm: the growth into maturity of the arts in Canada. Poetry is being nurtured in the outports as in the cities, and the strong flowering of this delight is what gives impetus to a magazine such as *CV/II*. Old and young alike are tasting its virtue. The response to poetry across Canada today is the response of a people longing for warmth and succour, a sense of community.

So be it. We have our poetry, pushing up from every crack and cranny. What we now lack is sufficient outlets for serious criticism of it. You can only criticize such wide, large, and various production, we think, by taking samples; and *CV/II* proposes to do this. We choose the task of finding poetry—whatever its genre—that best expresses our craving for confrontation with the real, with direct, day-to-day living. We aim to examine current poetry to see if some of its introspection—and how much of it—is really admirable as writing.

We need to ask how much of it is stale and self-defeating. What is true in metaphysical, linguistic, and absurdist strivings we shall endeavour to illustrate in ways that further appreciation. Is it amusing, but merely 'found' prose? Or is it just gamesmanship with pun and counterpun, a glittering skill in mounting maps of montage?

The poetry we want to praise and to print must have the authority of experience and action from all levels of society: the deprived, the enslaved, the sheltered, the brainwashed; as well as the fat, sleek, jaded. It must spring from all ethnic (and immigrant) sources, whose roots will nourish us. Where necessary, as with the literature of Quebec, we must translate and expound. And especially from all parts of the country we would like to explore the true feelings of women. Many women poets today are either looking into mirrors or speaking from behind masks.

The aim of poetry, which has the potential of surviving fashions and fads, is to illuminate the world and mankind's task within it. Thus, we need to challenge, in terms that are cogent, apropos, and informed, the writings of our avant-garde experimentalists, so that we may profit by what extends the bounds of poetry, and not be held back by sentimental revisitations of the scandals and astonishments of the past.

And now for details. First, our title, *CV/II*. *Contemporary Verse* was the name of a poetry quarterly published in Vancouver from 1941 to 1952 — years of drought for the publishing of poetry in Canada. Aside from Pratt's *Canadian Poetry Magazine*, sponsored by the useful Canadian Authors' Association, there were no outlets. Only the Ryerson Press Poetry Chapbooks worked bravely for the encouragement of poets. It was in the face of this situation that the critic and lover of poetry, Alan Crawley, a Winnipeg lawyer who had been stricken by blindness in mid-career, volunteered to edit a magazine and to call for poetry from across the country. The year was 1941. The response was electric. Poets then in their thirties — living in the east: Earle Birney, A. M. Klein, F. R. Scott, A. J. M. Smith; and in the west: Floris McLaren, Doris Ferne and myself — gave support through letter-writing and contributions. Younger, less well-known poets, such as Louis Dudek, James Reaney, Jay MacPherson, Daryl Hine, P. K. Page, Anne Marriott and Miriam Waddington, suddenly found themselves in print nationally, for the first time. Subsequent to the west coast activity, though of course independent of it, John Sutherland, Patrick Anderson and Irving Layton met the need for poetry outlets in Montreal. Thus began the publication of *Preview*, *First Statement*, and eventually *Northern Review*; and *Fiddlehead*, in Fredericton.

Although in 1975 "the times is different," with as many as 168 volumes of poetry published in Canada in one year (1974), and with a great proliferation of "Little Mags" in every part of Canada, it seems to us that there has been scant room for serious criticism except for reports in the elitist quarterlies (with a few honourable exceptions). "Reports" is the operative word. With so much to study, who can be an analytic critic? Moreover, what criticism there is has tended to concentrate on books published within our "golden triangle." We would like to have criticism from all the regions, about all the regions. For regionalism is the putting down of roots. A geographer does not look at a map of Canada to see what is good, better, best: he looks to see what is unique. Especially in Manitoba, keystone province, the far-reaching cultural and ethnic range has always been fascinating and productive, as a source for literary inspiration. We are centred here, but we are setting up a network of editorial scouts from Prince Edward Island to Vancouver Island: first, so that critics may come to know the work of poets better; and second, as added impetus for the fast-developing interest in Canadian writing in the high schools and universities. The main body of our magazine will consist of book reviews, review articles, taped interviews concerning "Perspectives." It will contain, as well, "Retrospectives" dealing with poetry and poetic criticism of the past (especially in areas which we feel have been neglected by our literary historians). Since this is not a poetry magazine the poems which we have room to publish must be chosen with thought and care. At time of publishing we have enough on hand to keep us warm for 1975! Perhaps, thereafter, *CV/II* will be in a position to publish "poetry supplements." In the meantime, the work of criticism must go on.

(1975)

from ROOTS

v

In Saskatchewan
    they seem to hate trees
they hate the finger upraised
to disturb the flatness
not   *The Wind Our Enemy* —
    but trees.

We drove and drove
    dust devils swirled
black puffs of oil wells
    choked
we drove in madness
yet eased   in the towns
to see one solid building
    brick (a city hall?) pivotal
among false fronts

And after the shaken blackened houses
twisted on a ditchside
gaping doorways   aching silos
we were surprised, in *Saskatoon*
by a green welcome.

    Whose wind?
    What enemy?

Spring lilacs hung down, dusky
scenting the river.

vi

So we came to the border
(a buffalo on signposts)
the black soil rippled
not yet green-pricked.
We stopped by the roadside
so we could run down amongst last year's stubble
to stoop, to discover
the furry and furtive
mauve crocuses:
a keen wind blowing
air so fresh we grasped it
in lungfuls, armfuls.

vii

In the brown-shingled house
(brand new in 1911)
battered by *Winnipeg* wind
he is the last, shrivelled, small-limbed
member of the family.
He hugs close the past
in photographs skew-gee
studding the walls —
his scrubbing brush worn to the quick
snuffs at the same linoleum
(World War I)
his pantry a mouse-nest
of fluff, nasturtium seeds, bent forks

a box of corks
all sizes, any bottle.
Only outdoors
tending his seedlings
in the black earth, May-awakened,
only setting out tomato plants
and Grannie's geraniums
(generations of fire)
only as he looks up suddenly
beyond us, out into the sky
his blue eyes
    terrify.

viii

I walk beside you down the oak-lined street
to the orange house, pitched roof
where I was delivered
and grew in darkness

overhanging eaves
snow-burdened
in summer the oak-leaves
sombre, olive
the garden a deep
mysterious tangle
poppies up to my shoulders
sweet-peas arching

in spring my father
poured the round seeds
into my hand—crusty and crooked.
Now! plunge finger in, and dig
a narrow hole, just finger deep

release your hold
bury the seed.

I followed awkwardly,
and when the orange bells
musk-scented
burst into air
I lay down in the nasturtium bed
sucked at the burning leaves
forgot the digging
and the coarse manure
never connected that wild birth
orange and bleeding
with black soil, ignorant
and sleeping.

I walk beside you where I grew
amongst the flowers
and retain
in the scent of the sweet-pea
my mother's scissors, snipping
in the musk of nasturtium
my father's thumbs, pressing

     heart planted then
     and never transplanted.

Writing West: On the Road to Wood Mountain[1]

Eli Mandel

The subject of regionalism in Canadian writing has come in for more discussion lately than one would expect in a predominantly nationalist atmosphere but it is probably worth going over the ground once again, if only to see where the confusions may be, or simply to provide a personal perspective. The theoretical basis of literary regionalism is rather less firm than the historical or geographical but a sense persists that writers work out of locale or area, boundaries of some sort defining sensibility. Whether it follows that personal experience can contribute to the discussion remains problematical but writers generally do insist on either the uniqueness of experience or at least the importance of an individual point of view and inevitably any talk of place gets mixed up with one's own sense of particularity. At any rate, it seems to me important to try to say something about my sense of where I stand in relation to place in poetry; maybe once and for all to find out in the very process of writing where and how the west, the prairies, Estevan, fit into a personal mythology, into the sounds and rhythms of a voice, images, definitions. And, of course, even to attempt to say this is to recognize one is not alone but part of a pattern, part of a cultural development. There could be no other reasons for making the attempt.

Some years ago Milton Wilson suggested that the real virtues of Canadian writing might very well lie in our often criticized colonialism and regionalism. Our perspectives, he suggested, have something to do with boundaries and contrasting patterns; not with place so much as with motion:

> The nomadic culture of contemporary N/A makes the wandering poet the norm, and in as varied a country as Canada he is always having to set his digestion on fresh images—from 'Dawn on Anglo-Saxon Street' to 'Dusk on English Bay,' 'from the ambiguous Avon flowing through Stratford, Ontario, to an equally ambiguous streetcar running down Main Street in Winnipeg, from the 'blue men of Saskatchewan' to the 'blue women of Quebec' and more than back again, from Newfoundland to the Last Spike. Indeed, the poet who moves west (or returns west) already has a niche in our gallery of poet archetypes right opposite the poet who can never get out of Montreal.

I must admit that before recalling Wilson's remark I was a bit uneasy about presenting myself as a *Western writer.* Ten years in Toronto, it seemed to me, hardly qualifies one as a poet of the prairies. But if Wilson can be taken seriously, it is not place alone that matters but a direction, an attraction—something like the movement of a compass needle; not where it is, but where it points matters. My image for the prairie writer then, at least as a point of beginning for this account, is not necessarily the one who is in the west, or who stays here, but the one who returns, who moves, who points in this direction.

I know this too can sound heretical or like special pleading but it fits very closely my own sense that it is not place but attitude, state of mind, that defines the western writer—and that state of mind, I want to suggest, has a good deal to do with a tension between place and culture, a doubleness or duplicity, that makes the writer a man not so much in place, as out of place and so one endlessly trying to get back, to find his way home, to return, to write himself into existence, writing west.

A lot of regional criticism, I know, concentrates on place: Laurence Ricou in *Vertical Man/Horizontal World*, Edward McCourt in that fine and important and early work, *The Canadian West in Fiction*, Henry Kreisel (despite the title of his article: "The Prairies: A State of Mind"), George Woodcock, who, in a recent article on Canadian poetry in the *London Times Literary Supplement*, concludes by noting how important place and land have become in Canadian and especially western Canadian writing, referring particularly to Suknaski, Marty, Newlove. Place and Land. I remember how moved I was when last year I first heard Andrew Suknaski read at Banff from his *Wood Mountain Poems* and how I thought: that's the book I should have written, its terrible authenticity, its powerful directness, its voices and places echoing in its time and truth. This is a book I'll come back to later. Just now, I note that Suknaski puts the point I want to make in his own comments about his work: "For me *Wood Mountain Poems* is a return to ancestral roots in my birth place, after seventeen years of transience and aberration in numerous Canadian cities — and of trying to find the meaning of home." He then turns to that doubleness I mentioned a moment ago, that divided sense in this writer that makes his vision not only complex but fascinating: "The poems also deal with a vaguely divided guilt; guilt for what happened to the Indian (his land taken) imprisoned on his reserve; and guilt because to feel this guilt is a betrayal of what you ethnically are — the son of a homesteader and his wife who must be rightfully honoured in one's mythology." Suknaski's "well-remembered story" then is built of all those complicated motifs; aberration, guilt, division, betrayal — not, in other words, folksiness, nostalgia, description, or even realism, but "one's own mythology."

It occurs to me how many writers 'writing west' are those who leave and return: Robert Kroetsch, for example, from New York State to the badlands of Alberta; John Newlove, from the badlands of McClelland and Stewart's office in Don Mills, Ontario, to the plains of Saskatchewan — at least in memory and desire; W. O. Mitchell, Adele

Wiseman, Dorothy Livesay, Margaret Laurence—the list can go on, despite, of course, those who stay and write, or move and return in a totally different sense. So it isn't place that we have to talk about but something more complicated and more compelling: remembered place —or beyond that—remembered self, something lost and recovered, a kind of memory, a kind of myth.

Writing about another novelist who returns west, Ann Mandel sees Wallace Stegner's "neglected history," *Wolf Willow*, as a work about a place that exists in a kind of frontier, not *in* Stegner's personal history or *in* the 'actual' history of the area, but "more accurately...*between* them, for it is the frontier between memory and history that attracts Stegner.... The frontier," she says, "runs through his imagination between the search for the self and the writing of a book. The 'ancient unbearable' moment of recognition belongs on one side, Stegner's mental geography on the other, and the link is literature: style." She quotes Stegner: "There is a kind of provincialism...that encompasses the most profound things a writer has to say."

I turn to Stegner's book, and Ann's article on it here, partly because Ann is writing out of our own experience of returning to East-end-Whitemud—Stegner's town; returning, I say, though we had never been there before, except in the book; partly because Stegner's own return to his childhood home sets up the kind of doubleness that is my own concern; partly because the book brings me closest to the kind of personal experience that I want to record in this paper—the muse of Estevan itself. For of all the things that Stegner's book is—and that includes a history, a memoir, a legend—a story and memory of the last plains frontier, as he puts it, an extraordinary account of a man and a writer recalling how it was to grow up, to be a boy in a small town on the prairies—of all this, it is most significantly an account (I use Ann's words here) of "the function of culture in a society and...his own role as a writer, a book in search of himself and his own identity." And for our purposes, there is among many passages, one that strikes most truly home:

...every frontier child knows exactly who he is, and who his mother is, and he loves his alarm clock quite as much as if it had feathers. But then comes something else, a waddling thing with webbed feet, insisting that *it* is his mother, that he is not who he thought he was, but infinitely more, heir to swans and phoenixes. In such a town as Whitemud, school superimposes five thousand years of Mediterranean culture and two thousand years of Europe upon the adapted or rediscovered simplicities of a new continent....If there is truth in Lawrence's assertion that America's unconscious wish has always been to destroy Europe, it is also true that from Irving to William Styron, American writers [I would add, Canadian too] have been tempted to apostasy and expatriation, toward return and fusion with the parent. It is a painful and sometimes fatal division, and the farther you are from Europe—that is, the farther you are out in the hinterlands of America—the more difficult it is. Contradictory voices tell you who you are. You grow up speaking one dialect and reading and writing another. During twenty-odd years of education and another thirty of literary practice you may learn to be nimble in the King's English; yet in moments of relaxation, crisis, or surprise you fall back into the corrupted lingo that is your native tongue. Nevertheless all forces of culture and snobbery are against you writing by ear and making contact with your natural audience....You grow out of touch with your dialect because learning and literature lead you another way unless you consciously resist. It is only the occasional Mark Twain or Robert Frost who manages to get the authentic American tone of voice into his work. For most of us, the language of literature is to some extent unreal, because school has always been separate from life.

It has been said before, of course. And in Canadian terms too. The gap between culture and nature, the European-American tension, these have been talked about from different, even opposite points of view by writers like E.K. Brown, Northrop Frye, Warren Tallman, and a host of others, but for my purpose, Stegner's version of it, like Robert

Kroetsch's later account, is the important one because it strikes so close to home, because he writes about the place and language and experience I know, articulating the west of my own experience.

The return from Toronto to Estevan is a long one, by way of Eastend, to Cypress Hills and Wood Mountain, and through time back some forty years. It is Sept. 1931. At the rim of the Souris Valley, a ramshackle green clapboard house rattles and creaks in the unceasing wind, the "pushing and shouldering wind," Stegner calls it, in those years always gritty with dust, the topsoil lifting, blowing away. My father is in Meadow Lake, or some other god-forsaken town, trying to sell, of all incredible things, Fuller Brushes. We have no money. The house groans. My mother is reading poetry to me—poetry!—from *Elbert Hubbard's Scrap Book:*

> When Earth's last picture is painted
>   and the tubes are twisted and dried,
> When the oldest colors have faded, and
>   the youngest critic has died,
> We shall rest, and, faith, we shall need
>   it—lie down for an eon or two,
> Till the Master of All Good Workmen
>   shall set us to work anew!
>
> And those that were good shall be happy:
>   they shall sit in a golden chair;
> They shall splash at a ten-league canvas
>   with brushes of comet's hair;
> They shall find real saints to draw from—
>   Magdalene, Peter, and Paul;
> They shall work for an age at a sitting
>   and never be tired at all![2]

'Envoi,' by Rudyard Kipling

It's enough, as W.O. Mitchell puts it, to give a gopher the heartburn. You have to know Elbert Hubbard's work to appreciate the extraordinary irony, the collosal disparity in the situation: the gap between literature and life. The *Scrap Book*, we're told in the subtitle, contains "the inspired and inspiring selections gathered during a life time of discriminating reading for his own use." The coalminers of Bienfait were gathering to march on the town of Estevan. Steel-helmeted RCMP posted machine guns at what they called strategic corners and streets. Jewish farmers like my grandfather abandoned the hopeless dry dying farms. And the publishers of Elbert Hubbard—that is to say Hubbard himself—tell us "He was merely gathering spiritual provisions for his own refreshment and dedication. To glance at the pages of his *Scrap Book* is to realize how far and wide he pursued the Quest, into what scented rose gardens of Poetry, and up what steep slopes of Thought To Alpine Valleys of classical literatures it led him, and through forests and swamps of contemporary writing." Beautifully produced, with its illuminated red capital letters, its boldfaced type, the book collects gems and flowers from a most astonishing variety of sources: say, to take a list at random, Dickens, John Quincy Adams, Israel Zangwill, George Horace Lorimer, Goethe, Robert Louis Stevenson, Theodore Roosevelt, G. Lowes Dickinson, Samuel Johnson, Cavour, Franklin, Joseph Conrad, Grenville Kleiser, William Wister. And it treats us to such aphoristic wisdom as J.C. Holland's: "Music was a thing of the soul—a rose lipped shell that murmured of the eternal sea—a strange bird singing the songs of another shore." Outside the green clapboard house, another Russian thistle bounded by. "Life is but a Thought," remarks Coleridge. Somebody carves *murdered by the RCMP* on the gravestone of a dead miner. "The nation that has schools has the future," remarks Bismarck.

There's more, of course. All those bad poems that somehow stuck in my mind and became the forms and language I would always have to work with: Henley's "Invictus"; Fisher's "I met her on the Umbrian Hills"; Bourdillon's "The night has a thousand eyes"; Dana Miller's "And This I Hate"; and the writers: Stevenson; Vachel Lindsay; Rupert Brooke; Alfred Noyes; Christina Rossetti; Alice Meynell; Tennyson; Bliss Carman; the whole panoply of 19th-century versification ranging as it does from the impossibly sublime to the intensely inane. But the point surely is that the irony to which I'm drawing attention now entirely escaped me then. In that poor shabby house surrounded by the devastated land and indeed in very peril of our lives, the high-minded sentimentality of those words moved across my mind like a vision of real human possibility. Never mind that, like Stegner, I wasn't even aware that "the information I was gaining from literature and from books on geography and history had not the slightest relevance to the geography, history, or life of the place where I lived," or that living in Estevan I didn't even know I lived there. The life of the mind and the life of the body had been radically separated, compartmentalized. Mentally, I was being brought up as a genteel Victorian boy, with a quaint though serious touch of middle-European Yiddish gentility to boot. Physically, emotionally, like Stegner and in his words, I was a sensuous little savage. The contradictions didn't strike me then; only later, only now, in the attempt to locate a self, a place.

Like others of that savage tribe I moved and lived with, along with them, I tortured gophers, scattered and smashed the huge co-operatives that ants built on the prairies, studied their wars, their cities, sucked wild onions and soured my mouth in chokecherries, masturbated in gangs, peered up the back of two-seaters in some wild scatological hope, pored over the corset ads in the Eaton's catalogue, all in the sweaty, thick closeness of the childhood dream. But if culture and nature were then hopelessly at odds, another division soon appeared as well, a rift within culture itself. I suppose its first manifestation was through radio: the language describing the Primo Carnero — Max Baer heavy-weight championship fight. Somehow I knew the whole of Jewish prairie culture was at stake in that collosally inept struggle. And other voices in other rooms: Eddie Canton, Lil Orphan Annie, secret codes, impossible adventures. Somewhere Graham Greene talks about his lost childhood, how it is that at one moment, one book *becomes* a metaphor of your own life, in some way perhaps even a determinant. Your dreams and images live out your life and though you never do become the heroic figure of *The Viper of Milan* (Greene's own fateful choice of books) or even the villain in that work, you act out the metaphors by your reticence, your evasions, your commitments, perhaps if you are lucky enough or obsessed enough, in the forms of your own imagination.

Alongside *Elbert Hubbard's Scrap Book* and its pernicious poems another book appears, this one of my own choosing, though try as I will, I can't recall how it came into my hands. What I do know is that once I began to read it, nothing could take me from it and that I would do anything to find the money to get another of the series. Elbert Hubbard could be read to me, but I would lie, cheat, steal, betray, do anything to be able to read another issue of *Doc Savage*:

> The golden man stood strangely silent at the end of his laboratory table. For a long while he studied the object under the crystal, his pale eyes flickering, gold flecks swirling oddly in them. At last he spoke to the ape-like figure beside him. 'Monk' he said, 'what is it?' One huge hairy arm gestured. The world's leading organic chemist looked over to his companion. 'I don't know' he said.

Northrop Frye, whose name is bound to come up in this discussion sooner or later, calls stories like those in *Doc Savage* romances and tends to talk of them as more or less pure versions of story, that is, form or imagination. "Form," he says, "becomes something more like the shaping spirit, the power of ordering which seems so mysterious to the poet himself, because it often acts as though it were an identity separate from him. What corresponds to content is the sense of otherness, the resistance of the material, the feeling that there is something to be overcome, or at least struggled with." As a theory, I suppose it is as good as any. For what I have been talking about is the shaping form and the sense of otherness, the resistant material. What isn't clear is whether the prairies themselves are a form that imposes itself on the resistant self or whether it goes the other way around: we possess these stories, not even our own, and try to put their shapes on a world which resists fiercely.

One last personal allusion and some remarks on contemporary poets and I will be through. In the summer of 1973, Ann and I stopped, on the road to Wood Mountain, some forty miles past Estevan, to which we had returned, at the Jewish ghost town of Hoffer, Saskatchewan, the remnants of a Jewish colony with which my family has remote connections. There's some dispute about its status. I've been told the real name is Sonnenfeld and it is still being farmed. But on that hot July 1st, as I stood looking at the traces of some fifty or sixty years of life — a door frame still standing, an iron bedstead and Quebec stove resting in the grass, two or three sheds, a shell of a house, a huge concrete vault, the colony's papers still there on the damp dirt floor — I was possessed not only by a troubling sense of transience, lost hopes, small human marks on a vast landscape, my own past disappearing, but by a question that had slowly been forming itself in my mind for the whole summer. Would this mute, intransigent place ever say anything? Was the only language one I imposed or whatever impelled my own speech? What *would* Doc Savage do in a crisis of these dimensions?

The answer, of course, was right there before me — and it constitutes everything I have been trying to say in the paper. The writer's subject *is* his own dilemma, writing west. For myself, it is the impossible divisions of gentility, vulgarity, Judaism, romance; a mixture not unlike the one (with some variations) you can find in Alice Munro writing about her childhood in Wingham, Ontario. Or in its poetic form, again with variations, in Suknaski's "West Central Pub":

> we smoke white owl cigars
> and drink white wine —
> john moneo says:
> lil jimmy rogers —
> now he made some fine lil records
> the lil bugger could sure sing —
> was a fine poet

(they'll never touch him
in a thousand years)

a young buck we know
walks in with a girl
none of us have ever seen—
moneo quotes service:
there are strange things done
in the midnight sun…

                              of wood mountain

adds lee soparlo

then a man from kildeer enters
wearing a pair of pants
that seem nothing but seams and patches—
i remark to john and lee:
in first year university
if you take philosophy
the dizzy fuckers talk about an ole ship—
the boards are replaced board by board
till a question plagues the mind—
is the ole ship there anymore—
at what point does the new ship
replace the old one?
then i talk about those pants
with patches seeming three layers deep—
wonder if we ever become something else
completely changed

the man with patched pants has overheard me
and asks:
where the fuck did you get your education?

i guess it begins now
i reply

The poem is about identity, change, process, the poet. And it deploys with beautiful subtlety several prairie motifs: the beer-drinking or wine-drinking philosophers; the beer-parlour as seminar and place of initiation; the poem as parody. But it also locates the poet for us in a striking use of an old image out of Gilbert & Sullivan: a thing of rags and patches, the wandering minstrel, ineffectual lover and singer, prince in disguise. And it's that sense of identity or patchwork, a *now* patched up of *then* and no longer the same, that gives Suknaski's work its authenticity. Al Purdy, in his introduction to the poems, says rightly, "This book is in no sense a history of the area, although it does deal with Wood Mountain people and history. Nor is it an auto-biography of Andy Suknaski, although his own life is both marginally and centrally involved." For Purdy that means the book gives us, as he says, "a clear look at people and places," and exploration of the territory of time, a sense of place unequalled anywhere else, an over-riding sense of sadness, and nostalgia and affection as well. Fair enough. No one, I think, in this country is more sensitive to voice and tone in poetry than Purdy, in his own poetry, in his critical remarks. And he means only to introduce the book briefly. What I hear in Suknaski's work differs from Purdy's version only in emphasis, I think. Purdy chooses the metaphor of territory or place for time, the double sense of time in Suknaski's poems. Place, then, is in Purdy's phrase "Multi-dimensional" so that whatever a clear look at place means, it is by no means a simple matter. To change the metaphor, if *Wood Mountain Poems* is about roots at all, these are a tangled and complicated mass, and more than anything else, it is the poet's unease, his deep-rooted embarrassment, as he touches on, reveals, the tangle, that comes through to us — not sadness, not nostalgia, not affection, but shame, everything implied in his own use of words like "betrayal" and "guilt."

I don't know how one describes an art of embarrassment. There's a moment in Alice Munro's *Dance of the Happy Shades* when a vulgarly refined group of middle-class ladies suffer excrutiatingly because they have to sit through a recital played by idiot children. And Munro doesn't let us off the hook easily. The idiot child plays effortlessly "something fragile, courtly, and gay, that carries with it the freedom of a great unemotional happiness." How can that be? "What do you write?" she is asked; "Fiction" she replies, and she goes on, "Bearing my humiliation by this time with ease."

Nostalgia, sadness, memory, even affection—these are not difficult, nor are they necessarily the source of poetic power. Language and form are other matters.

As Purdy says, "There is nothing flashy or sensational" about *Wood Mountain Poems*, "no verbal surprises or gymnastics (apart from the elasticity of time)" but there is an exceptional sense of dialect, of voice, as if Suknaski were hearing sounds carried by the wind: fragment of speech, the way it *sounded* to be there, what was said. Why *that* is important I leave it to you to sort out, but it is true that wherever the diction of poetry radically alters, unusual things are happening, both in sensibility and culture.

> *geez*
> *all the time slim/ting*

says Jimmie Hoy in one of Suknaski's poems; Hoy, owner of an archetypal, mythical real Chinese Cafe, an immortal prairie place:

> *all time talkie too much*
> *makie trouble summa bitch*
> *wadda hell madder wid you?*
> *geez clyz*
> *all time slim thing*

Voices, like Johnny Nicholson's grandfather: "Johnny...hiss too cold here in Siniboia/hiss be different from Wood Mountain/i think mehbee me n babah...vee go back to farm in spring/orr mehbee propperty in mooz jow." Or the modulation from Ukrainian to Yiddish English, the old Jew commenting on furs he is bringing: "deez one is primarry/deez one is ordinary/ and deez one is jewst a fooking doog" or to use native speech: "before I beg/I will cut willows for my young men to use/while killing mice to survive," or most chilling of all, a father's words in that incredible opening poem "Homestead": "When these things happen to me/do all you can and help one another save yourselves/from me."

The last words speak, to me at least, of a profound sense of betrayal in the word itself. After all, how and why should we turn others, especially those closest to ourselves, into poetry, as Suknaski does in the confessions of "Homestead"? Why write and re-write the past? It's always the past. Why relive the "unbearable moment" of recognition?

On the road to Wood Mountain, we saw petroglyphs, signs carved into the rock. Long ago men wrote pictures and words into the land. A curious impulse. It seemed to me then when I saw those, as now, that like the lost home of Estevan, the lost language of the petroglyphs were definitions of the prairie and that it would be in the voice of poets we would hear those definitions again. Divided men seeking to make themselves whole. Men out of place here—or anywhere. Andy Suknaski writes:

> leaving home having arrived
> at the last of all follies
> believing something here was mine
> believing i could return
> and build a home
> within the dying
>
> leaving home and shugmanitou
> the cry of the hounds
> drawing nearer

(1977)

---

1. W.H. New's *Articulating West* informs more than the title, and a comment in Ann Mandel's "The Frontiers of Memory" in *The Laurentian Review* provided the necessary memories and form.

2. Compare the Kipling quotation from Hubbard with these lines from a song composed in 1932 about the Estevan strike.

In a little mining village
Scarcely noticed on the map
Bourgeois guns were turned on workers
And their life's blood there did sap.

No one dreamed of such a slaughter
In that town of Estevan,
That armed thugs with guns and bullets
Would shoot men with empty hands.

Just a protest from the miners,
And boss bullets then did fly,
Caring not who was the target
Or the number that would die.

Blazing forth, nine hundred bullets
Bodies full of lead did fill,
Murdered three, and wounded twenty—
But the Cause they could not kill.

Three more martyrs for the miners,
Three more murders for the boss
Brutal laws, to crush the workers
Who dare fight in Freedom's cause.

As those miners lay a-dying
In their agony and pain,
Whispered, "Though we die for freedom,
Yet we do not die in vain."

The song, entitled "Estevan," appeared on p. 2 of the *Canadian Miner*, published in Calgary January 30, 1932. The lyrics were composed by Cecil Boone and the tune is that of the old Irish Rebel song, "Kevin Barry." The song is quoted in *Towards a New Past*, "An Oral History of Industrial Unrest in the Estevan—Bienfait Coalfields." Department of Culture and Youth, Government of Saskatchewan, p. 47.

Poetry as Communication

Miriam Waddington

Myself when young, did eagerly frequent
Doctor and Saint and heard great Argument
About it and about; but evermore
Came out by the same Door as in I went.
                                   (Omar Khayyam)

When I started to write at the age of ten or eleven I had no thoughts
at all about poetry. By the time I was sixteen I had both thoughts and
theories, and models as well. I knew I wanted to tell something to
somebody, even if it was only to myself. So I tried to say it as clearly,
as freshly, and as simply as possible.

In my youth I was impatient with language. I felt it should be as
unselfconscious and unnoticeable as breathing, that the meaning and
the sense of the poem should shine through beyond its language.

This, of course, was a naive and unlearned view. Later, at university,
I met the doctors and saints referred to in Omar Khayyam's *Rubaiyat*,
and most of them—during the late thirties and early forties—were

believers in the new criticism. Some of the so-called new ideas that floated around in those days are by now clichés: that literature is a world unto itself, that a poem should not mean but be, that the form, the pattern itself is meaning enough, and it is therefore irrelevant to search for a deeper human core. There was also the notion—very widespread—that the poem should be detached from all personal experience, that the writer should be distanced and objective, that the 'I' should not intrude too often or too passionately. Also, the more easily you could relate the poem to myth, theology, or other traditional works of literature—but not to politics or social issues—the better and the more universal the poem. And if the poem was, in addition, rich in the kind of symbolic allusion that suited the critical strategies of fashionable academic theories, so much the better.

Being of independent mind and rebellious nature, I never accepted the academic denigration of meaning even before I had read I.A. Richards. And now, after fifty years of writing poetry, and nearly as many theoretical digressions and explorations, I find I have come out by the same door as in I went.

I still believe that language should *seem* to be simple but of the kind of simplicity that contains complexities; and also that the poem should tell us something we didn't know before we read it. The something which it tells us should have a source in the poet, and his view of the world, and a threefold impact on the reader: physical, emotional, and intellectual. This, in one sentence, is the sum of all my wisdom, such as it is.

The problem with most poetic theories is that they focus on and emphasize only *one* aspect of the poem—be it the physiological, as in sound poetry, or the visual as in concrete poetry, or the emotional as in confessional poetry, or the intellectual (either for or against) as in surrealism and dada.

Language is symbolic[1] and works on several levels. In poetry we take the presence of more than one level for granted. Language is also contextual and full of collective cultural associations as well as personal ones. The poet's job is to use language so as to synthesize all its physiological, contextual, and emotional aspects in a compressed and heightened way. His poem must make sense and communicate at the conscious level, and simultaneously, it must also communicate and make hitherto unarticulated sense at the unconscious level. The poet addresses his whole unified self—physical, emotional, and intellectual —to another whole self. If his poem works, it will also unify the reader's physical, emotional, and intellectual selves.

Towards this unifying purpose the poet employs three linguistic tools or structures. The first is rhyme and rhythm; I am not going to talk about tone, voice, measure, breath, notation, or ritual chant, since they are all contained by the terms, 'rhyme' and 'rhythm'. The second is form, and the third, which is the most important of all, is metaphor. The term, 'metaphor,' is also the most inclusive, since within it you will find all varieties of symbol and image working in the service of making human meaning and order out of non-meaning and chaos.

Let me stress that the three structures—rhythm, form, and metaphor—are never separate in the poem—they always work together in mysterious and unpredictable ways. Don't ask me how, but they do.

Form is not separate from content or meaning. It never was and never will be. It has always amazed me and still continues to do so, when I read in some critical article or other, that a writer has not 'distanced' himself enough from his subject; or that a poem is 'too personal'; or when I come across the term 'objective correlative.'

If a work has a shape or a form at all, you can be certain that two elements have already gone into it. One is intellectual, for there is no form, only chaos, without intellectual direction and control. The other is transformation. Lived raw experience is quite different from written, or painted, or musically composed experience. To create a work of art at whatever level and in whatever medium, the experience has to be transformed through a process, much of which is technical. If it is not transformed it is journalism, or diary, and even journalism and diary deal with a reality that has been transformed in its own way.

One of the problems surrounding form and language has to do with the reader's expectations. He picks up a poem expecting something new, strange, complicated, or possibly something noble. It was against such rhetorical expectations that we find George Herbert in "Jordan" asserting himself.

> Who sayes that fictions onely and false hair
> Become a verse? Is there in truth no beautie?
> Is all good structure in a winding stair?
> May no lines passe, except they do their dutie
> Not to a true, but painted chair?

And in the same poem Herbert goes on to argue with the modern academic myth-finders, and archetype-hunters:

> Is it no verse, except enchanted groves
> And sudden arbours shadow coarse-spunne lines?
> Must purling streams refresh a lovers loves?
> Must all be vail'd, while he that reades, divines,
> Catching the sense at two removes?

Now to go back to rhyme and rhythm. I want to stress that the writing and reading of poetry is physical or physiological, in the same way as our pulses and breathing are physical. We do not notice all the inevitable rhythms of living. The very medium we live in, time, with its diurnal and seasonal comings and goings is rhythmic. The earth's turning is rhythmic, the position of the constellations is rhythmic, and all our hearts beat to a universal yet individual rhythm. In the same way, each poet invests language with his own individual rhythm. Often he does not venture beyond traditional rhythms and conventional forms because rhythm, like language itself, contains unknown and unpredictable forces.

Finally we are left with metaphor. The imagists of the early twentieth century, under the leadership of Ezra Pound, raised their rebellion against metaphor to a movement, that of imagism. They opted for a denotative rather than a connotative surface. Gertrude Stein's fine prose work is the best example of this anti-metaphoric stance carried to its limits. Today there are still schools of poetry that believe metaphor intervenes between the poet's experience and the reader's sampling of it in all its immediacy. My own belief is that since metaphor is so closely linked with meaning and the discovery of meaning, there can be no substitute for it, nor can there be any real poetry without it.

What is metaphor? Metaphor is a linguistic construct that strives to come as close as possible to the heart of creation. Otto Rank, a psychologist, understood metaphor as an extension into infinity. Koestler, a novelist, believed it was essentially a method of discovery. Winnifred Nowottny, in her fine work, *The Language Poets Use*, patiently explains metaphor as "...a set of linguistic directions for supplying the sense *of an unwritten literal term... we should note that metaphor directs us to the sense, not to the exact term....* By not using any of these exact terms, metaphor allows us to supply an uncontaminated image from our own experience of the physical world." The poet, then, initiates a process, and "the reader pieces out the metaphor by something supplied or constructed from his own experience...."[2]

What does metaphor discover? According to Nowottny it discovers unnamed and hitherto unarticulated experiences. Coleridge believed that metaphor primarily discovered or uncovered the relations between ideas, and also between these ideas and our own selves, thus relating us to all that is universal in human life. Beardsley, in his *Aesthetics*, attributes to metaphor the power to create new meaning: "Sometimes we invent or hit upon a metaphor and find that it gives us a new idea. The reason is that the connotations of words are never fully known or knowable beforehand."[3] Wolfgang Kayser in *The Grotesque in Art and Literature* is getting at the same thing when he shows us that language, especially in relation to the grotesque, releases certain unknown forces that can be terrifying.

Owen Barfield[4] attributes to metaphor and poetry the unifying power I spoke of earlier. The unity which existed for primitive man was lost when man perceived himself as separate from his environment. The poetic metaphor restores this lost unity.

Thus, through synthesizing elements from all the resources of language, physiological, emotional and intellectual, the poet succeeds in finding a new combination of words that gives meaning to the experiences everyone feels. Ultimately that is the function of metaphor, and through metaphor, of poetry.

(1981/86)

---

1. See Edward Sapir's essay, "Language," in *Culture, Language and Personality*, ed. David G. Mandelbaum (Berkeley: University of California, 1970), 3-44.

2. Winnifred Nowottny, *The Language Poets Use* (London: Athlone, 1960), 59.

3. Monroe Beardsley, *Aesthetics* (New York: Harcourt, 1966), 143.

4. See Owen Barfield, *Poetic Diction: A Study in Meaning* (New York: McGraw-Hill, 1964).

The Artist
Then, Now and Always

Margaret Laurence

I have to speak about how I feel as a writer. I don't like calling myself "an artist," but I guess I am, and would join with my tribal sisters and brothers in many ways. I believe that as a writer...an artist, if you will...I have a responsibility, a moral responsibility, to work against the nuclear arms race, to work for a recognition on the part of governments and military leaders that nuclear weapons must never be used and must systematically be reduced. Throughout human history, artists have affirmed and celebrated life. Whether we work in words, in music, in painting, in film, in bronze or stone or whatever our medium may be, the artist affirms the value of life itself and of our only home, the planet Earth. Art mirrors and ponders the pain and joy of our experience as human beings. In many parts of the world, and over many centuries, artists have risked and even given their own lives to portray the society around them as they perceived it, and to speak out against injustices. Since the most ancient times, artists have passed on to succeeding generations the tales, the histories, the songs, the sagas, the skills of their trade. Can we conceive of a world in which there would be no succeeding generations? A world in which all the powerful works of the human imagination would be destroyed, would never again be seen or listened to or experienced? We must conceive that this is now a possibility, and one not too far in our uncertain future, either. We must not, as artists, or so I feel, stand by and passively allow this to happen. The death of the individual is the end which we will all one day meet, but in the knowledge that our children and their children will live, that *someone's* children will go on, that the great works of humankind will endure in art, in recorded history, in medicine, in the sciences and philosophies and technologies that our species has developed with devotion and a sense of vocation throughout the ages. The individual is the leaf on the tree. The leaves fall but the tree endures. New leaves are born. This concept has been the mainstay of our species from time immemorial. Now the tree itself is threatened. All art is a product of the human imagination. It is, deeply, an honouring of the past, a perception of the present in one way or another, and a looking towards the future. Whatever the medium of any particular artist, art is reaching out, an attempt to communicate those things which most concern us seriously in our sojourn here on earth. Artists, the real ones, the committed ones, have always sought, sometimes in ways prophetic and beyond their own times, to clarify and proclaim and enhance life, not to obscure and demean and destroy it. Even the so-called literature of despair is not really that at all. Despair is total silence, total withdrawal. Art, by its very nature of necessary expression, is an act of faith, an acknowledgement of the profound mystery at the core of life.

As a writer, therefore, I feel I have a responsibility. Not to write pamphlets, not to write didactic fiction. That would be, in many ways, a betrayal of how I feel about my work. But my responsibility seems to be to write as truthfully as I can, about human individuals and their dilemmas, to honour them as living, suffering and sometimes joyful people. My responsibility also must extend into my life as a citizen of my own land and ultimately of the world.

I do not claim to have done this well. There are no personal victories in those areas. The individual, here, becomes part of a community and only as a part of that community can one person ever be effective and true to herself or himself. There has to be the resolve not to give up, and to join with all others who believe that life itself is more important than our individual lives, important though these certainly are.

Dr. Helen Caldicott speaks of "psychic numbing," the temptation to shut out from our minds and hearts all the terrifying things in our world. To think that the problems may just possibly go away if we ignore them. To feel that we are totally helpless, and so...why bother trying to do anything? What Dr. Caldicott calls "psychic numbing" I would call "despair," and although I would take issue with the early Church Fathers on many things, I would agree that despair is rightly placed as one of the deadly sins. The problems of our world will not go away if we ignore them. It is not all happening on TV. It is happening on our earth, and we, humankind, are the custodians of that earth. We cannot afford passivity. We must take on responsibility for our lives and our world and we must be prepared to make our government listen to and hear us. Our aim must be no less than human and caring justice, and peace...*for all people that on earth do dwell.*

(1984)

The Golden Eye

Miriam Waddington

I have always thought of myself as part of nature—one item in a whole series of plants and creatures. Therefore, to me, poetry is not something outside of nature. It is one particular aspect of nature, both in it and of it, even though it must be shaped and transformed before it becomes a poem.

The poem is an ordered selection from the many words, images, symbols, and collective relics that lie asleep somewhere in the fluid pool of the self, conscious and unconscious. Until these elements are awakened, drawn together, sketched out, whittled down, shaped and re-shaped, they lie inert in some kind of dark shimmer of chaos.

The process of selecting and shaping is a bloody struggle, at least for me. Bringing forth and expressing whatever needs expressing is full of pain, destruction, and countless little defeats as well as pleasures. For that reason I am often reluctant to start working at anything, and all too often I experience what Otto Rank calls the artist's fight with art (in *Art and the Artist*, his book on the psychology of the artist).

I first started thinking about the golden owl about a year and a
half ago. I don't know how it got into my mind, but it was suddenly
there, a wonderful consoling image of stillness and permanence.
Whenever I summoned it, the image was an anchor that kept me safe
in the world. It was also a personal space which nothing could touch,
spoil, or destroy.

But the poem always knows more than the poet, and once I
started to write the poem, the world of today with all its negatives
pushed its way into it. And how could it be otherwise? We do not live
in stillness, there is no assurance of permanence, and there is no space
into which we can retreat from outer destruction and danger. The
most an artist can do is to create for himself and for others a few
instants of time, some fleeting glimpses of permanence. And
occasionally, there appears in the guise of some natural object or
other, a manifestation of life that glows and shines and continues in
spite of everything.

(1984)

Aspects of Owls I

1

Certain owls are golden
you can see them
sometimes
asleep at the bottom
of very deep wells

It is comforting
the way they wait
for a pebble to fall
through the many
transparencies
that tremble

the countless arches
that rise
always in the water

2

Owls wait
for the pebble to fall
into the absolute region
at the brink
of their stillness

3

It is startling
to watch the single
zigzag shiver
of motion
that both announces
and delivers
its own birth
from the golden point
in an owl's golden
eye

4

The golden eye
flickers
at the bottom
of every deep well

Aspects of Owls II

1

It is necessary
to respect owls
they are aspects
of future
odd little fragments
of feeling

2

They are
drowsy messengers
they send us downy
letters and soft words
they whisper
of our lost seasons

They write us
about the white weather
of the nineteen-thirties
sealed now
under canals heavy
with plutonium

They write us
about twentieth-century
skating rinks
flooding the fields
with vapour

Also about deserts
of frozen ash
heaving now

with the blind cries
of the unborn

3

Under the feathers
of this new darkness
the unborn lie
and the owls sleep
their uneasy days
wrapped in our own
endangered sleep

4

Somewhere perhaps
muffled rumours
and faint traces
of the golden eye
flicker
in the bottom of
an old well.

The Blindman River Contradictions

Rudy Wiebe

INTERVIEWER: *Maybe you could begin by telling me where you were born and where you grew up?*

WIEBE: There's a story around that I was born in Saskatchewan to a Mennonite family but that's not true. I was really born in Alberta quite near Edmonton, a tiny hamlet which has now disappeared. My father was the son of the Inspector General of the British Army and he came here to homestead when my grandfather got tired of him sitting around home: he was 19 years old and still had no idea what he wanted to do, so grandfather said, "Go out to the colonies and see if you can make something of yourself." My father ended up in Nova Scotia while his father was going to Bermuda to inspect the British military installation there. From Nova Scotia he gradually worked his way west, like everyone else.

How did a Mennonite end up in the military?

There was no Mennonite. I'm not a Mennonite.

You aren't?

I'm British, I'm English. I never had anything to do with the Mennonites; that's a fiction I made up because of course in Western Canada there's much more point to being ethnic than to being English. Actually, a Canadian writer has enormous disadvantage in being English, as you perfectly well know, rather than Ukrainian or Greek or Icelandic, or Mennonite. I had the races of the world to choose from and I made a really bad choice; I should have chosen to be Jewish, which would have given me tremendous literary contacts in ways that I can never have as a Mennonite (Mennonites generally don't read and never buy books — at best they borrow them) but really, I'm English, and I was telling you about my father who detested militarism but his father was the Inspector General of the British Army, a professional soldier who kicked him off the family estate in England and so he ended up on a homestead near Falconer, Alberta. Of course, Falconer didn't exist at that time but he rode up the Blindman River trail from Lacombe to Buck Lake I guess, and he found a homestead easily enough.

Really? What was Falconer like as a place to grow up?

Well you see, my father and his cousin created that hamlet because they were such terrible farmers. They were archetypal Englishmen, they chose homesteads for the scenery they wanted on their estates and the Blindman River valley is really beautiful, but the place they chose had the worst soil in the entire district. If they had gone just a bit west of Lacombe where the black soil is two or three feet deep, they'd have done well, but they had to have a rippling stream, scenery an Englishman could appreciate, wooded river banks, hills, ravines, and they didn't bother to find out that three inches of good soil is all that covers the clay. So they couldn't make any living as farmers, especially gentlemen farmers; they had to do something else. They were perfectly literate, they could keep accounts well, so they ended up building a general store on the banks of the Blindman River. There were several families living nearby already so they named the place Falconer after one of the families.

Your name wasn't Falconer?

No.

What was it?

Are you the police?

Of course not.

Exactly.

Am I to assume that you went to a one-room schoolhouse?

Of course I did, but the reason I became a writer was because I sat on the knee of the Governor General of Canada. You see my grandfather, this general above all British generals, finally got perturbed about what his son was doing in the wild Canadian west and after thirty years he decided to visit him. I was born in the middle thirties, that is a fact, and was still too young to know what was really going on, but when my aged grandfather visited us he brought the Governor General along—it was John Buchan, Lord Tweedsmuir. By that time Buchan had written several novels, *The Thirty-nine Steps, Greenmantle*, which I read a few years later—I was reading by the time I was three or four though I wasn't old enough to do that at the time he showed up—but I knew he was a very famous man and he came to have tea in Falconer one afternoon when my grandfather finally visited my father, the one and only time either came to Alberta. Lady Tweedsmuir came along with a huge vice-regal party and Lord Tweedsmuir picked me up, I remember this with absolute clarity, he put me on his vice-regal knee and patted my head and said, "You know, there's certainly good stuff in this boy; just keep him growing," and then he drove back to Edmonton because the tea was over. History was made in Falconer that day. The house still stands where it happened, you know. It was very exciting; everyone had such English accents.

Was it a house filled with books?

No. My father rebelled against all things English. He detested the English military tradition of the nineteenth century and basically he hated English books because they propagated that militarism. I did go to a one-room school, that's a fact, but my father became secretary-treasurer of the school and he went through the library and took out all the books like *Tom Brown's School Days* and *Great Expectations* and *Rob Roy*, all those classic books that describe English life—*Winnie the Pooh* and *The Wind in the Willows*—and I wasn't to read one of them so of course I read them clandestinely. I almost burned the house down because I was using a match to read, if you can believe this, a match to read *Tom Brown's School Days* under the blankets! He punished me for it of course, but beating simply made me a more compulsive reader than ever.

Did you have any favourites that you especially enjoyed reading?

I really liked reading the nineteenth century novel where everybody knows exactly what they are doing. You have an ordered sense of the world in the great novels of the nineteenth century: you must get married, and get married well. You start with Jane Austen—I also read Scott but he's too romantic, so far away in chivalry and honour and impractical principles like that—the thing I loved about the English novel was its simplicity: money and marriage. Of course George Eliot messes it up by having Miss Brooke marry well and then the problems start, but basically Dickens, Thackeray, Trollope create a work that makes total sense: once you have married rich you are set, the story is finished. I liked that.

Were you a prose reader all along or did you read some poetry too?

I liked poetry a lot, famous poems like "The Highwayman" and "Sheep" and "Dover Beach," that enormous English melancholy of tides rolling endlessly up and down the naked shingles of the world. I loved that perhaps because I never saw an ocean; my father wouldn't take me anywhere near one. He himself returned to England to fight in various wars that England always has and Canadians always feel obligated to help them but he would never take us there, me or my sister. He always said, "See an ocean and before you know it you'll be standing at attention, saluting something," and he didn't want us to be corrupted by the English genteel world either so we didn't eat with napkins on the table. Now I knew that English people really do eat with napkins on the table, and fine bone china, they always have that and any amount of silver cutlery. It made me angry because the one time I met my grandfather and his friend the Governor General I experienced this clear sense of class, of *correctness*. You know? The contradictions of my father were very strange; he hated the army but he served in two world wars, he wasn't any good at farming and he wasn't so good at business either. But he did know how to write speeches and he ended up being a member of the Alberta legislature here in Edmonton. The thing that got him elected was building the railroad between Lacombe and Breton; he worked on that for twenty years, around wars, and the M.L.A. salary certainly helped keep the store going and then when he got the railroad built he lost his seat. Typical of Canadian politics of course, but it enraged my father even further. He got kicked in the teeth again and again for the kind of person he was; he sort of lived his life seething. On the other hand I really did like the liberal melancholy I found in Tennyson and Arnold. Tennyson's great question standing in Westminster Abbey, that magnificent structure built to faith and the state church, "But God, what if it is not true? What if there is nothing up there?" Is Darwin really right, or the Bible? That kind of liberal melancholy — focussing the human need for doubt — it's heady stuff.

Your father was a politician and a great speaker, he must have been a pretty good storyteller too.

Well, he controlled himself when he was at home. My mother often said to him, "Don't bother, so much control!" but you know my mother was Ukrainian and he did this again in defiance of all things English. I mean what Englishman would marry a Ukrainian peasant girl, eh? And that she certainly was. My mother was the warmest, most loving person who had a far better knowledge of everything human than my father, and her blood was the rawest, bare-footest, most up-to-your-ankles-in -the-cowshit kind of peasant that could be. This ancestry really gave me my dichotomy; I mean I go in two different directions: I don't mind calves and chickens wandering around the room and at the same time I long profoundly for white linen on the table. I can't imagine a better

start for a novelist. But I felt I had to disguise this basically unbeliev-
able dichotomy when I began writing so I invented this Mennonite
persona that I'm known by, now.

*Did your mother sing Ukrainian peasant songs, and tell you anecdotes,
proverbs, enrich you from the treasury of Ukrainian folk culture?*

She certainly did. But she had to do it clandestinely or my father would
swear at her. Every time she started singing one of these beautiful lyric
songs, getting all weepy the way Ukrainian people do when they get
into the old songs, he would come in swearing and cursing, and if he
hadn't truly been an Englishman he would have hit her. Of course he
didn't; as an Englishman he could just yell at her or slice her fine with
cold sarcasm, but he never touched her in anger in his life. I would sometimes hear them through the bedroom walls, "You know, Charles, if you
would hit me sometimes you might get over it." I understand this now.
I didn't then, that if couples really love each other, sometimes if they
fight physically they can settle things. My father could never do that;
an Englishman's sense of fair play will not allow him to beat women or
children. It's impossible, so they lived this kind of profound, almost
terrifying contradiction unresolved.

*Did you have any teachers that made any lasting impression on you,
that helped you develop the promise the Governor General saw so
intuitively?*

What can I say? I was the archetypal Canadian prairie kid who always
has to walk three miles to a one room school; always through deep
snow at forty below, always poor and during the depression. Well, we
were poor. My father and his cousin owned a store but it was a terrible
business. People think that storekeepers have lots to eat, but they
don't unless they eat their own wares and then they're just making
themselves poorer. And the multi-racial 'ethnic' Canadians all around
us never believe you can possibly be poor if you spoke English like
my father. You should have heard his accent when he was mad.

When did you get bitten by the writing bug?

I had a good childhood to be a writer because I had all these contradictions at home and I longed for a world out there that I believed
must be really attractive. It was, and so I read more and more. Reading
is a way of ordering the world better than the world that surrounds
you. If you can say that a critic is a reader of a text, that a critic takes
a text apart and orders it more clearly, then the writer takes the world
apart in effect and orders it according to his thinking. And that was
always appealing to me. The world I lived in was such a miserable
world; why not make a better one? You couldn't make it any worse.

So you picked up the pen to do social work?

No, no writer is a social worker but one of the effects of writing, of
thinking and putting stories on paper is that you do create a particular
world view, if people are patient enough to read it all, carefully. Most
of them aren't, of course. Many readers just want a diverting story
but if you write serious fiction, as I hope I do, then eventually you
do create a particular world view; it is there in your work, hidden,
and reading uncovers it. A good reader has to be willing to follow
wherever the writer leads. Many people aren't; if the trail is too tough,
they'll just go off and ride easy on some railroad track laid to somewhere else. But if they have to walk and cut their way...you know,
following a good writer is like following a good scout through Alberta
bush. Maybe the trail is half-disguised and you even have a hard time
finding it. Most people would rather sit in airplanes and circle around
the world that way, looking down serenely on everything and actually
feeling nothing much at all except comfortable.

Were you a child prodigy in the literary world of Falconer?

No.

*Do you remember some of your earlier stories? Were you shoved up
in front of the class to read, or be the star performer at the Christmas
concerts?*

No, no, I had a lot of miscellaneous ability...I was fairly well coordin-
ated so I could play sports quite well and I could sing pretty well, I

could tell stories pretty well. It would have been much more convenient if I had one particular ability, you know some people really have a voice and that's good because then all your choices are limited: either you sing or you're dead. Some people have good logical minds and they know they're going to be lawyers or doctors and of course every immigrant offspring wants to be that because they make money. But if you have a miscellaneous mind that goes in all kinds of directions you've got no help. I could have done about fifteen different things and been sort of average at any one of them. I had problems.

When did you decide you were going to be a writer?

I am still not sure if I am one. Every book you write, you're still trying to find out if you can write it or not. I've been involved with publishing fifteen or twenty books, but that still doesn't mean they're very good or that I'll be able to write another one. You're always trying to find out, well, can you or can't you? And every time I start again I—I mean I don't even think in some ways that I *write* a story; it seems to me rather that I'm finding it. I don't know if I'll ever find another one. How can you tell?

When did you write your first story? How old were you?

Oh, probably about the time my sister died. That was right at the end of the war. It wasn't a story, actually it was a poem. Or a song. I made it up riding to school. Falconer was so small the school was in the country and I...this...thing had nothing to do with my sister who was lying in a coffin in our storeroom because there weren't any undertakers around to take away the body of a person you loved and bring it back packaged like they do now. My father was in England of course, training soldiers, but it was spring luckily so the body stiffened up nicely and didn't smell too much among the leather harness and barbed wire. I made it up...it was a kind of a song I guess, I was riding my horse to school. I was about eight years old, and crying.

How about your first publication? Was it in the Falconer Gazette or where did you publish first?

Well you could hardly call it publication, a local newspaper article. The write-up of a school party which I disliked so much...I didn't like parties even then so I was the perfect reporter. I stood there and watched kids my age, fourteen or fifteen, going through the charade of a party and it gave me the perfect kind of writer's stance. I was standing back and watching everyone, including a goofy, long-boned kid like me ladling out the punch, watching the older boys trying to pick up girls and the girls simpering and giggling and some of the sensible ones I admired not knowing what to do because being silly is really the only expected behaviour there. That experience gave me a sense of distance, of being an observer at the same time as a sort of participant...this sense is a necessity to any writer. In one way you are totally involved and in another you are quite apart, watching. That's a fine thing about being a writer. You're split. It helps if you're a Gemini.

Are you a Gemini?

No. I wish I was.

From what you're saying, it must have been quite traumatic for you to go from Falconer into the big city. Was it a difficult transition to make, have you ever really left Falconer?

I don't know. I'm a Libra and I balance two things at least, all the time. All my life I'm holding two things or more in my hands. Now the fact is that I've never literally lived on a farm; on the other hand Canadian newspapers have sometimes had agricultural journalists review my novels. All my adult life I've lived in cities, yet I like the land, I like farms. But I can't stand the thought of myself being a farmer. It's ridiculous.

Do you enjoy going back home?

Where's home?

Falconer.

No, I never go there. It doesn't exist. I know this is a cliché but really, you can't go home again.

What else would you still like to do? Do you have any second careers in mind outside of writing?

No. Writing is one of the great arts and anybody can spend a lifetime at it and still not be satisfied with what he's done. I suppose it's that way in making the other arts too, say music, painting, but those arts aren't quite so close to daily life. Nobody naturally uses musical sounds all the time, nor makes pictures or designs, but everybody uses language. Language, both poetry and fiction — it's so close to the way we conduct our lives in one sense and in another so far away that there seems to be no connection at all with what a marvellous writer like James Joyce or William Faulkner does with language and what we do, writing letters or talking, and yet in a mysterious way there is a connection. Far more so than what Picasso does with images, or Stravinsky with sound. Story is always a living closeness; there's an endless fascination in making them. Anyway I don't even think I write stories; I find them. I'm more archaeologist than inventor. You never know when, or where, but you're always looking and suddenly you unearth a marvellous archaeological site and then, if you're smart, you dig very carefully indeed.

Do you think your awareness of language or your appreciation of it is heightened by the fact that you grew up in a community with so many central European kids, people talking so many languages?

Oh, that is certainly true. I can't imagine myself being a writer without my mother who spoke to me only in Ukrainian or her mother in German. My father had been sent to one of the best schools in England, not exactly Eton but close, because his father had military plans for him. But the polyglot world of languages in which I grew up gave me a magnificent start and my mother always said that the first word I ever uttered was "Baba," it wasn't anything else; it was Ukrainian.

Then why have the Mennonites laid claim to you? What's in it for them?

Oh well, heck, they're just glad to grab any publicity they can get. I mean, they have so little artistic reputation, until my generation they've never had a writer writing in English in this country worth reading twice.

Then how did they end up with you? Couldn't they have chosen someone else?

They've certainly thought so many times since, I assure you, but after my first book came out the die was cast. They couldn't do anything about it and they just have to put up with it, now. As Osip Mandelstam says, no more than you choose your own parents, do a people choose their own poets.

Thank you very much.

(1984)

Canadian Poetry Today: An Overview

Dorothy Livesay

When asked to present my views on the state of Canadian poetry in 1985, I began thinking of all the hurdles there have been since the League of Canadian Poets and the Canada Council first initiated a policy of poetry readings—a policy that really started functioning during the 1970s. And I had to ask myself the painful questions: Do you truly believe that the quality of published poetry has been raised? and equally vital, that the quality of poetry criticism has improved from its low level? As to the first question I can give a whole-hearted "yes." As to the second, I mourn.

Back in the 1920s when I was still at school, there was a great wave of interest in Canadian culture and along with it, of attention to our poets. Without government help the poets Bliss Carman, C.G.D. Roberts, Duncan Campbell Scott and Wilson Macdonald did tour the country, offering readings, especially to private schools and to public libraries and literary societies. I fear that no statistics exist, no research is available; but I do remember that newspapers like the Vancouver *Province* gave full page attention to Canadian books and their authors;

dozens of anthologies appeared in the Twenties, with critical prefaces; and branches of the Canadian Authors Association sprang up all over the country. We certainly believed in free enterprise and although satirists of the Thirties Modernist movement like F. R. Scott took pot shots at the "Maple Leaf School" of poetry, nonetheless these were the sole organizations still functioning during the depression. Lorne Pierce, Ryerson's editor, was the only publisher giving poets an outlet by means of his slim poetry chapbooks, which presented poems by Louise Morey Bowman, Annie Charlotte Dalton, W.W.E. Ross and Lawren Harris. Therewith, the then modernist movement, largely "imagist," began to flourish in Canada. It blossomed further during the Forties with the publication of the first *Contemporary Verse* edited on the West Coast by Alan Crawley (1941-1952) and followed soon by *First Statement* (Irving Layton), and the later *Northern Review* (John Sutherland). But none of these editors were from the academic establishment nor were their efforts supported by government. That development did not take place until the Canada Council was set up in 1957.

Some of us were doubtful about the idea of writers or artists depending on grants rather than their own individual efforts to make a living. What I believe happened was that as grants proliferated, poetry was raised on a pedestal. Poets became the pet progeny of a select clique. Reaction was predictable. So it was that in the Seventies, what I term as "grass-roots" poets appeared, led by the forerunners, Birney and Pratt. The new voices were Purdy and Acorn, Lane, Friesen and Trower. Their successes, it must be admitted, were largely due to the Canada Council, whose policies of aiding publishers and stimulating poetry reading tours created a new climate. Even the CBC responded, through Weaver's program, "Anthology."

As a result, never in our Canadian literary history have there been so many published poets as in the decade 1975-1985. Some graduate student might find the time that I do not have to count the yearly titles, but I am sure my findings are plausible. Just this year the short list of six poet candidates for the Governor General's Award (1984) could have been augmented to ten, all eligible for first prize. Even so, bookstore basements are jammed with unsold, unpublicized poetry. Books are given to friends or sold by the poet at readings. Readings proliferate. Small specialized bookstores are being pushed to the wall by the chains who, themselves, are gobbling the best-seller market and ignoring the need for quality literature in paperback.

I would like now to look for the causes of this sprawling, uneven dog-fight. More importantly, I would like to ask some questions: Is today's poetry merely fashionable, trendy, elitist? or is it meaningful, sound as a bell in structure and message? Politically speaking, is it indicative of a determination on the part of the Canadian writers to be a voice *against* the television and video invasion which is a frightening threat to our cultural sovereignty?

Rather than give casual responses here I feel it is time to recall the period at the beginning of this decade: the year 1975. Then, there were few publications open to poets or critics of poetry. When I was appointed writer-in-residence at the University of Manitoba I felt it was incumbent upon me to help fill this gap by publishing a quarterly magazine devoted to poetry and poetics. The Canada Council would subsidize such an effort once we had proved our value in the first three issues. These I guaranteed financially, and *Contemporary Verse Two (CV/II)* was born. Our aim was, first, to erase from Canadian poetry the blight of elitism. We wanted to publish poetry from all levels of society and from all ethnic sources. Second, we wanted criticism from all the regions about all the regions; and third, we wanted to explore "the true feelings of women."

Now, ten years later, with *CV/II* still a survivor and under new management, we must begin to assess the poetry scene once again. The question now is: did *CV/II* succeed in fulfilling its aims? Throughout the decade *CV/II* appears to have published a much greater representation of poetry by women than one can find in any similar journal. Women's poetry has received critical attention and appraisal, yes; but not enough women have come forward as critics. And it should be remembered that *CV/II* was meant primarily to be a journal of poetry criticism. Certainly a great effort was made to break down regional and elitist barriers. This was aided by appointing regional representatives right across the west, into Ontario, and eventually into Quebec (Montreal) and the Maritimes. As well, the culture of every province was highlighted. Regional issues of *CV/II* were edited by local poets and critics.

In my opinion the magazine's aim to get the regions of Canada better acquainted with each other's culture has had some unpredictable but remarkable results. Ironically, the stimulus to make regionalist poetry so widely known has created a volume of local publishing almost beyond belief. A registration done by *CV/II* for 1984 shows that of magazines publishing poetry, Nova Scotia had six; New Brunswick, two; Prince Edward Island, two; Quebec, 17 (six of these in English); Ontario, 40; Manitoba, five; Saskatchewan, five; Alberta, five; and British Columbia, ten. (Sadly, figures for the Yukon and the Northwest Territories are not given. Yet poets there do contribute to B.C. and Alberta outlets.) What are we to make of this? How much cross-fertilization has been achieved? I have to reply: precious little. Rather than having, for example, Maritime books reviewed by Saskatchewan critics, we see a proliferation of snug local reviews. This is true right across Canada. Well, though I am now sitting on the sidelines, I am so concerned about this turn of events that I dare, herewith, to offer my own analysis for consideration. It is my contention that Canada as presently constituted is comparable to ancient Greece. We are a nation of city states. Therefore, we would flourish much better economically, politically and culturally if, instead of preserving ten parts of the jigsaw, we could establish ourselves like the five fingers of a hand: a handful of city states. Recently I have heard politicians airing this idea. By organizing Canada into five regions they suggest we could reduce the many redundancies. There could be five legislatures instead of ten; five lieutenant governors; five ministries for the protection of the environment, etc., etc. Indeed, further support for this concept comes from provincial governments themselves. They are demanding and seeking much greater powers for their areas, howbeit still living under the umbrella of Ottawa.

This plan would suit Quebec, would it not? And the Atlantic provinces do have more in common, economically and culturally, than they have differences. Ontario, I agree, is a law unto itself; but Manitoba, Saskatchewan and Alberta are *prairie* provinces. So, ring-around-a-rosie! This leaves us with the whole of the Pacific Coast communities, North, South, East, West, with their own very differentiated economies, their own cultural interchanges. Above all, inauguration of this program might result in the chance for Canada as a whole to take that great leap into cultural sovereignty: a five-fingered nation.

Such is my theory! Apply it to poetry and what would be gained? Fewer publications but higher standards; and a climate of self-criticism as fresh as the bite of an apple.

(1985)

Part Two

Part Two

Clearing the Field: Some Notes on Recent Poetic Theory

George Amabile

Art is an open concept.
(Wittgenstein)

Why does a poem have to *mean* anything? Why can't it just be a
beautiful thing I've made out of words?
(Kroetsch)

The Democratization of Poetry, Direct Speech, The Prairie Voice,
Mythologizing the Past, Avant Garde, Experimental, Open Form,
Modernist and Postmodernist. For the past decade or so, these
cultural passwords have been invoked with increasing frequency.[1]
More often than not, they are used to forestall critical discussion,
rally support, define allegiances, and so on. They have the force of a
shorthand expression of unassailable concensus, which, of course,
does not exist. Thus, they inhibit thought and perpetuate a number
of unproductive illusions about poetry and its relationship to the
world. Instead of discussing the merits or shortcomings of individual

poems, we tend to talk literary politics, to categorize, define trends and movements, or invent rationales.

There are reasons for this. Poetry (in Manitoba, Canada, the USA, England, and much of Europe) has had to live with a rapidly shrinking audience. And yet, the number of serious and accomplished practitioners has increased sharply. As a result, poets find themselves competing more and more intensively for a diminishing "general readership," for magazine space, book publication, reviews, Arts Council and Canada Council grants, for the critical attention of universities and scholarly journals, for inclusion in important anthologies, for readings, residencies in libraries and colleges, for Artists in the Schools programs, and other kinds of recognition. Such "professional" competition tends to change the character of poetic theory. Instead of an open-ended exploration, it becomes a kind of sophisticated sales-talk, attempting to validate one literary manner at the expense of all others. Under such conditions, serious discussion disintegrates into polemics, rhetorical stands, dead (or dying) metaphor, exaggerated claims, and a compulsive adherence to this or that poetic mode. The brief commentaries I offer below represent my own attempts to re-subtilize part of our theoretical vocabulary.

The Democratization of Poetry. This phrase is often invoked to validate a variety of poetic practices, including "the poetry of prose," direct speech, and poetry written in "the vernacular." The rhetorical strategy is succinct and effective. A powerful political buzz-word is (mis) applied within a literary context. Given our infinitesimal, mostly well-educated audience, however, such a term, grandly egalitarian though it is, can only refer to a shift in fashion among a very minute elite which includes poets and aspiring poets, academics who get paid (as I do) for (among other things) explaining poetry or coaching its production, students who must endure at least one English course in order to pursue their careers, and a few unusual people who include poetry in their lifestyles. Poetry in Canada (and elsewhere) is not only an elitist activity (like almost every other activity in our fragmented, nearly granulated culture), it is also a privileged one, protected from the rigours of the marketplace by government subsidy. And yet, though it is grossly inaccurate (in any populist or grass roots sense), this pseudo-political buzz-phrase continues to operate as an effective bit of sales-talk because of its hidden persuaders: If you don't write like us, it says, then you are: 1. Elitist, 2. Right Wing, Conservative, Reactionary, Fascist, and 3. Out of touch with "the people" and the times. Of course, "the people" couldn't care less, and those who most often invoke the phrase are usually thoroughly repulsed by Kilmer, Prather, McKuen, and the endless anonymous authors of greeting cards and golden moment memento books whose junk is grotesquely "traditional," clichéd, gives poetry a bad name and sells like hell.

Nevertheless, in another sense, within the very small world it has become, poetry *is* more democratic. Not because it has reached a "common level" of language, not through plainness, ordinariness, everyday reality, or any other homogenized concept of "the people," but rather, through a rich diversity of individual achievement. What we need now, and what we are beginning to get, is a climate of clear, open-minded attention to new work apart from the regimentation of literary cliques and camps. I think Canadian poetry, with its vast multicultural frame of reference, is at the threshold of a new era which will see the development of a truly planetary sensibility. I think we will continue to move away from the concept of the "great poet" who speaks for everyone, and toward a pluralistic reality in which most serious poets will produce a few "great" poems within the context of a small but uniquely constituted audience.

Direct Speech. In a utilitarian society, efficiency is greatly admired. But efficiency is not the only quality suggested by this phrase. Like its cousins, Plain Talk and Unpretentious Language, it implies honesty, modesty and thrift. Thus, conventional wisdom is brought in to validate a literary style which is often incredibly restricted in what it can say, evoke, or suggest, grounded as it is in a literal sense of language which is one of the central precepts (and practices) of industrial society: one word, one meaning. Language as abstract information. Facts. Linear thought. In this view of things, plain talk is true while subtle or complex talk is weak, feminine, deceptive. But these assembly line truisms can be deeply repressive because they reduce all the immediate particularity of experience, thought and feeling to a limited number of acceptable expressions and ideas. "Common" language is a symptom of the collectivization imposed by our system of State Capitalism through media, education and peer pressure. It is narrow, thoughtless, automatic, conformist and predictable. I am not interested in the way "everybody" talks, but rather in the way individuals talk, their specific, pungent quirks of expression. Of course, simple language can support an enormously subtle and complex vision (Cavafy, Seferis, etc.). But that is another story.

The Prairie Voice. As the infinitely resourceful "ground of being" keeps changing when we probe it in sub-atomic physics, so the single "voice" we strive to hear and establish on the page eludes us. I think we are deceived here, by a very attractive metaphor[2] which takes the intensely regional nature of Canadian writing as an absolute. Without question, regionalism is a source of literary vitality and has produced truly distinguished work. But, in its passion for isolation and self-definition, it can become, like Nationalism, vehemently conformist and prescriptive, assuming, as it often does, that there is already a fixed Prairie (or Canadian) style, and that the writer's primary responsibility is to stray as little as possible from its imperatives. It is also inaccurate to assume, as we sometimes do, that literature is determined by landscape, as though we were all sedentary, 19th-century agrarians who rarely travelled further than the nearest town. Most of us are very mobile, and many of our best writers have lived elsewhere (in Canada and the world) for years or decades. A purist definition of what does and does not constitute Prairie Literature or The Prairie Voice could easily, as it hardens in the minds of readers, writers and critics, destroy what it hopes to encourage.

Mythologizing the Past. This is an increasingly attractive poetic enterprise. It is looked upon with great favour by Ministries of Culture because it is easily justifiable to the public and to other governmental bureaucracies; and it gives the writer the rare pleasure of feeling that he or she is making an important contribution. Shaping the "received" identity of a nation (or part of a nation) is an exhilarating task but it is not without pitfalls.

When I expressed, at a recent workshop, my lack of wholehearted reverence for the past, a colleague snapped back, "You're so American." A conventional, clever perception. But is it true? The fact is, there is no country on earth which makes so much of (and lies so much about) its past as the USA. But it was precisely my discovery of the actual, de-mythologized, brutal, greedy, class-ridden, racist and altogether inhuman history of that country which curtailed whatever sentiments I might have had about its stature or value. Better to dismiss the past altogether than invent some glib, cosy, self-aggrandizing substitute. But of course that can't be done. History is very much with us and will not go away. Our stupid, vicious treatment of indigenous peoples and the environment continues to plague us, as it must, and I am wary of poems that are little more than fantasies of glory and conquest and pioneering and other heroics, which, at bottom, were often motivated by avarice and depended on various forms of slavery, violence or deceit for their success. If we are to have a mythologized past, and I think we should, I'd like to see one that doesn't flinch and fake it.

I am not against myth, nor do I wish to minimize the importance of the past. What I find troublesome is the way we attempt to "mythologize" a past which only goes back a few hundred years. We do not want to look beyond that, we do not include in our mythologizing the whole field of time, and so our "past" isolates us and sets us against the "pasts" of other cultures and nations. Time is not divided, except within "the psychosis which is human history" (Northrop Frye). It is precisely the addiction to aggressive, destructive, technologically justifiable "progress" which I find unacceptable in "historical consciousness" because it has proven itself hostile to creative intelligence.

Avant Garde. More sales-talk. This time in the form of a quaint, traditional, military metaphor which invokes the masculine mystique, and attempts to validate certain works merely because they are unusual. Not that original, eccentric work should be discouraged. We need to continually try and fail and try and see. It's part of the larger process of literary growth. What I object to is the way the term is used to confer (or co-opt) special status and to claim a spurious superiority. It is especially inappropriate when used by those who present themselves as radical, anti-establishment outlaws while sitting firmly and comfortably in the seats of power, holding national awards, residencies, professorships, and so on, having enjoyed, for years, the success they pretend to dismiss as indecent. Now that their once innovative poems and theories have become a tradition, the revolutionary rhetoric they used in order to win recognition is used again to maintain power and the *status quo*. Thus, young, talented and truly original writers who do not conform to established "avant garde" practice are attacked for their reactionary, modernist, and regressive tendencies. And that is how young turks become old farts.

Experimental. This time the metaphor taps the religion of Science. But scientific experimentation is a procedure which has specific, inter-related parts: data, hypothesis, experiment, control, and result. It is often inconclusive, and the actual experiment, the test set-up, is value-less by itself. "Experimental" poetry (and art of all kinds) is almost never accompanied by the aspects of scientific inquiry mentioned above, and so we are at a loss to know what is being tried, or what it is attempting to prove. In contemporary literary usage, "experimental" usually means, "I don't know what I'm doing, do you? and why should it matter?" or, "Don't look too closely at this, I was just hacking around." Actually, insomuch as they are the results of trial and error, most poems are the products of "experimentation." To single out any one work or author as having special "experimental" status is pretentious and absurd.

Open Form. Honest, sincere. But also, that each work, like each person or blade of grass, has its own unique and unrepeatable form. So far so good. But it is not enough to simply spread words around on the page. That is only "symbolic" openness. What we need is to open the poem's frame of reference, toward a planetary, cosmic, perhaps timeless, context for our personal, regional experience, so that what we write can become resonant in the widest possible field of attention. Open form without open consciousness is nothing more than a superficial mannerism. Once we write it down and print it in a book, the "open" poem closes just as stubbornly as a sonnet or a sestina.

Modernist. Postmodernist. Cops and Robbers. Niggers and White Folk. Nazis and Jews. But there are no good guys and bad guys in poetic theory. Or there shouldn't be. These terms, aside from designating approximate periods of literary history, are worse than useless because they polarize and set into conflict diverse but valid approaches to the poem. As stylistic categories, as definitions of aesthetic or linguistic practice, they stink. That's why, though I experienced a brief attack of dutiful solemnity, I was greatly relieved when Ed Dyck, at a recent conference (*The Death of Realism,* St. John's College, University of Manitoba) told us the news. Postmodernism is dead. *R. I. P.* And may it soon be joined by all those other *isms* which continue to provoke us by trying to narrow our field of attention so as to satisfy their insatiable desire to categorize, diagnose and prognosticate. As a description of the poetic mode that has dominated Prairie Poetry for some time, I prefer the term Laurie Ricou used in his lecture at the same conference: The Poetry of Prose. I think this is a much more accurate way of conceptualizing the theoretical framework within which most Prairie (and Western?) poets have worked.

But do we *have* to work within a theory in order to write good poems? Maybe not. The technology of poetry, unlike the technology of industry or medicine, does not replicate and is not transferable. What works for you most probably won't for me. That's why, when I am involved in the writing process, I need to clear my mind of principles, rationales, and justifications. I want, more and more, to write from a state of absolute stillness and clarity, beyond will, or ego, or theoretical programs. That way, maybe each poem, each impulse, will find its unique resolution. I no longer see any point in trying to develop a neat, predictable signature style. Perhaps because it is extremely unlikely that any poet or group of poets will be able to speak, as Yeats did, for an entire society, I find myself more and more interested in the individual poem, rather than the poet or school it has come from. Maybe we should refuse to sign our little masterpieces, let them speak for themselves beyond favour or reputation, theory and rhetoric and hype. It might free us a little from the rigours of salesmanship, and remind us that, in a very real sense, we have come to the end of history. Now that Science has understood its limitations, and Nature is clearly an exhaustible resource, what I look for is a poetry, whatever its mode or theoretical persuasion, which will express and help us to participate in the wholeness of life. And I think we are beginning to get that in the work of many young writers, in Bowering's *Kerrisdale Elegies*, in the modified ghazals of Patrick Lane's new book, and elsewhere. Canadian poetry seems to be moving away from the projective (projectile?) verse of Charles Olson with its linear drive, its Post-War masculine ethic, and its fear (hatred, distrust?) of the "eternal present of the psyche" (Jung) or "the paradise of the archetypes" where time "is recorded biologically without being allowed to become history" (Eliade), and toward a more lucid awareness of "the unity of experience" (Joseph Brown). I think this is part of a larger, and I hope inevitable, development in Canadian society toward a trans-cultural, planetary tradition which supersedes nations and even languages and has its roots in the vast psycho-genetic resources of the human species.

I've also detected a climate of renewed mutual interest and support among poets here in Manitoba, and a softening of theoretical boundaries. After all, it's the same no matter what theory you fly by: The enthusiastic mess. The confusion. The work. Not a mechanical application of principles and moves, like assembly-line work, but the slow, lively inter-play of meanings, shadings, rhythms, textures, balances — all under the temporary roof of a thing you think you're saying or letting happen — the process, the continual adjustments, discoveries, rightnesses. The fact is, we all know how to write. But it takes time, and patience, and energy freed from public ambition for a while. So what if our grand quest for The Prairie Voice fails? If the shaman finally arrives in a suit of saran wrap? So what if our theories and movements and rationales are little more than throwaway shelters built out of buzzwords and dead metaphor? When the bandwagons crash and the structures totter around us, what we walk away with is the small excitement of some possible poem, and the quietness in which it might begin to breathe.

---

    1. Like theology, poetic theory tends to harden into belief, then crystallize into dogma, while the poem itself gets strangled at the source.

    2. By the mechanistic model which dominated physics until Einstein and Planck. As the Greeks were by the idea of an irreducible "atom."

Story Forming

David Arnason

(Interviewed by Robert Enright)

DA: I'm interested particularly in solving narrative problems. How you can tell a story that has certain restraints, certain limitations. Then I start to write and whatever story comes, comes. So, the ideas for the stories come after the form for the stories. The idea is secondary—it doesn't matter what it's about. I have no idea what story it's going to be when I start and I have no idea where it's going to go. As a matter of fact, perhaps a slight confession, one of my principles of composition is to eliminate possible endings. If I'm writing and I think of a neat way of ending the story then I automatically exclude it. I'm a real believer in the process of writing.

RE: How do you know when you can trust your instinct for not using a certain ending?

DA: Well, what happens is that you throw away a lot of stuff. I never do a revision of a story. I do polishing, I make small alterations and changes. But if a story needs revising, it goes in the garbage. If it doesn't work, it doesn't work. There's no way I can recast it. For me, that would be hopeless. I just crumple it up, throw it away and start another one.

RE: Let's talk about "The Marriage Inspector." Give me some sense of its form and why the story takes the narrative turns that it does.

DA: Well, in that story I was interested in a particular kind of voice, and it really came out of the notion of this character who is singing a happy little song. And that's where I begin. I begin with the notion of this character, who's vacuuming and he's singing a happy little song. I didn't know the Marriage Inspector was going to arrive in the story until he did and I suddenly thought, "Hey, that's okay, there's a Marriage Inspector now," and what worked out was a role reversal, where suddenly you reverse that whole business that all men are animals and rapists and murderers and see the male figure as essentially human. So I just tried to keep his voice as gentle and as loving and as kind as it could be.

RE: But very early into the story, as this guy's vacuuming as a proper househusband would do, there's a knock on the door and there's the Marriage Inspector, this preposterous figure who informs him that they can't have children because they don't have a permit. How did this guy come into the story?

DA: I think in the ends of my fingers when I'm doing that sort of thing and he just arrived. I opened the door and there was the Marriage Inspector. That's as much as I can say about it, he happened to be there. Take another story for instance. A story like "The Boys." What I set out to do was to write a story in which I had a couple of characters sitting in a bar. I set myself the limitations that nothing could happen and I couldn't allow them to use any direct speech. Now how can you write a story in which the characters say nothing and nothing happens? How can you play a narrative across that? And the fact that some of my friends say they can identify these characters has nothing to do with it. If they fell into the story, well, that's fine, but that wasn't my concern. I wasn't telling a truth, I was making a thing.

RE: I get a strong sense, though, that you never really give up on story. That in some ways, despite your formal sophistication, you're an old-fashioned storyteller. Now, am I wrong in perceiving that there really is a recognizable story every time one picks up a piece of your short fiction?

DA: Oh, of course. There has to be, that's the contract with the reader. The reader has to be entertained and there are ways of doing it. The thing about reading is, as soon as they close the book, that's it. You're not there and they don't have to be polite. They're sitting in their own living rooms and when you bore them, they close the book. I'd gotten into the habit of reading books and skipping through the dull places to get to the good parts. So I figured, why not just write the good parts and leave the dull parts out? Who cares how they got from here to there anyway?

RE: I notice that one of the narrators in your book has an untoward fear of dogs and another has a bottomless desire for praise. It strikes me that those are characteristics that you probably share with those narrators. I gather these stories relate to you in some inescapable ways?

DA: Well, obviously you don't have a lot of choice. About all you've got are your own memories, your own life to work out of. I'm not very keen on autobiographical examinations of the soul. But the small details are the same details that you know; you're intimate with them, you pick them up here and there. In the end I suppose I don't believe in the notion of the self as some individual generating system pumping these things out. I think of us all as composed of those chunks of discourse, those little observations we or our friends have made at various times. And I think you can pick them up whole hog and use them. I want my readers to be interested, to enjoy these things: they're fragments of other stories, stories caught within stories, anecdotes told inside anecdotes. All the boxes you can open and try and unfold.

RE: Have you always been intrigued by the ways in which stories are told?

DA: I grew up in a family where people loved to tell stories; where my father and his brothers would get together at Grandpa's every Sunday morning and they'd drink coffee and for three or four hours they'd tell stories. The loudest storyteller, the one who could throw the best hooks, kept his story going. If the story didn't work somebody else would drown you out. So if you wanted to get your stories in you had to learn what are the hooks, what are the ways of catching people, how do you maintain suspense, how do you keep from giving away the secrets until you absolutely have to. What are the narrative traps where you can get lost? So, I'm very concerned about craft, about technique, about knowing what it is you're doing.

RE: As a fisherman's son it's right that you would use the idea of hooks. But unlike your earlier books, *The Circus Performers' Bar* is not about the kind of experience that you had as a child growing up on Lake Winnipeg.

DA: No. I think any writer has a duty to explore his past. But for the sake of the reader, he has a duty not to pummel it forever. I'm no longer a fisherman's son on the shores of the lake. I live an urban life, I'm engaged in a world of people whose fears are not whether they'll be drowned in a storm, but whether they'll be blasted by a nuclear blast. Or more likely, whether they'll suffer some minor urban humiliation of the kind we all run through from day to day.

RE: There's a lot in the stories about the lives of people that you seem to both like and despise, simultaneously, and I can never quite figure out what my reaction to these characters should be. In that sense, they're puzzling stories.

DA: I hope they're puzzling stories. I hope that nobody swallows the hook completely. The characters are mostly genial; some of the language I intend to be seductive. My ideal as a writer would be to write every sentence so that the reader would want to read the next one. That's accomplished largely through narrators who are graceful or good-humoured or self-effacing or self-mocking. So I play off these gentle characters, who are sometimes real monsters. I often work them in a kind of a confessional mode. There's a way when somebody appears to be confessing his innermost thoughts that you feel you have to be kind to him. But, if you stop and think about it, some confessors are really monsters too.

RE: Yes, in fact, what a lot of these characters have to tell us we don't necessarily want to hear. Are these stories about very discrete grotesques?

DA: Yes, I think so and I think part of that comes out of my sense that we're all discrete grotesques in one way or another. Beyond that though, there's a literary tradition that I find a lot more exciting than the normal canon of literature. Henry James, frankly, still bores me silly. But Rabelais, on the other hand, I find incredibly exciting. I'm interested in a tradition of writing that takes you from Chaucer to Rabelais to Sterne to Don Quixote and then to a lot of really fascinating South American literature. It's a tradition that's separate from the mainstream of realist writing.

RE: In fact, you're really talking about the picaresque in a way. And you're basically talking about a fictional world where anything is possible, where the conventions of reality, including gravity, are not terribly useful to you as a writer. Does that give you more freedom? Do you feel any limitations?

DA: I don't think so. There are no rules. All that matters is that it works in the long run. What you have to avoid is being self-indulgent, avoid losing control. Even though I try to abrogate control on one level, on another level, I'm always very concerned about it and about where the reader fits into all of this.

RE: You really talk as if you have the fictional world completely in control. You use the story as a way of creating hooks that can hold the reader so that they're forced to follow your fictional line. Are you really talking about an act of coercion? What is your relationship to the reader?

DA: Oh, it's certainly coercive, no question about that. What you want to do is to both seduce and bully the reader at the same time.

Again, I'm not there to make the reader into a better person, or to reveal the fundamental human truths. If the reader finds them there, that's good for him, but that's not what I'm aiming for. What I would like to do would be to release joy. Write things that would make people, when they were finished, happy. That they would think this was too short, that they would like to have had more of it.

RE: I don't get a sense of lingering in "description," to use a phrase that comes up in the book. There's not a great deal of description in this book, is there?

DA: No, I'm not very concerned with that. The stories are short, some of them only two and a half pages. But they're as long as they have to be. When I get a book of short stories I always read the shortest stories first before I decide whether I'm going to read any more. So I thought, well, I'm really going to have to work at getting some really good short ones if they're going to read the long ones.

RE: Do you type out loud in a sense? Do you have to hear the words on the page or is it sufficient for you to see what you're typing?

DA: No, I don't hear these things. And I don't even see them; what I see are my fingers working. I sometimes make mistakes for that reason. I don't even glance at what's written and then I go back and find that I've misspelled 'the' and words like that. But I neither read nor hear what's going on. It's a matter of feeling what you're writing.

RE: I'm not sure I understand how you mean that. You talked earlier of your fingertips dictating the story. Do you mean something as physical and visceral as the touch of the fingers on the keyboard having some kind of catalytic effect?

DA: I can't even write with a pencil anymore. It would be hopeless for me to take a pen or a pencil and try to write a story. I've tried it and they're dreadful. They just don't work. Thank God for the electric typewriter and the word processor, because otherwise I wouldn't be writing.

RE: Let's talk about your re-writing of inherited stories. I'm thinking here of the way you transform the *Little Red Riding Hood* story in "Girl and Wolf."

DA: Yes. It's a rewriting of *Little Red Riding Hood* from the point of view of the wolf. I'm interested in fairy tales because it seems to me there are truths in them other than those which appear on the surface. "Girl and Wolf," by the way, is closer to an authentic version because I've based it on pre-Grimm patterns.

RE: It's not just told from the wolf's point of view. After all, this wolf sees the world as a place of open and endless possibilities. It strikes me that you do too.

DA: Well, he does until he meets the girl who, as it were, defangs him.

RE: I don't want to get too simple-minded about this, but what's the point of taking this traditional story and really giving it an entirely different cast?

DA: Okay, there was an article in the *New York Times Book Review* that actually set off this story. The original versions were not intended for children. They were told by 18th-century French peasants during working parties. The erotic implications of the story were not disguised. They were quite openly and directly present in the earlier versions. I wanted to pick up the actual patterns. In the early story, she does a kind of strip-tease, which she does also in mine, but I wanted the kind of reversal where the predator is not the wolf at all, but Little Red Riding Hood. And that seems to me to be not completely untrue about human relationships.

RE: This is coming from a man who finds a drunken woman singing in his office?

DA: Well, if Ulysses could come upon sirens, why can't a businessman? He's got to go off to his office to work, why couldn't he encounter a siren? There are few enough of those opportunities. Like Ulysses, he turns her down.

RE: We're talking about fairy tales and Greek myths and it's quite clear that you will lift the germ of a narrative from pretty well anywhere.

DA: Yes, anything is grist for the mill. Again, what I want to escape are the traditional patterns of the mimetic storyteller who tells the same thing. It's tough enough coming from the prairies where everybody who picks up the book assumes that a young man growing up in a bitter windswept prairie town will earn his manhood by facing a railway train on a trestle. It's just about time the country grew out of those assumptions.

RE: Although it's something you could probably work with if you really set your mind to it. There must be a reversal in that: the train runs over the sucker and kills him dead.

DA: That would be a nice idea, I hadn't thought of that. Maybe I will run over one of them.

RE: The Circus Performers' Bar is an inspired title. Where did it come from? From more of your rummaging around in the fairy-tale attic?

DA: The title story of The Circus Performers' Bar is one of three stories in the collection that is a rewriting of Snow White and the Seven Dwarfs. In this case the story is set in St. Petersburg at the time of the abortive revolution of 1905, and the seven dwarfs are all performers in the circus of the Western Region. I got fascinated with the story of Snow White because it's one of the oldest fairy tales; it goes back to much earlier fertility myths in which Snow White represents spring and the mother represents winter and the seven dwarfs of course, in mediaeval lore, were the seven planets. So what I wanted to do was re-write these stories and in this case, steal a fair bit from Crime and Punishment as I went along.

RE: I couldn't locate the time of the story and it's a wonderful confusion. Now, are you after that kind of ambiguity, where the reader can't even settle into the time or place of the story?

DA: It's full of anachronisms anyway. Yes, I desperately do want to blur those kinds of notions. Lord forbid that anyone would think I had provided an accurate picture of St. Petersburg in 1905.

RE: You don't ever have any worry about using a story up in any sense? I was going to ask you whether you think of writing as a way of taking all of your literate experience and somehow eventually getting it all out. Is that what the process of writing is for you?

DA: Well, I think that in real ways all literature is about literature, so I don't feel in any danger of running out of it. If it's your own life that you're dealing with, then maybe someday you'll have told all your stories. I tried to get rid of those as fast as I could and now I've got all the stories in the world to tell and I'm quite prepared to tell them, to re-do them.

RE: I want to get back to this sense of what writing can do and throw an accusation at you that sometimes gets thrown at writers who aren't working in the great tragic mode. You know, comedy can never be as good as tragedy, even with Shakespeare. I suppose the same kind of distinction could be raised with your fiction, that it doesn't deal with the great themes—life, birth, death—in a direct enough way.

DA: That's fine, you go and read all those dull things. I'm interested in the comic vision. Quite clearly, the last thing I would be remotely interested in writing is a great tragedy. In fact, as far as I can understand it, tragedy, and the ability to respond to tragedy, is essentially a narrow, elitist sensibility of the upper classes that allows them to feel superior to the people in the pit. I'll cast my lot with the people in the pit.

There's a Trick with a Mirror I'm Learning to Do

Pamela Banting

Given that the model of the penis-pen writing on the virgin-page participates in a long tradition identifying the author as male and the female as his passive creation,[1] then what kinds of changes in the body of literature itself are we witnessing now that more and more women are taking up the pen? Have women writers bought the package deal — have we taken up the penis with the pen? Have we in fact appropriated the phallus? Apparently there exists a fifth-century B.C. Greek vase which depicts a woman "marching off with a giant disembodied phallus tucked under her arm."[2] What kinds of inscriptions are now being made? What kinds of writing emerge not from the anxiety of influence but from the "anxiety of authorship"?[3] Are these inscriptions being traced on masculine bodies in the same way that men have tattooed women?

The phallic economy within which we all live, and read and write, doubly derives female identity through the productions of the penis and the pen. A woman represents the master's piece, she herself *is* the masterpiece. In Judith Fetterley's words, the female reader, taught to identify with a male point of view, is the "immasculated" (not emasculated) reader. Intellectually male, sexually female, one is in effect no one, no where, immasculated. Fetterley poses the question: "What is it possible for a woman to read in these conditions of efface-ment and estrangement; in a universe...where the rules of aesthetic reception and indeed of the hermeneutic act itself are mapped onto a phallomorphic regime of production?"[4] One must also ask, what is it possible for a woman to write? Is it at all possible to write out of one's "femininity" if your reading and the very structures of language itself are trapped within this phallogocentric economy? Is it even possible to posit the existence of "femininity," striated as the concept is by phallic logic, by peckertracks?

In fact, there is very little utility in the categories of female and male. Feminine desire is not the exclusive property of women, nor do men have an exclusive listing with masculine desire. Desire is multiple, beyond the limited parameters of heterosexuality, homosexuality and even bisexuality. Desire is an "indeterminable number of blended voices," a "mobile of non-identified sexual marks whose choreo-graphy can carry, divide, multiply the body of each 'individual,' whether he be classified as 'man' or as 'woman' according to the criteria of usage."[5]

However, although desire has the power to dissolve binary opposition, there is no abolition of difference(s). It is possible to make provisional speculations about writing which is sexually marked. On this occasion I wish to speculate about writing marked as "feminine."

For example, in feminine writing, knowledge, rather than being transmitted as an object, is often interrogated at its foundations. Although masculine writers are also involved in this project, they are not in quite as "advantageous" a position as feminine writers. As the repressed, the censored, the debarred, the derobed, the deranged, the delayed, the deterred, woman is in a uniquely "privileged" position as interrogator. That is to say, since writing derives from the locus of struggle between the emergent repressed instinctual drives of the body and the symbolic structures of language, and since women's unconscious desire has been more effectively repressed than men's, there is greater potential in women's writing today for a shift in the linguistic system and an escape from the binary prison. "At the bottom I am really a questioner," says the French writer Hélène Cixous. No longer the oracle, the one who answers, the assuager of hermeneutic anxiety, no longer the allegory of truth, woman is the one interrogating, posing the questions.

Another quality of writing from the feminine border is that such writing is never singular but always at least double. A new metaphysics, or an alternative to traditional metaphysics, is inherent in the woman's position. Verena Andermatt Conley suggests that this may be because woman is habitable:

> ...able to contain and to be contained at once, in an endless process of birth, hence as being able to think the other, to feel and not just to see the other and to have a relation to other(s) different from "man" . To "woman"...things happen from the inside, a child for example, whereas to "man" they always happen from the outside. "Woman" therefore would have a relation to inside and outside (and to others) different from "man". This double feminine, of feminine voices, could introduce a dissymmetry in any relation which would not come back to a closed binary opposition but which would let the other(s) enter and leave in infinite play.[6]

Sharon Thesen's second book of poems, *Holding the Pose*, displays on its cover three identical snapshots of the author, herself holding the pose. Traditionally, it is the artist's model or the woman who plays the role of the muse who holds the pose. Sharon poses as her own muse. She is split: as woman she is a muse. But as a writer she is not amused. In *Artemis Hates Romance* she talks back:

> To 'honeybunch', you stupid fucker, you never thought I'd do it did ya, you slimy hogstool, I hope you rot in hell you no good bum with your big mouth and your endless threats about breaking both my thumbs. What a joke, it was just a lousy way of shutting

me up and you knew it. Well you can take your finger out of your
ass and shove it up your nose for all I care, because it's no
goddam thanks to you, hiding my typewriter and always wanting
fancy dinners all the time, well why don't you get one of your
girlfriends to make your dinner eh? and now we'll just see who's
going to incapacitate who from now on. So eat your heart out
shitface, and just for the old icing on the cake, you remember
how I told you that big black guy was 'just a friend'? Well, he
was considerably more than a friend and furthermore has a whang
the size of a Coke bottle. So go wipe out on a freeway, creep,
cause I'm not taking anymore of your CRAP.[7]

But of course, even the sass and backtalk trade in masculine cliché
and thus point to the female writer's aporia of discourse. She can only
speak out against him in his terms, in his language. She is a mimic, and
the very act of speaking her own desire simultaneously alienates or
distances that desire behind a barrier of language not her own.

The strategy of mimicry *can* reserve a portion of feminine desire,
but such desire would seem to remain extremely marginal, even further
estranging the female body. I quote a poem from my own manuscript,
Pamela:

between our bitter
silences

i observe you, obsessively
imitating my gestures and speech

writing your body
over mine

i mime
myself

for the perversion of watching
you repeat

my body
my disguise[8]

The French psychologist/linguist/philosopher Luce Irigaray describes mimicry as a form of subversiveness. She defines it as

> ...an interim strategy for dealing with the realm of discourse (where the speaking subject is posited as masculine), in which the woman deliberately assumes the feminine style and posture assigned to her within this discourse in order to uncover the mechanisms by which it exploits her.[9]

> [To play with mimesis] means to resubmit herself...to "ideas," in particular to ideas about herself, that are elaborated in/by a masculine logic, but so as to make "visible," by an effect of playful repetition, what was supposed to remain invisible: the cover-up of a possible operation of the feminine in language. It also means "to unveil" the fact that, if women are such good mimics, it is because they are not simply resorbed in this function. *They also remain elsewhere.*[10]

Irigaray reasons that women employ the mimetic strategy with ease because they have always nourished its operation through their reproductive capabilities. After all, what is mimesis but reproducing from nature? In these terms, mimicry is not at all a disappearing act. Rather it can convert a form of subordination into an affirmation. There is a surplus, a supplement, a residue, left over when a woman mimes femininity. The strategy is essentially a deconstructive one.

The chief proponent of deconstruction, Jacques Derrida, describes the way this "unresorption" functions in the operation of mimicry. He writes:

> There is no imitation. The Mime imitates nothing. And to begin
> with, [she] doesn't imitate. There is nothing prior to the writing
> of [her] gestures. Nothing is prescribed for [her].[11]...We are faced
> then with mimicry imitating nothing; faced, so to speak, with a
> double that doubles no simple, a double that nothing anticipates,
> nothing at least that is not itself already double. There is no
> simple reference. It is in this that the mime's operation does
> allude, but alludes to nothing, alludes without breaking the
> mirror, without reaching beyond the looking-glass.[12]

The mime is the mirror of a mirror, a ghost that is the phantom of
no flesh. The mime who is a woman writes herself on the blank page
that she herself is. In miming the "feminine" identity imposed upon her
she imitates nothing. She reveals this identity to be the copy of a copy.
Like a vampire, it casts no reflection. (For an excellent example of this
mimetic strategy, see Patricia Young's book of poems based on the life
of Jean Rhys, *Melancholy Ain't No Baby*.[13])

Another very useful model for describing the writing effect of the
feminine is Julia Kristeva's elaboration of the split subject. For Kristeva
the subject-in-process is engaged in a dialectic between two dispositions
which she calls the semiotic and the symbolic. The semiotic is that
which precedes the imposition of the symbolic and the formation of
the "self" at the mirror stage. It is the region anterior to language; it is
the pre-verbal stage, where the body is governed by instinctual
drives, rhythms and intonation. The semiotic is prior to value and
exchange. The symbolic, on the other hand, is associated with language,
powers of representation, abstraction, substitution, deferral, identity,
the Law of the Father, and the phallic order. Irruptions of the semiotic
cause displacements along these fixed axes of the symbolic, challenging
existing linguistic, social, psychological, and philosophical systems
and producing change, renewal.[14]

Another poetic text which writes itself along this cleft in the split
subject and which bears a feminine signature is *in the second person*
by Smaro Kamboureli.[15] Smaro's text participates in this interplay
between the masculine desire for mastery of the tongue and the

feminine desire to refuse mastery. "Playing hide-and-seek with one's mother tongue is one of the many ways of adopting a second language, of entering into the labyrinth of Language....English words put together in Greek syntactical patterns."[16] Doubly removed as a woman, and as an immigrant, she lives "beneath language," or in "that realm of language where words as signs are not yet divided into signifiers and signifieds....the stage where words are beings in themselves prior to becoming the proper names of things."[17] She is the occupant of an underworld of language. Disembodied in her own body. She is, like Eurydice, twice removed. Or like Lot's wife in the Bible, who looked back to her lost city and lost her self, her life. A mute marker in the landscape.

Reading *in the second person* we enter a textual labyrinth panelled with mirrors. The entire book makes gestures as if it might retreat behind this barrier of silence. That is, the book at hand is the double of the burned diary, the diary of silence, incinerated in the kitchen sink, the scene of the mother. That shadow text is/was the text of the mother—written in the mother tongue. The present text (the present tense in the diary) is written in the language and the Name of the Father, the language of symbols and abstraction. The poet's literal father is very much a presence in this book. And his voice, demanding submission to his will, is echoed in the censoring and censorious voice of the writer in which she addresses her Other. This Other, this anterior self, a previously fully functioning and sufficient self, has by default been exiled to the semiotic, that region of unnameable drives and impulses of the body. Simultaneously, though not contradictorally, the Other has been dislocated outside the body and transferred onto a lost polis. The loss recorded in this book is the alienation of the semiotic self, condemned to a perpetual wandering among lost shades. The aporia of the female self.

However, the burned diary *is* articulated through the present one, creating a braided text in which the writer comes to locate the place of language in herself. Like many feminine texts, Smaro's writing is a writing toward the Other (even if that Other is another part of the multiple self). Women's writing is a re-enactment of the mirror stage, where the split subject rediscovers itselves and language.

So what happens to the model of the poet when she rejects Orphic dismemberment but loves the split in herself? Writes a long poem to the split in herself? What happens to parameters of the writing self when someone writes her autobiography in the second person? What happens when writers such as Betsy Warland and Daphne Marlatt have transferences onto the dictionary—that genealogical table of phallo-cratic culture—and begin to insinuate that parole is not enough? What will be the results of women writing like women? Will men's writing become more "feminized" through the inevitable spread of influence? Will there be a burst of androgynous writing? Will there be a utopia of texts, a textual utopia? Or textual clashes, textual warfare? A dialogic relationship perhaps. Or an overdetermination and specialization of texts—male, female, gay, lesbian, bisexual, and so on?

I am no Cassandra, no oracle. But I do place my trust in the logics of mimicry, discontinuity, disruption, deconstruction, seduction, excess, and incest. When the goods get together, the goods get going, and there is a concatenation in the market-place. Scheherazade no longer tells stories to save her life. She speaks her own pleasure in the act of storytelling. She has ceased speaking to an exclusive audience, has walked out into the plaza, and joined her voice to that of her Others. Hester Prynne has gone into the textile business and operates a stall in the market. She is into the warp and woof of things and has no time for those who would exhort her to speak the name. There are acrobats and entertainers in the market-place these days, and a great sound of laughter. Jouissance spills from the skins of the very market tomatoes, *"fresh from the garden gathered by hand tomatoes for fiiiiilliiiiing."*[18]

---

1. Susan Gubar, "The Blank Page and the Issues of Female Creativity," *Writing and Sexual Difference,* ed. Elizabeth Abel (Chicago: Univ. of Chicago Press, 1982), 77.

2. Mentioned in Peter Schwenger, *Phallic Critiques: Masculinity and Twentieth-Century Literature* (London: Routledge & Kegan Paul, 1984), 80.

3. The term derives from Sandra M. Gilbert and Susan Gubar's book *The Madwoman in the Attic: the Woman Writer and the Nineteenth-Century Literary Imagination* (New Haven and London: Yale Univ. Press, 1979, 1984), 48-49.

4. Quoted in Nancy K. Miller, "Rereading as a Woman: The Body in Practice," *Poetics Today*, Vol. 6:1-2 (1985), 291-299.

5. Jacques Derrida and Christie V. McDonald, "Choreographies: An Interview," *Diacritics*, Vol. 12 (Summer 1982), 76.

6. Verena Andermatt Conley, "Letter to Jacques Derrida: 31 October 1982," *boundary 2*, Vol. 12, No. 2 (Winter 1984), 73.

7. Sharon Thesen, *Artemis Hates Romance* (Toronto: Coach House Press, 1980), 35.

8. Pamela Banting, "Selections from *Pamela*," *Prairie Fire*, Vol. VI, No. 3 (Summer 1985), 41.

9. Luce Irigaray, *This Sex Which is Not One*, trans. Catherine Porter (Ithaca, N.Y.: Cornell Univ. Press, 1985), 220.

10. Irigaray, 76.

11. Jacques Derrida, *Dissemination*, trans. Barbara Johnson (Chicago: Univ. of Chicago Press, 1981), 194.

12. Derrida, 206.

13. Patricia Young, *Melancholy Ain't No Baby* (Charlottetown, P.E.I.: Ragweed Press, 1985).

14. Julia Kristeva, *Desire in Language: A Semiotic Approach to Literature and Art*, ed. Leon S. Roudiez, trans. Thomas Gora, Alice Jardine and Leon S. Roudiez (New York: Columbia Univ. Press, 1980), 6-7.

15. Smaro Kamboureli, *in the second person* (Edmonton: Longspoon Press, 1985).

16. Kamboureli, 7.

17. Kamboureli, 9, 10.

18. Kamboureli, 34.

Open/Entrance:
'Raw' notes towards poetics

Douglas Barbour

How to write of writing. I do love to talk about it, but talk is free, thats one of its glories, & what I say now I can always say another way another day. Writing remains. And though I dont really disagree with what I thought before, I do prefer not to be pinned down to just one way of expressing my thoughts on poetics. So: notes, because it's never really *a* poetic but poetics, various ways, always in transformation, of approaching the act of writing; & '*raw*,' because my thinking on this matter is never fixed. Still, much of *how* I write is based on the concepts of poetics I first engaged reading Robert Duncan, Charles Olson, Ezra Pound, Denise Levertov & Phyllis Webb, especially; yet I continue *to discover* influences, that is actively seek them out. Nevertheless, I know that the work of those writers, plus, a short while later, Margaret Avison, Robert Creeley, Daphne Marlatt, John Newlove, bp Nichol, Michael Ondaatje, Al Purdy, & later still Robert Kroetsch—the names proliferate—continue to affect my writing. I believe a committed writer never stops learning; that texts of other writers continually offer insights, possibilities, to the writing mind seeking to expand its range. bp Nichol has spoken of himself as "an apprentice to language," & I believe the attitude expressed in that phrase: we can always learn more about our craft. Yet I also believe that each writer eventually makes a unique subject matter in whatever he or she writes. The notes that follow are just that, notes, on some of the possible ways I view the poem, the book, the writing, & the reading too.

*

Never knowing quite where to begin. Always beginning. Where. And with what in mind. Whats in mind now is always what we begin with having always already begun & never reaching back to beginnings but beginning   again   with words where we always begin. To write. What. It changes, always. It changes/we change/& so does our writing: where we always begin [I wanted to *say* something] again.

*

We say
What we say we see
&
What we say we see
We see

A recent mantra of sorts, perhaps. But it goes back a long way in my thinking: to early days agreeing with at least the metaphoric validity of the Whorf-Sapir Hypothesis. It speaks not simply to the act of art but to all acts of language, from which our art comes, as language is that place where all saying/seeing takes place. Perhaps. I can never be absolute about these things, about anything, for language itself is duplicitous, duplicating the world or duping us into thinking so. Other theories of language say that it is purely self-referential, always has been, a network of relationships. If thats the case, our writing must be, too. And what does that mean. I am never sure in these spaces of inquiry & exploration. Language is perhaps no more than free-floating signifiers, a system of differences, yet we take significance from what we read, & perhaps even more from what we write. We go on. Writing.

*

And writing, it appears, always occurs in the presence, in the context, of other writing. Not that we dont write out of 'experience' [whatever we mean by that term] but that 'new' writing is always begotten out of other writing, as well as 'experience.' Indeed, it sometimes seems we cant comprehend 'experience' except through what has been written about it. 'New' writing is usually not truly *new* but some extension of, some breaking of the bounds of, what is already known, already written in our understanding. The history of writing as continual marginalia.

I doubt if there was ever a time when writers were not already aware of other writers, or at least of other 'writing.' 'Homer' created his epic in an already present tradition. And what 'he' 'wrote' then became the ground of European epic: how self-conscious is the *Aeneid* as it insists within itself on the presence beforehand of the *Iliad*, out of which its text emerges. The great romances always write themselves into a long tradition, without which context they would have so much less power. *Don Quixote*, the first great realist novel, is also the first great self-conscious novel, already calling attention both to the ways it transcends the romances it parodies and to the ways in which it is inventing a 'new' tradition. The poems that count have always been written in the shadows of earlier poems. Which is to say that writers have always been conscious of their art & craft *within* their art & craft (or at least the most interesting of them have).

And yet, today, the whole situation appears more complex than ever, & one reason is that we know, or can know, so much more. It is simply no longer possible to be a naive poet & a good one. Poets must be learned (in some sense or another), if only to have learned what they can ignore & discard. Certainly so that they will recognize conventions which are dead or dying & avoid them in order that their work will not be stillborn — out of date before it even reaches a reader. Here we begin to touch on what (to me) is the core of poetics: language itself, & the poets relation to it. "Language itself is alive," says Daphne Marlatt, & I agree. I agree: we write out of an engagement with it — which is willy-nilly an engagement with life, what else could it be. But language is a huge living structure of structures, a structure which exists spatially so to speak in time. Because we live towards the end of a long & full tradition, the words we say we know others have said before. Because we read them in the pages of the history of writing we cannot speak wholly new. 'Moon' can mean so much because we have *read* so many moons. Because so many words & phrases contain a full history of previous appearances, the writer listens while writing for echoes of those appearances, hoping the writing will thus have greater resonance for the reader who also hears those echoes, those other voices singing each to each [I note the unavoidable synaesthesia of my argument: writing to be heard, listening for what has always been inscribed in previous texts which stretch back through time; this is what comes from paying attention to textuality in the world].

Where do the words come from, then [where are the voices coming from]: they come from all those other texts surround us as we write [taking the term 'text' in its fullest possible sense]. Thus intertextuality: it is the space we inhabit as we write, the place we speak from. For some writers the knowledge that we live & write in such a fully inscribed space apparently leads to despair. But why. It is in fact exciting to work *with* your language, a language full to brimming with its own history & pre-history — & to go further, to push at the boundaries, to open the field. [And, perhaps, as many feminist writers insist, an important way to open the field is to interrogate, blast, subvert the previous writing, when its conventions prove to be wholly phallogocentric.] I am a Heraclitean: you can never step into the same poem twice, yet the river of discourse continues to flow & you have to enter it. Swim, not drown. Language *is* shared, even in the midst of deconstruction. We have to live with these paradoxes, it seems; & I do, joyfully, for in their midst writing continually begins again.

*

The stance is receptive. It is not one of mastery. The world, events & emotions, the Other: these *enter*. The writer. The writing. Through language, via language, *with language*. Which is not to say there is no discipline; there is. But it is a discipline of waiting, of opening the writing self to what comes. And what comes comes as words, no matter how it also comes from the world. To sidestep the ego (with its need to order *a priori*, to organize from mastery, to *control*), & let the wor[l]d *in*. All that space to be filled. But not by 'me.' By the writing.

*

One reason I so enjoy the spaces of the new poetry could be that I grew up inside space[s], on the prairie. It's possible that I enjoy what is called minimalist art because the prairie trained me to respond to the smallest shifts of perspective/perception. Yet while this may be true of me, it isnt true of many of the poets I admire who also work their changes with minimal effects. Still, I find the slight shift breathtaking, & a poetry which uses few of the traditional resources of 'poetry' terrifically exciting. To eschew conventional metaphor (not to mention my *bête noire*, the simile) is to push oneself to write true in some freshly limited, freshly minted way [& yes, I know, it isnt possible to eschew metaphor wholly; language is metaphorical, as are the large structures of poetic discourse—the *form of lyrics* is a metaphor, but we cant always be sure of what, which is its great power]. Over the years, then, I have slowly come to a sense of the radical possibilities of a language simplified, stripped of many of its traditional rhetorical forms. Perhaps the nature of the horizon on the prairie affects my perception, for it writes edges, boundaries, & the limitless possible beyond them, hidden (yet moving towards us as we move towards it). The vision of horizon tends to encourage an attitude of looking beyond, over the edge. Cumulus there, accumulative, the potential additions of metonymy. It opens. To mystery, to what comes, breaking, in the heart of the world. Since I love that mystery, I seek, however well or poorly, to engage it in the words & rhythms of my writing. I worry less & less about what it means & care only for how it happens. I began writing poetry in an attempt to say what I saw, the physical landscape I perceived. That landscape has become the languagescape, out of which I write. Perhaps the two are layered sheets of experience, wholly inscribed as I come to them, waiting only to reinscribe themselves in another writing/reading of what is there — on the page, in the next line approaching, a kind of horizon heralding the space where we read the world as the wondrous mystery it is. So now I listen more carefully than ever to the words, as they come, as they seek a shape of being there which cannot be pinned down, a dance of possibilities comprehended only as a dance of possibilities continually in flux.

*

Is an engagement with words an engagement with the body. The body of language. The body of life. How can it not be. Words body themselves in the writing, the speaking of them. Poetry is, for me as writer anyway, an act of rhythm, & it is in that act that the body emerges in action. I am a jazz fan, & I write for rhythms sake. To make the words dance. Across the field of the page, the stage they play upon. But in the ear, listening, too. Free, & easy, sounding, pounding out the rhythms of life as we breathe it. [Still, as bp Nichol's *The Martyrology* says, "love me for my mind as well."]

But all this also points to words opaque presence, their mysterious being, their refusal to be only transparent windows on 'reality.' The words are real; & writers have to deal with them as objects in themselves, wholly attentive to their presence as utter [& uttered] being. But what we therefore (& paradoxically) listen to as we listen to the words is our own being, our bodies rhythms, our own encounters with the real, the 'out there' which we only know insofar as we can name it. Poems are acts of naming.

*

Sound. Sounding. The body of language *heard*—orality *performed*. Body language expressing itself. There are many ways to create sound poetry, ranging from the equivalent of carefully scored classical music to folk blues cries & mumbles. For me (solo, or in Re:Sounding, with Stephen Scobie), it's always a form of improvisational play, vocal play, on a base text which exists simply as pre-text for performance. Textual space I enter to immediately enlarge (upon). Expression transcending words, syntax, etc. An attempt to open language up—even in the pieces which are wholly written out. I/we never do a piece the same way twice: the jazz influence here, for sure. Moving, in the pieces which play further with pure vocal sound, into rhythm, something *like* music, though not exactly music. Performance art takes place in a performing space where poetry, music, drama, etc. meet & join. For me it moves to rhythm, rhythmning, making it swing. Let it go. To make a joyful noise. Sounding.

*

I read fantasy & science fiction, but my poetry seldom attempts to be speculative in the way those genres are. Yet I know that my reading in them has had its effect upon my writing. Some people think of sf & f as paraliteratures (I agree) of little intrinsic value (I disagree), & also find their (often) strange &/or technocratic language antithetical to what they expect of poetry. I don't believe that has to be the case. Some of my favourite tropes come from sf & f, for one thing. For another, I tend to agree with Samuel R. Delany—possibly the most

consistently interesting & demanding contemporary sf & f writer —
when he argues that "the vision (sense of wonder, if you will) that
s-f tries for seems to me very close to the vision of poetry, particularly
poetry as it concerned the nineteenth century Symbolists." Ah: 'vision.'
What do we mean by that term. Or by 'spirit' or 'essence.' I am not
sure, but I feel it when I encounter it, & in poetry I tend to encounter
it in poets who offer me those wonderful words (& they can be any
words at all; it's how they come together that does it) which bespeak
mystery, which stop me cold & hold me, rapt, before them. I have
sometimes found such vision in sf, & I have certainly found it in many
of the poems I most love & admire. And, I have attempted in my play
with language to create patterns of words which might just offer
vision to my readers (& sometimes I have played through sf & f tropes
because they give me that thrill of recognition & cannot be avoided
at that point in the poem: they belong).

*

Of course, its easy enough to say we must be open to language but what
do we mean. It involves trust, I guess, and trying to be open to everything. It means paying attention to words, phrases, speech, everything
in language you encounter, all the possibilities ["that first you listen
/then begin to speak"]. Rather than worry about ideas, I listen for first
lines (& sometimes I have quite happily stolen them from others).
Language generates more language. Writing generates more writing.
Once I find a line, then I try to pay it the closest attention possible,
following its lead, letting it lead me on, deeper into the poem. Of course,
& this is the kicker, the more youve practised this, the harder youve
worked at understanding rhythm, sound patterns, the play of various
tropes, possibilities of form, & all the other aspects of the craft, the better
able you are to let the language speak through you, to let the poem happen. And — the other kicker — what works for me may not work for you.
I believe the attitude of openness is necessary, but it will appear very
differently in different writers. Whatever produces a good poem is right.

And, finally, I cant really analyze it; I try to let it happen, I wait for it, & I hope. I do know that forcing a poem does not work. I have written poems out of ideas, out of particular incidents which seemed like things to write about: they are poor poems at best; non-poems more likely; they do not breathe.

*

In *Seed Catalogue*, a longpoem which is only part of a 'life-lost poem,' Robert Kroetsch quotes Rudy Wiebe in a now-famous statement: "You must lay great black steel lines of fiction, break up that space with huge design and, like the fiction of the Russian steppes, build giant artifact. No song can do that...." Well, not exactly, & certainly not as Wiebe infers 'song' for his purposes. But *Field Notes*, by its very existence, proposes an alternative to Wiebes 'necessary fiction.' That kind of longpoem, which stretches up & out, a high/way grounded at one end only, moving ever onward & outward, over the particularities it bespeaks, provides as interesting & valid a way of engaging & interrogating this vast space we call prairie as any novel can (though of course both forms of writing have their place, & Im grateful for every piece of writing which adds to our 'place/meant' here). And it does so partly by inscribing space itself in the poem, all those absences which write the empty presence of this still not fully imaginatively inhabited place in which we live. But I will go further & say that I believe even 'songs' can do something with prairie space, if only in a kind of choral counterpoint with other 'songs,' both those of other writers & ones own. I am speaking of short poems which, in various ways, display spaces [or silences] in their complex formations, those spaces re/presenting something of the spaces outside which surround us [see, as prime examples, the poems of John Newlove, most especially those paradigms, 'Ride Off Any Horizon' & 'The Double-Headed Snake']. And when, as is often the case, these short poems connect with others so as to make a larger whole [through sequencing or by serialization], then a book emerges which, like the longpoem, inscribes aspects of the vast which surrounds us as well as any fiction can.

*

Most of my books are precisely *books*, conceived as something more than just a collection of independent lyrics. On the whole I tend to write either longish poems or poems-in-a-group, something which will make a book-length whole that can be read as such. Im not sure when I began thinking in terms of the poem as book, but I recognize the influence of so many major 20th century poets who went for the long poem in one form or another, & especially bp Nichol, who has always argued the holistic concept of the life work as one poem. I tended to work in smaller forms but I wanted to incorporate them in larger ones, & somehow began to do so without really theorizing about it at the beginning. More recently, I have become much more conscious of taking this direction in my work, & have seen the possibilities that the conception of the book holds out as one more way to avoid the [to me] negative (egotistic) connotations of the traditional lyric. One way to evade the ego-demands of lyric is to create a system in which a series of lyrics comment on each other & offer the possibility of voices rather than simple voice: to play through the serial poem or the sequence, where the voice speaking is not simply ones own. Another way is to seek intertextual voices to interact with ones own, sometimes partly there in counterpoint, sometimes as utter pre-text for the new poem ('homolinguistic translation' is an example of the latter). I like the idea that it is the poem, with any number of possible voices, which is speaking rather than just me. And Ive found that the more I pay attention to the language, the more what the poem says is not simply some 'thought' 'I' had turned to verse. At least, it seems that way.

*

Of course, in the end, one can only say what Robert Creeley once said: "I am *given* to write poems." I write what I find I *have* to say. As I explore the particulars of each poem as it is given to me, as I follow the line of language leading me on, into the poem as a field of possibilities, as process itself—the world of language is *at least* as Heraclitean as the world of sense—I hope to discover possibilities of speech (heard, overheard, heard again) I didnt even know I knew. Ursula K. LeGuin presents a non-religious religion in *The Left Hand of Darkness*: it has only one prayer/non-prayer: "Praise then Creation unfinished!" I can think of no better statement of the deeper meaning of open form. One of the major arguments of such a poetry discovered & heard in openness is the value of such human openness before the world as well as the word. In an open-ended world, then, the open-ended poem. Offered, as always to *you*.

Robert Creeley, "'I'm given to write poems,'" *A Quick Graph* (San Francisco: Four Seasons Foundation, 1970).

Frank Davey, 'The Language of the Contemporary Canadian Long Poem,' *Surviving the Paraphrase* (Winnipeg: Turnstone Press, 1983).

Frank Davey & bp Nichol, 'The Prosody of Open Verse' *(Open Letter*, 5:2 [Spring 1982]), 5-13.

Samuel R. Delany, 'About 5,750 Words,' *The Jewel-Hinged Jaw* (Elizabethtown, NY: Dragon Press, 1977).

Robert Kroetsch, 'The Continuing Poem,' & 'For Play and Entrance: The Contemporary Canadian Long Poem,' *Essays (Open Letter*, 5:4 [Spring 1983]), 81-82, 91-110.

Denise Levertov, 'On the Function of the Line,' *Light Up the Cave* (New York: New Directions, 1981).

Daphne Marlatt & George Bowering, 'Given This Body' *(Open Letter*, 4:3 [Spring 1979]), 32-88.

Ezra Pound, 'How to Read,' *Talking* (Montreal: Quadrant Editions, 1982).

Phyllis Webb, with Douglas Barbour & Stephen Scobie, 'Talking the Line' *(Writing*. 4 [Winter 1981-2]), 22-25.

And the poems, the poems, the poems, by these & others, where the deep truths of personal poetics lie.

From the Bottom of the Lake

Sandra Birdsell

When I was enrolled in Robert Kroetsch's Creative Writing class at the University of Manitoba (I think this must have been 1976 or so), I was still casting about, searching for that "thing," my thing, or what I would write about in the years to come. At that time I had written about fifteen short stories which came out of interesting ideas, or anecdotes. And they all seemed so contrived to me and wooden. But one very short story, which I submitted to gain acceptance into Robert's class, came a little closer to the bone. This story would later become the base material from which the stories in *Night Travellers* and *Ladies of the House* evolved. It was a story of dislocation, of isolation: a young girl cut off from her family during a time of grieving. I was surprised and very pleased when I was accepted into this course and then amazed and a bit frightened when Robert Kroetsch called and asked if it would be all right to use the story in the first class. When the students discussed it, they were asked the question: what writer does this story remind you of? Someone said, Margaret Laurence.

I scrambled to read Laurence and in the process discovered other Canadian authors, including a small collection of stories, Gabrielle Roy's *The Road Past Altamont*. I read *Seed Catalogue* at the same time. When I read *A Jest of God*, *The Road Past Altamont*, and especially *Seed Catalogue*, it was a kind of spiritual experience for me. Most moving. I had made touch, I suppose, with what was inside me. My origins, my people. (I can recall reading *Anne of Green Gables* in school, but Prince Edward Island was really another world away.) I must admit that the discovery of *A Jest of God*, and of these stories, the recognition of place and the people, gave me courage and made me realize that I could write out of my place as well.

About this time, I was sitting out on the patio one summer day, reading. A man walked into my back yard. A friend, a neighbour. We talked. I confessed my skeleton. I wanted to write. He was a Book Store Man by profession. Knew all about books. And he said, "What makes you think you have anything to say? You haven't travelled, had adventures. You've been a housewife for eighteen years." Well, I was glad that I had read those pieces by Margaret Laurence and Gabrielle Roy. I was glad, because his comment touched a personal fear. But the works of those people supported me and gave me a hard kernel of belief that I could and would write about my place, my people, and that it was important to do that.

So it was a great liberation for me when I realized that it was possible for me to write out of the prairies, about small-town people, and for that writing to have a universal appeal. This has proven to be true for me as I constantly meet people from different provinces who know that I have written about them, about their place, their communities.

I have always wanted to tell a story about a family, since about the age of twelve. It's probably because I come from a very large one. Family has always been important to me and still is. There's much drama in a large family! Everything that happens in the world, happens in a family. What struck me was the stories we'd tell at family gatherings, at Christmas, or Easter, on Mother's Day, or Mother's birthday. It seems all our gatherings centred around our mother. But what struck me

was that someone would begin to tell a story about a particular inci-
dent and someone else would jump in with their version of it, and then
a third and fourth version. And all the tellers had their own perceptions, their own reasons for telling or shaping the story the way they
told it. And so that's why I wrote *Night Travellers* the way I did.

I must confess that when I was putting *Night Travellers* together
I didn't realize that there was any kind of historical precedence for
"linked stories." I hadn't read any. I hadn't read *Lives of Girls and
Women*. It was later that I became hooked on Alice Munro. I think at
that time I was reading *Short Story Masterpieces*, and authors such as
Sherwood Anderson, Katherine Mansfield, Faulkner, and Eudora
Welty. The structure of *Night Travellers* came out of a growing sense
of frustration with what I perceived to be the restrictiveness of the
short-story form. It seemed to me too neat, too compartmentalized
and unrealistic to capture and contain a character as you see happening
on television every day in thirty or sixty minutes. You almost had to
impose some kind of resolution on a character, just to end the story.
When I came to the end of a story written that way, I'd find myself
saying, "yes, but." I kept seeing that same character later on in life. The
character didn't want a sixty or thirty minute treatment. And so I kept
bringing the same characters back into new stories, because I wanted
to see them again, working with new problems, at different stages in
their lives. I was saying to them, I guess, so you think you've found the
solution, eh? What about this situation? What about when you become
less idealistic and must compromise? And why invent new characters
to do that?

When I began writing *Ladies of the House*, the same working
method applied. I wrote one story, which led to another and another
and I couldn't send them out to magazines because I needed them
around me, to remind me how these characters were not finished, but
still had something to say or learn further down the road. I still
feel that you just can't tell the whole story in one story. Or that the
"whole story" can ever be told. I don't write stories which are complete
in themselves and which I can send out. There are a few exceptions.

No, the one I've finished leads into the third one or the sixth one, and so I don't want to part with them because I know they don't often make a lot of sense without the resonance of what came before and after. I once referred to them as "beads on a string completing a whole necklace."

I'm usually not at all happy with the endings of my stories. If I could go back, I'd like to take the scissors to them and cut the last three or four sentences off most of my stories. I still haven't been able to trust the reader totally and often I tack on things to make certain that they haven't missed the point. I regret that now, but doubt that it will change. There's a strong temptation, because you work so hard on the story, you know, and you think it would be a shame if the point was missed and so you tell the story and then you tell them what the story was about in the end. I don't really know when the ending is right. I rework endings to death. Once I wrote a story, "Judgement," in fact, and I read that story on three different occasions. Before I read it, I would rewrite the ending! I have a St. John's College ending, a Book Store ending, and another which I forget. But after a year or so, the ending presented itself to me and while I still don't think it's the "right" ending, it was the most acceptable one for me at the time of publication. When I read that story now, I think it works. But I think my ambivalence for endings comes from my ambivalence with the form. I feel as though I'm imposing something on the story just to end it. In fact, the one novel I've written just falls apart at the end, the last ten pages or so. Sometimes, in the end, it doesn't make much difference whether the character lives or dies, survives or gives up. They could do either and it wouldn't change the story much. I suppose I'm more interested in the process than the conclusion.

In both collections of stories, I think that Lureen is the character who best reflects the typical Manitoban person who is born of multiple cultures. We have such identifiable pockets of cultural communities here. At least when I was growing up this was so. And when you are part of many, you walk around looking to see where you fit in. And historically too, you look at the place where you've grown up and wonder what influences it has had on your subconscious.

Being told when very young that I lived at the bottom of ancient Lake Agassiz had a great influence on me. Because I lived beside the Red River which flooded the town and my own home frequently, I began to wonder whether that lake was going to come back. And then, I also was aware that people from my father's family had always been here, probably coming down into the Grasslands once that great lake receded. And I was aware of my mother's origins, in Holland, then Germany and finally Russia. Both my parents told us stories. My mother's were stories of suffering, life and death kinds of stories. My father's stories were often tales of trickery, or Red River carts and Louis Riel. He told stories about magic and medicine.

In *Night Travellers*, I write the rural story. In *Ladies*, most of the stories are set in a city. I found the city stories particularly difficult to write because there seemed to be a paucity of images, such sharp corners, and a starkness. I think that's because the city was new to me. That it's easier to write about a place from a distance. One can make magic out of a place if you have the luxury of distance and time. The retelling of the story becomes coloured. But I think, for me, the rural story has more appeal because of the green spaces, the accessibility of our rivers, the uncluttered sky. I don't really want to move to the city, but I'm afraid that's where the stories are now. And the characters are isolated, and have a feeling of dislocation. They are trying to get in touch with the values, the family thing of small communities, but are still glad to have the freedom that anonymity affords in the city. And yet they long for that close family thing. In the last story, in *Ladies*, Dee,the grandchild of Mika, stands and listens. And I thought at the time that perhaps Dee would go to the country and live there. But I'm not certain of that yet.

I said that I still have a strong sense and feeling for family and I do. But the family is under much stress and strain right now. Usually, in the traditional family, someone must give too much. And usually, it's the woman. And often to the detriment of her own development as a human being. My women believe there is safety in the familiar and the known even though that may be restricting. But it's real, tangible, what they can deal with. It is safer to hide behind a role, for the sake of security and family. Sometimes I would like to think that these are noble people who give their lives to serve others, and sometimes I think they are frightened people, afraid of the unknown and afraid to take a chance.

The Process: I usually begin a story with a character in mind. I seldom begin with story. When I do, I'm sometimes presented with problems. How to impose that story on a person who in the end may not want to be in that story. So, people are the thing for me. Sometimes I walk around with a person in my head for a long time and then suddenly I get a line of dialogue in that character's voice and then the story will just rip off by itself. Sometimes I fiddle around for a long time, searching for the voice. Usually that means that I've begun to write too soon and haven't got a complete picture or feeling of character yet. When I choose the point of view, it usually has to do with the voice of the character. If it's a flamboyant, cheeky character, then they usually want to tell the story in their own voice. If a character is a contemplative type, or hides behind words, then usually I will write in third person. I love that cheeky, rollicking voice, but first-person viewpoint does have its limitations. But when it presents itself to me, I feel as though I'm blest and let it rip. And usually these are the best stories.

I'm a lazy writer. And I would love to tell my stories like Rodin's statue, "The Thinker." Have my character sitting there, motionless, thinking deep thoughts. But, unfortunately, a writer has to move people around, put them into a setting, make them speak and meet other people, and this is hard work. It's so much easier to write great long paragraphs of deep inner thoughts and so difficult to make the character speak and move about. But this is fiction. This is drama. I often think about going to a play and sitting in the audience and waiting for the play to begin. A man comes out and stands in front of the curtain for two hours, and this man tells us what happens in the play, what the characters are thinking. And never once do I get to see them play the story. I would kill anyone who did that. Or at least become irritated.

To tell the story instead of letting the story tell itself is much easier, I'm sure, but not as satisfying. It's very tempting to avoid the "nuts and bolts" of writing.

The blank page is a fearful thing. My friends know me well. They know when I'm confronting that blank page, better than I do. They say, "Oh Sandra, you're into a new work, I can tell." I can't tell, except that I'm extremely sleepy all the time and pacing and full of pent-up anxiety. I only know that when I'm into the third or fourth page of a new work I'm laughing and skipping about, happy and full of so much energy that people wonder if I've been on a vacation and rested, because I look younger and happier. This is usually when I'm working the hardest. When I have too much time, long stretches without a new work, then I'm haggard, feel bad and guilty. That blank page is a scary thing. I think most writers must be very religious people. Because writing is a supreme act of faith. You fear that you will be empty. That the words won't come. Sometimes I pray before I confront that blank page. There are oodles of things we do to avoid the page. But after you've done them all, you just have to sit down and do it. Two weeks later, you may have three pages, but the mind has been scuttling about the possibilities and so when the three pages are set and firm, you already know what's going to happen in the next twenty or so. And there is immense relief, that the story is there. That you've been able to do it once again.

Some Principles of Line Breaks

Dennis Cooley

In the absence of metre you can break a line in several ways.

1. grammatical unit

This is probably the simplest and the most common principle. It readily suggests itself since it is already in place as a unit for other forms of discourse, especially the prose we are accustomed to reading. And writing. It seems so "natural," being so common. This is probably also the most popular line with readers since it asks the least of them: if we can't have metre, at least we've got grammar. Here the line boundary equals the syntactic boundary, and we get limited uncertainty at lines' end. You can see it in, say, much of Al Purdy:

> this is the moment you'll always remember
> this is the wind-blown instant of time
> that swings you into the future
> oh heavy as the heavy cellar stones of the world
> but hammering on the gates of the sun[1]

2. the bardic or oracular line

Built on chant or incantation or, more modestly, on listing, stock-piling or cataloguing, the line leans heavily on repetition. It works largely by accretion, returning again and again to a base. Hence its essential anaphoric quality—emphatic parallels in sounds or grammatical units. Whitman pushes in here:

> Voyaging to every port to dicker and adventure,
> Hurrying with the modern crowd as eager and fickle as any,
> Hot toward one I hate, ready in my madness to knife him,
> Solitary at midnight in my back yard, my thoughts gone from me a
> > long while,
> Walking the old hills of Judaea with the beautiful gentle God by
> > my side,
> Seeking through space, speeding through heaven and the stars,
> Speeding amid the seven satellites and the broad ring, and the
> > diameter of eighty thousand miles,
> Speeding with tail'd meteors, throwing fire-balls like the rest,
> Carrying the crescent child that carries its own full mother
> > in its belly,
> Storming, enjoying, planning, loving, cautioning,
> Backing and filling, appearing and disappearing,
> I tread day and night such roads.[2]

A line that thrusts forward, almost unstoppably, that builds not off nuance or hesitation, but off exuberance, adding on, turning on its heady fervour. Again, you will notice how the boundaries of the lines exactly coincide with the boundaries of syntax. This model is not going to cause any great problems for modern readers, either. True, some of them might still find Whitman a bit rough, but no one is going to find these linings strange or impermissible. And why should they? They've got the sanction of the Bible behind them, and the reassurance that they are not left up in the air as the line ends. There's that comfort of having things tucked in as you come to the juncture, not having to face any great insecurity.

3. Ogden Nashing

There are other versions of this sort of thing, but you all know Nash: the crazy distribution of (often polysyllabic and absurd) rhymes at the ends of long rambling lines that are 'prosaic' in their rhythms. The nashing of teeth. I take his practice to be representative of related twists to the traditional line.

4. Marianne Mooring

Again, there can be many other versions of this strategy, but Moore has made her lines famous. She counts out lines by syllable, each line of a stanza having its own count, which is then repeated in subsequent stanzas. Each of these lines becomes part of an intricate end-rhyme. But neither the lengths of the lines nor the pattern of rhyme exists prior to the poem itself. Moore finds a pattern for each of her poems. The effect, as she writes, is like pulling a snake through a maze—the sentence sinuously threads its way through the stanza.

5. physical limits

This, too, enjoys a reasonable acceptance among poets and readers. I'm thinking here not simply of butting up against the typewriter bell or the furthest reaches of the right margin, of stopping before you fall in the gutter. I may be wrongly inserting some psychological principle, but I'm also thinking of poets who will simply stop at some edge that is not defined by the printed page but possibly by some sense of not transgressing an invisible vertical. Eli Mandel seems to do this in his latest books.

6. arbitrariness

This may at first appear to be no principle at all, but clearly it is. If I choose to write out of randomness—and I may do so for several reasons—I have the basis for an erratic line. Not one that will please everyone, of course not. But one that can generate some nimble reading. The reader can't nod over the page, confident in the linings, in any simple correspondence between the limits of the line and the limits of meaning. The lines will constantly shift under your eyes, not let them come to rest, come to an expected conclusion. Margaret Atwood uses something like this principle a fair bit in her early poetry—setting up brittle irregular lines to reveal all those anxious figures who step warily through the poem. As if afraid of making one false move. Tense, Atwood's lines. Snapping off like twigs, so jagged they can stab you.

7. freeing up parts of speech

You can see the nervousness in these lines as the grammatical units separate out and are distributed over the lines, breaking the containment of the single line. Working at cross purposes, purposing cross moments. You will have noticed how stretching across lines (stretch marks) throws loose some words at the ends of lines where they lie, speak in forked tongues. Doubling, dealing in duplicity. Words attaching, detaching, reattaching themselves in various configurations. As a word points back to the line it completes or forward to the line it anticipates, a hanging at the end it leaves you hanging, way out on a limb, it does double duty: a noun in this line, then by god an adjective in the next. Here intransitive, there a transitive. e-i-e-i-O. You don't hurry over the lines, insisting on one grammar that obliterates all others. It's not monogamy we're into—it's infidelity, fooling around, promiscuity all over the place. A mad series of erotic attachments and reattachments. I've grown attached to you. In so many ways. Perverse. Polymorphous/ (there's more for us) perverse. We trace several paths through the lines, *one* of them defined by its own intact standing— *this* line, entirely by itself. Self-possessed, that too. So language begins to slide, meanings to proliferate and to undermine themselves. Lines that meander & refuse to be pinned down by one grammar or one meaning. A grammatical doubling.

8. syntactical ambiguity

This case might be considered a larger or more extended version of #4. Whole phrases, even whole lines, can serve to complete *and* to open a unit.

$$\text{like a dog}$$

you lope off

with it

my love

a chewed T-bone

in yr jaw

Where does that "my love" fit in the sentence? Appositive to "it": with it, that is, with my love in your jaw? As apostrophe: you, my love, run off with it first chance you get? As opening of a new 'sentence': You lope off with it; my love is a chewed T-bone? You see how it goes.

It's evident that the line is freed up for overtime because none of the lines is conventionally punctuated. The insertion of such markers would force us onto a more determined trajectory. This is most obviously and irrevocably true in the case of terminal punctuation but it also holds for internal punctuation. Both practices would hive out and insist on the integrity of each designated unit of syntax.

9. "false" or premature closure on buried idioms

yet id be

short with you then short

bread shouting

luv me luv me

i can make you

feel good inside

A variation on the power of idiom to alter our parabolas—the idiom that sets its expectations. And then the betrayal:

does this mean

i am not

a loaf of bread

large with love

                    the eyes big & liquid with it
                                    me gassing up for
                a shy brunette for
            man cannot live on
            alone

When the line edges coincide with expressions that seem to stop at those same boundaries, the subsequent discovery, after that first falling into place, is unusually capricious.

10. word play
    If you're gonna divvy up grammatical units like that, why not words themselves? Chip off a syllable or two and let the pieces fall. Lay the pieces apart, carry a piece way over to the next line and see what happens.

                        yup
                    getting up
                pity

                    making
                        just bare
                    ly mak
                            ing
            it
                                (up)

This kind of poetry can get pretty uppity all right. Atwood, who gets a loghouse and a houseboat simultaneously by cracking the words across the lines:

    If he had known unstructured
    space is a deluge
    and stocked his log house-
    boat with all the animals[3]

A lot can be done when that right margin becomes more than a physical barrier or a place to rest. Wit for one thing. To wit (to woo):

                            such making
            believe
                                making it
                up
                            yup
                        making it up
                            im making it
                up
                        all right
                        its hard
                            making
                it up
                                up &
                making
                        it
                            making
                                up

Wit as it sits in syntax works in metonymies & away from the
metaphor we've come to prize. Those little jags at the end, gags, they
sometimes set you up—drop false clues along the trail. Aha, this is it.
But the path turns, re/turns in verses/versus—betrays us to new com-
pletions, awareness of false closures, the inadequacies of single-minded
readings. Second takes. Takes a second. Take a chance. Beware of the
buried idiom, the 'complete' syntax, certain to go off on the curious,
the unwary/unweary. The short line that can tip you/through dizzy
openings & closings, off quick takes,) trip you/up) lures, springs. Exits
& entrances. We stand (I can hardly stand it) en/tranced/at the
entrance. Quite a line-up. Where do we enter? I can tell you where to
get off. Get on with it.

11. breath units

Time to catch your breath. I've held onto this one for awhile because by now almost everyone's heard of it. Some think this is what line breaks *are* (and they *are* for one school). And, like it or not, these units can be done. Have been. Has been among lines by now. We all know the argument as it originated, largely with Charles Olson, and that it means stopping a line where the poet would stop for a breath, presumably when speaking (I'm not sure the manifesto is precise on this point).[4] Contrary to common prejudices, the practice can take you in a lot of directions, since each poet will tromp a different path through the words, depending on the moment/the movement and the poet's whole make-up of sounding/taking soundings.

12. tentativeness

The American poet, Robert Duncan, describes how William Carlos Williams came across the revolutionary phrasing of his 1920s poetry.[5] Counting out his lines to ensure he got ten syllables as some semblance of iambic pentameter, be damned if he didn't find many lines ending at odd places. Sure, there were many nouns and verbs — traditionally thought to be the proper parts of speech to announce the line is finished ("strong" endings they were called. Still are, so far as I know). But what Williams was finding, often as not, were pronouns, articles, conjunctions, prepositions: all the wrong words, which could be heeled back into the line only by restructuring the syntax. What Williams discovered — the telling juncture — took him in new ways. The line, suspended on those grammatical openings, became an amazing thing, offering all sorts of possibilities never before available. No longer a neat tucking in, it became an opening out. Less assured, this new line would not fold in, like a mother putting a kid to sleep for the night. Now it would declare itself in all its uncertainty. A new aesthetic: not fluency but clumsiness — an awkward turning/on frozen feet. Clumsy, if need be, clumsy as all get out. As if for the first time. *What's the matter with you?* my uncle said. *Cat got your tongue?* "Stutter," from the same base as "study" — to pay attention. Ear tuned to a new music. It would register a mind in motion, suspicious of glibness or smoothing things over. Working the edges, putting us on/ edge. The syntactical unit, opened, would hover over its moment, waiting on its yet unknown fulfillment: nervous/nervy. Ondaatje: a blind lover, doesn't know what he likes till he writes it out. Sends it out, casting a line into the stream. You don't know what the outcome will be, how it will all come out. Or at least you create that effect.[6] (The distinction is not so crucial as sceptics may suppose. Certainly not if, as I am doing, you weight the conventions not to the moment of composing — always a dubious enterprise since that moment can never be available to anyone but the poet, if even her — but to the moment of reading.)

Doug Barbour:

> under   moon
>
> earth turns
> blue & green &
>
> terribly true
> to where its been
>
> & we turn too /
>   we do
>
> turn under its light
> white in the cold
>
> or warm night we hold
> on to / here
>
> where   planet
> still breathes in
>
> its orbit   still
> breathes[7]

The stanzas here become an active part of the punctuation. There is the apparent closure of "still breathes in" (the planet drawing in its breath), and then — its breathing in orbit.

13. speech models

This line works with greater speed. Draws on narrative, idiom, anecdote, repetition more than #12 does or can. Think of the breezy, almost smart-ass form it takes in writers like George Bowering and Robert Kroetsch, you'll see what I mean. Check Anthony Easthope on the hegemony of iambic pentameter in the English tradition. He argues it is historically constituted in the Renaissance at the expense of an earlier accentual tradition. By promoting syllables between accented syllables, and by spacing them out fairly evenly, iambic pentameter helped to entrench the " 'Received Pronunciation' of Standard [British] English....It does so because it legislates for the number of syllables in the line and therefore cancels elision, making transition at word junctures difficult."[8] It eliminates from 'serious' literature, other than for comic purposes, the radically elided voices of working people. Quickly elevated to ruling status, blank verse delivered a canon that

> asks for a clipped, precise and fastidious elocution. Such pro-
> nunciation — one thinks of Laurence Olivier — signals 'proper'
> speech; that is, a class dialect. Pentameter aims to preclude
> shouting and 'improper' excitement; it enhances the poise of a
> moderate yet uplifted tone of voice, an individual voice self-
> possessed, self-controlled, impersonally self-expressive.[9]

The argument, which Easthope works out exquisitely, is compelling. Once established, blank verse

> becomes a sign which includes and excludes, sanctions and
> denigrates, for it discriminates the 'properly' poetic from the
> 'improperly' poetic, Poetry from verse. In an unbroken continuity
> from the Renaissance to 1900 and beyond, a poem within the

metrical tradition identifies itself (in Puttenham's words) with
polish and reformed manners as against poetry in another metre
which can be characterized as rude, homely, and in the modern
sense, vulgar.[10]

Much the same can be said for other elegant and privileged
phrasings, the anapest in particular. Pick up the argument on our end
of history, in our place, and you've got big trouble. Fluent phrasings
of whatever kind silence a more radical vernacular. Combine eloquence
with the cache of metaphor (they stick together, in the privileged line,
like expatriate English), and you leave no room for other forms or the
other realities they carry. All forms are historical, all are ideological
—produce certain possibilities, shut down others. All you have to do
to see how crucial these things are is imagine Al Purdy's experiences in
iambic pentameter. Can't be done.

And so we write off speech models. And the line-ends give first
that dramatic hesitation and, then, the *bam!*—hitting the next word,
like bumpers when you're pushing a car, when you run into the following line:

> you can give the
> whole damn thing away
>   far   's
> im concerned

It's *WHOLE* and *im*, the stress doubly registered by the pauses after
"the" and, less emphatically, after " 's."

A note: the rhapsodic line is not based on speech models, generally generates a longer line, bound & determined to observe its
analogs, to return, spellbound, to home base. Anaphoric.

14. as a separate unit of meaning

This condition is, for the time being, I think the least appreciated,
at least among readers. The old convention of enjambement, which

partly countered the convention of the line as a self-sustained metric unit, still tells us to push on, with little pause, for meaning: this next line completes what I now am in. That convention of reading leads us to blunder over contemporary lines, however troublingly set, as if they too were defined only as parts of grammatical units that subsume them. But if we are willing to entertain the line as a unit of meaning in its own right, *quite apart from whatever words precede or follow it*, we are on to some new effects. Try reading the second line in this as an intact unit of meaning:

> am a lantern   feeding on
>   what lies below me

Forsaking all others, the line begins to offer itself in new ways, not simply as a noun clause answering to the preposition "on." It also speaks, declaratively, of discovery: "What lies below me!" I have found, where "lies" operates not as verb but noun.

The new conventions offer subversions of more determined readings. They can even leave us in states of contradiction—the syntax as it strings through the lines saying one thing, the individual lines something else. Make up an example: "I am certain I will never know." Now divide the one (yes, you've got it) after "certain":

> I am certain
> I will never know

We can even describe the grammatical condition that obtains. The removal of the subordinate conjunction "that" and the insertion of a negative into one of the lines, so one line asserts, the other denies. Working in uncertainties, refusals to nail things down.

15. visual effect

Recognizing that *printed* poems come to us only in a visual medium, some poets have played with that. Not just for semantic or phonic effect (though these concerns can be closely connected). To let

the eye enter, wander, enjoy the shapes, the clean empty spaces. To let
the sprinklings & the saturations take shape. Loopings & threadings.
line [ME. *line*, merging OE. *line*, a cord, with OFr. *ligne* (both ɩ L *linea*,
lit., linen thread, n. use of fem. of *lineus*, of flax ɩ *linum*, flax)]

               inklings
       come what may

    In its most radical application the poem becomes graphic art. But
in this argument I'm still thinking of poems that use words and that
observe, however sub/versely, some form of syntax and sematics.

             zodiac

                       tarnish of night
       sky
                     dip
      into the   tank

                             of dark
                                  ness

              emerge:
                       :   clean
                as silver
     jewelry   :
                    dripping cold
                                  as memories
                    your memories
        :
             of me

The principle is fairly simple: the further the eye must travel, or the more stressfully it must move, from one word to the next, the greater the silence. The holes are silent, measures of waiting. Wanting? White holes in space (watch out watchout, you might fall/ in), emitting. Admitting. Listen to them. "Blank space surrounding a word, typographical adjustments, and spatial composition in the page setting of the poetic text—all contribute to create a halo of indefiniteness and to make the next text pregnant with infinite suggestive possibilities."[11]

In seeing the poem as a configuration, through whose trajectories our eyes flick, we engage in language as visually presented, as writing which, following Jacques Derrida, we might oppose to speaking. Writing *on* the page, exists as its *own* transaction, not as some storage system for 'real' language previous to the writing, even if only "discrepant by the time of a breath."[12] Writing enjoys its own conventions, enjoins us to them.

16. lines that defy left-to-right, top-to-bottom reading

The transaction here is to put into question, even more drastically, our presuppositions about how we negotiate our way through a text. To insist on the materiality of language, to foreground the very means by which we constitute a language event.

                    Death
                                    is it
            dark
            is it   black
                                    is it
            black   is it
                                    dark
            is it   dark?[13]

Where do you start? Where do you end? Maybe if he hadn't put that question mark in there. If only he hadn't. But you get the point.

1. Excerpt from "What It Was —," in *20th-Century Poetry & Poetics*, 2nd ed., ed. Gary Geddes (Toronto: Oxford, 1973), 204.

2. Excerpt from *Leaves of Grass*, in *Complete Poetry and Selected Prose by Walt Whitman*, ed. James E. Miller, Jr. (Cambridge, Mass.: Riverside, 1959), 50.

3. Excerpt from "Progressive insanities of a pioneer," in her *The Animals in That Country* (Toronto: Oxford, 1968), 38.

4. The article, "Projective Verse," has appeared in many books, including his own *Selected Writings*, ed. Robert Creeley (New York: New Directions, 1966), 15-26. The piece originally appeared in 1950.

5. "A Critical Difference of View," *Stony Brook* ¾ (1969), 362. The piece (360-3) is a brilliant statement on the Williams-Pound tradition.

6. Paul Fussell, in his *Poetic Meter & Poetic Form*, revised ed (New York: Random House, 1971), 8, has written to the point:

> if constant enjambement takes place — that is, if the sense and syntax of one line run on into the next so that a hearer would have trouble ascertaining the line breaks — we have a very different kind of free verse, a kind we can designate as meditative and ruminative or private. It is this kind of vigorously enjambed free verse which has become a common style in the last twenty years or so as a vehicle for themes that are sly or shy, or uncertain, or quietly ironic, or furtive.

7. From "Moonwalks," in *Draft: An Anthology of Prairie Poetry*, ed. Dennis Cooley (Winnipeg/Toronto: Turnstone/ECW, 1981), 29-30. Barbour has a gorgeous set of moon poems that work off an adept line: *Songbook* (Vancouver: Talonbooks, 1973).

8. *Poetry as Discourse* (London: Methuen, 1983), 68.

9. *Poetry as Discourse*, 69.

10. *Poetry as Discourse*, 65.

11. Umberto Eco, *The Role of the Reader: Explorations in the Semiotics of Texts* (Bloomington: Indiana U.P., 1984), 53. The quotation comes from a useful article called "The Poetics of the Open Work," which is well worth reading in its entirety (47-66).

12. *Of Grammatology*, trans. Gayatri Chakravorty Spivak (Baltimore: Johns Hopkins, 1974), 18. Derrida insists in this book that writing is based on spacing.

13. In W.W.E. Ross, *Experiment 1923-29: Poems by W.W.E. Ross* (Toronto: Contact, 1956), 17. Ross is my nomination for the most underrated poet in the history of Canadian poetry. Interesting that date of publication, 30 years after the poems were written.

Searching for the Poem

Lorna Crozier

Where the poems come from, where they're going. Poems, when they happen, are magic and staring too hard at magic will make it go away. You may discover it's all a trick with mirrors, but then Calvino says a series of mirrors can multiply an object to infinity and reflect its essence in a single image that contains the whole of everything. I want the poem to do that, not reflect nature but contain it and everything else that exists, is dreamed or imagined.

*

Mandel writes about Houdini, MacEwan about the escape artist Manzini. I sit in my living room and look at the wall-hanging above the couch, think about the way the weaver broke the border in the lower corner so the spirit could escape. It's a subtle change in the pattern and easy to miss like the opening in the poem where the poet slips away.

*

Auden said poetry is a search for form. I used to carry that line around in my head a lot. It seemed to sum up what I had to say about the process of writing. But does it any more? Every poem looks for wholeness and integrity of the line, but it's also searching for something else. Maybe Baudelaire's universal analogy, maybe a state of grace, maybe something as simple as a memory you didn't know you had, a blood memory, Rilke called it, something you've known and forgotten and glimpsed again because it decides to let you see it.

*

Patrick reads the galleys of my new manuscript, says, you love the word *white*, did you know that? No, but there it is: white rushes, the senses like five white cups, white gardens, the white between words, between breath and breath

*

Is the poem searching for the one behind it, the poem you're not ready for, the one that's writing you?

*

An old rancher I once knew said you see animals in the bush because of their eyes, not yours. It's their gaze fixed on you that draws you to them. What you have to learn is how to let yourself feel that, then you'll find what you're looking for. *Magic Animals.*

*

Ondaatje says he's trying not to write about dogs any more. There are too many dogs with promiscuous tongues licking their way through his poems. I must avoid the word *white* and birds, especially white birds that make no sound.

*

If a poem could walk, it would have paws, not feet. Or hooves, small ones, leaving half moons in the sand. Something to make you stop and wonder what kind of animal this is, where it came from, where it's going.

*

MacEwan says, "Its name is the name you have buried in your blood."
Crazy Jake. Ona Moen. Shorty Turnbull. Emerson Crozier. I was born
in Swift Current, Saskatchewan. The highway sign at the crossroads
said *Medicine Hat, Saskatoon, Moose Jaw*. In every direction I could
go was a name I loved the sound of.

*

On the windowsill of my office, a postcard Patrick sent three years ago
from China. A man tattoos a woman's face on her pale back. She is
watching him in a lacquered mirror. When I turn the card over to read
the words, they have faded, the ink eaten by the sun. But if I look
closely, I can see the imprint of the pen on paper. I run my fingers over
the intaglio of missing letters, reading from memory, from touch,
touching white. Somewhere there's a poem here. Looking out.

*

The Muse that is the Mother of Memory

First memory—how clearly I recall it. Going down the wooden steps
into the dirt cellar (was I four?) to get a jar of pickles. A dark and
frightening place, always damp, alkali growing through the walls like
a poisonous mould. My hand reaching up for the jar when suddenly
on the earth floor, a lizard. I run upstairs and down she comes, Mother,
me close behind, a butcher knife in her hand. She steps on the lizard's
tail and stabs it in the back, opens the furnace door and throws it in.

But Lorna, Patrick says, it wouldn't have been a lizard in Saskatchewan.
More like a salamander. Remember you were four and it would've
looked big to you. Your memory's playing tricks.

How I argued for memory, that green body writhing on the knife, my
mother's strong hands, the flames from the coal licking the furnace door
as she opened it, slammed it shut. A lizard. At least a foot long.

*

Phone your mother, Patrick says. Ask her how big it was.

*

My mother says, What are you talking about? I never would've done that.

*

Blood memory. The muse that is memory. Blood on my mother's hands. Does the first memory shape the poems that come in a lifetime the way the first dream shapes a life? One of Jung's patients remembered hers—a dream of sunshine, of floating in water, everything warm except for one cold spot on her belly. Forty years later, she pushed the muzzle of a gun into the flesh just below her navel and fired, the dream unravelling from that dark hole.

*

In Montreal I meet a poet who says writing is an escape from the mother. She is trying to write poems in English because her mother's language is French. No, I tell her, writing is not an escape. It's a return, a going back to the first words, the round vowels of breast and belly, the mothering/mother tongue.

*

You must have been dreaming, my mother says.

*

Patrick says, You're beginning to sound more and more like your mother every day.

Why does this bother me so much?

*

Another memory: the world is white and cold (white, again). Saskatchewan. Walking with my mother, the snow crackling under our boots, the cold, cold air. She opens her coat and pulls me to her, then buttons it again. My back pressed into the front of her, my feet between hers, we walk home like this, leaving the tracks of a strange four-footed animal in the snow.

> Father is gone again,
> the streets empty.
> Everyone is inside,
> listening to radios
> in the warm glow of their stoves.
>
> The cold cries under our boots.
> We wade through wind. It pushes
> snow under my scarf and collar,
> up the sleeves of my jacket.
>
> Mother opens her old muskrat coat,
> pulls me inside.
> Her scent wraps around me.
> The back of my head presses
> into the warm rise of her belly.
>
> When I lower my eyes, I see
> our feet, mine inside hers,
> the tracks of one animal
> crossing the open,
> strange and nocturnal,
> moving towards home.

Maybe this happened; perhaps it didn't. The tricks of memory, but memory itself is not a trickster.

*

It is the animal we know is there but cannot see. The lost limb the body remembers, reliving its love of sun and movement, its itch in a spot long gone. Memory is what we know by heart, a journal of dream and waking, read in that strange light of winter giving way to spring, when time itself stretches like a shadow, connecting everything.

*

"The years are a patience," Patrick writes, "as if in my mind I am always/ there with a language/I can never understand."

*

When daguerreotypes appeared in the mid-nineteenth century, they were called mirrors with a memory. My mother's face: a mirror, a memory. My own face, the way my mind shapes it, the way my words shape it. "And our faces, my heart, brief as photos."

*

The strength of my mother's hands. How they glowed in the light of the furnace. This memory that was mine, now yours. To make it whole. To make it real, again.

*

Though you never see the animal, always, there are tracks in the snow.

Going Forward and Backward Standing Still

E. F. Dyck

Take language as a primitive, a basic human capability, and writing as the exercise of this linguistic capability in its graphic medium: then, poetry is writing whose referent is ultimately itself. (No point in roaming the prairie looking for buffalo chips when the mega-chip is at hand!) It's been said often enough and well enough: poetry is writing distinguished by its delivery of a golden world, by the interpenetration of matter and manner, by its (con) fusion of metaphoric and metonymic poles, by its charged meanings, by its recursive imping of the impossible. Poetry is language about language: beginning, middle, and end. Amen.

The art or science of language, which is never the language of an art or a science, nevertheless also refers to the great Other. There's nothing magical or even poetic about this doubleness; it is, simply and fortunately, one of the natural properties of language. But writing which exploits only half of this duplicity is not poetry, whatever else it may be. Example: a great deal of prairie writing, taking its anti-literary tone ever so seriously, trying deliberately to be a window of references to the Other, is smudged by the pat formulas of the plain style and fails to make full use of its own resources. Example: an anti-literary tone, held rhetorically, is one of the most literary attitudes possible. This game of high seriousness has been played by the masters of literature in English from then till now. Amazingly enough, the poet her/himself plays only a weak hand—language, so to speak, holds all the aces. Or, more faddishly, language is the meta-program which guides the computer of poetry programmed by the individual. Example: the astonishing, experiential fact that poetry is capable of ecstasy is less astonishing than the fact that the capability of ecstasy is a natural function of language which happens to be accentuated in poetry.

> quick jump
>   & a kick
> loose jointed he leaps
> from syntax/a trap
>   for the truth-teller
>   jumping jack
> oh/the bite of teeth
>   ("Lo—How Od Looks," *Odpoems*, 1978)

Thus, the power of language to formulate unprovable truths, to transcend system, to achieve ecstasy (compare Sidney 1595 to Goedel 1931)!

The poet's job is to write and read and....Why not *use* The (In) Complete Poetry Book, from antiquity's quilled scratchings to yesterday's computer print-outs, continuously being augmented, revised, rewritten, and in which (willy-nilly) every poet is a contributor? This is not a rhetorical question: Poetaster, thy sin is sloth. The only thing worse than a lazy reader is a lazy writer, and they deserve each other. The writer must know more about her/his writing than any other reader; though this does not excuse the reader-critic from knowing enough, it does indict many a writer for knowing too little. Some say that prairie poetry is necessarily flat: if so, it is flat necessarily because its writers and readers are too lazy to climb up and too scared to climb down.

I stand accused of living entirely in my head. After all, there is heart, there is belly, there is person, there is reality—right? I say re-read your Coleridge and your Jung! Yes, there is an unconscious poetics which is pre-linguistic, and the connections between it and the poetics of writing (that conscious making, of words) are many and profound. Example (one track, backwards): symbol, synecdoche, rhetoric, The (In) Complete Poetry Book,...Whence comes the particular symbol? Aha, you say, who knows! Endorphin, anyone?

> I have sought you, dolphin,
> and have found you not.
>
> According to your royal command.
> The canticle of canticles, remainder
>
> upon division of division into twos,
> a canon of canons encoding a canon.
>
> Your art is the art that delays,
> your art is the art that defies.
>
> To seek and not to find is
> to seek to seek the dolphin.
>> ("Ricercar," unpublished, 1985)

This is a strange figure—to escape from only by returning to! Poetry is a list of examples of the same: form and content; god is dead or alive; formulas made to be broken; the hope for a formula of formulas is hopelessly persistent. This is our human condition—Eros, flying up forever falling down, making a strange loop pierced by a two-headed, standing arrow moving very fast.

> Riddle of life   :riddle of noodle
> We crawl at morn, stand at noon, crouch at night
> Ready in minutes   :for eating and dying
> In every place   :the winds are blowing
> Every summer sun shines on banners waving
> Propellers turn in every White Dove Cafe
>   (Stanza 64, *The Mossbank Canon*, 1982)

So it is necessary and dangerous to indulge in fads. For example, phenostructarchism, a curious oleo of phenomenology plus structuralism plus archetypalism, now safe enough to be studied at learned conferences, is no longer a problem for most writers. Once considered new and dangerous, it is now recognizably a formula. For example, post-phenostructarchism, an even "curiouser" mix of phenostructarchism and deconstructionism, is the current poppy, already fading, of the opium trade of the avant-garde. But a *post*, as every prairie boy knows, implies a *fence*, and a *fence* implies *barbed wire*, and its purpose is to keep cattle in or out. Meanwhile, the heifer and bull of language escape to return. For example, schools of writing are an affront to imagination and thought because they deny the former and substitute for the latter. Do we want to exclude apprehension and comprehension (O, Theseus) from our poetry? Then we must attend perfectly to our schools. The day-school of male-chauvinist writing is losing its accreditation; the night-school of feminist writing is about to be officially sanctioned. We shall soon all be much better educated. For example, technology continues to realize more and more of the formulaic aspects of the human linguistic function. Unfortunately, computers and word-processors are exactly that—and not imaginative, thinking, writing human beings. These machines are unable to encode language's capacity for ecstasy; in the lingo of computer science, the halting problem for computing machines is demonstrably unsolvable.

Writers—keep writing! For a last example, information theory has replaced thermodynamics as the dominant metaphor for our age. This change is being heralded with shrieks of (mostly uninformed) delight by the literati. But who has taken the trouble and time to study Shannon's beautiful theorem? Which of language's properties (or poetry's insights) does it render precise? Perhaps we will misconstrue the possibility of increasing the "information" load of a set of signals as we once misconstrued the second law of thermodynamics. Perhaps the doomsday interpretation has already been replaced by the eminence of salvation.

The reader deserves to know where I stand: on, in, under, and with language. Not just utterance—or speech, or communication, or system. All of them, new (old) paradigms. Everything (nothing) changes (recurs). The same but different. Suppose feeling were chemistry. Suppose thought were a function recursive in imagination. Suppose matter (particle) were a manner (wave). Suppose language.

Desire and Prayer:
Notes on *The Shunning*

Patrick Friesen

Sitting at the typer, a blank sheet before me; the finished book, published some years earlier, beside me. How to begin the process of adapting the book to a workable stage play.

It is already a play for voices. In language it's a natural for radio and, when I close my eyes, I can see it as a film; not a wide-screen landscape film, but a film of tight shots wheeling around the characters as they walk in and out of events, talking and worrying with their gods. As a stage play it is not entirely clear to me.

I need to discover what the theatrical possibilities are within what is already written. I need to see to what degree I can work my cinematic imagination into theatre. Film, I've always thought, is essentially a matter of close-ups, of understatement in acting; not so the stage. At least, not from what I know of it.

It makes me go back to what it was I was working with, what I was trying to do when I began the book in 1978. I had left home long ago. In 1978 I was at the end of another line. Teaching, after six years, had drained me, was driving me to breakdown. It was another of the prisons one puts oneself into. I think the emotions in me at the time connected with the memory of my desire to get out of the hot-house religious atmosphere of my home town. It brought back the suffocation. Not the anger or the bitterness, not even the sense of injustice, but the suffocation and claustrophobia, like a small room on a muggy day.

I was going to write a book. It would say something about Mennonites in southeastern Manitoba. This much was conscious. Inevitably, it would say as much about me as about the community, but the aim was to begin the process of writing the experience I had been born into. Previous efforts, including my first books, although touching on that experience, were more in the way of rehearsal.

I had many false starts. Mostly I wrote individual poems, thinking that eventually there would be enough for a book. There were self-conscious poems about betrayal and theology. I wrote many poems. Some good ones, some awful ones, and mainly average ones. Only occasionally did a poem seem true.

Looking at the batch I did notice that the poems overlapped each other. There was something about the experience I was writing about that led to this kind of layering. Nothing was two-dimensional; no one event, no person, stood out as separate, not fully separate. Each carried within it the past and the seeds of the future.

Desire and prayer: blood, idea, the pursuit of money. Life does not consist of separate moments; they run into each other; they leap back and forth amongst each other. Life is neither linear nor cyclical. Yet we live with strong concepts of history and time, and we explain all the nuances of our lives in terms of these concepts.

I could write a layered book. It wouldn't be a story or stories, but rather bits and pieces of what later could be seen to be story. At any one point, if events stopped, if someone died, you could look back and decide on what the story had been. We tend to look for conclusion to make sense of the process. This is what we do with history. It's also what we do with form in our writing. Even the so-called "open-ended" approach is another form a writer imposes on his work.

I have never enjoyed the sense of being an onlooker in a book. I believe in inspiration; breathing in and out; the leaping and graceful deer and so, the jump of the writer's heart as he stands in a meadow, or in his house.

Richard Hildebrandt, a friend in whose house I was working, called me downstairs one night to watch "Man Alive," a religious television program. We watched a story on the purging within the Holdeman church in my home town. The young bucks, not old or wise enough to hold their positions of responsibility in the church, were out to clean up what was, as far as any outsider could see, the narrowest, cleanest church in town.

Everywhere they looked, outside of themselves, they saw pride and corruption of purpose. Especially, they seemed to see it in people older than themselves. The spiritual violence began. People were banned and relatives and loved ones ordered to shun them. Business people were asked not to do business with those considered "non-Christian" by the church hierarchy. Otherwise their businesses would be shunned. Censorship, the heavy hand of self-righteousness, took over the church.

There was really nothing new here. Intellectually I had known about this kind of thing. When my former neighbour appeared on the screen, a neighbour who had been a friendly, faithful Christian, and explained, with sorrow and pain in his voice, how he had been banned for pride...when his wife told how she was asked to shun her husband, and how she refused, then I knew my focal point for the work in progress.

Here were a people who had been founded on several principles, including pacifism; who had separated themselves from the world and its courts; and yet, some were imposing most violent punishments on their own brothers and sisters. Where would these banned people go for human comfort?

The community had always been tight and self-sufficient; to leave it was a wrenching experience. I hadn't been banned because I had never joined in the first place; not formally, at least. If I was shunned by anyone, and I was, well, I shunned right back. I had resources as a willful, cocksure young man, who did not believe much of what the church taught.

*

I went back to the wads of paper on my table. I found a poem about two pages in length that had the whole story within it. A kind of overture. There were the slaughtered chickens; there was the rifle and the single shot beside the creek.

Especially the image of a man lying beside a creek, one hand in the water, one boot off, the other untied, a rifle beside his bare foot, especially this image had been with me for some time.

But the man was just a man, no one in particular. It took a few more days to come up with the character of Peter, and he came by way of Johann, his brother.

A few weeks earlier I had had trouble falling asleep, wondering how to approach this book. I hit upon the idea of an old and a new Mennonite meeting at the graveyard. The new, the young Menno, would be sitting on a gravestone when he would hear a voice. It would be a long-buried Menno speaking from his grave. It seemed pretty far-fetched, but I got up and quickly wrote out eight or nine pages of rough poems based on conversations between these two Mennos.

I saw that the old Menno from those pages, I had called him Johann, was a natural. He had humour, self-criticism and warmth. I liked him. I had to use him, even if I didn't use any of the poems about him that I had written. But this was not the kind of man who would be banned from his church. He was too resilient and lacked pride. Well, then, it was clear there would have to be a brother.

Things fell into place quickly, before I could write everything down. Johann would be another side of his brother Peter, a suppressed part of him. They were really two aspects of one person.

Other people came to mind. My grandfather had a twin brother. Their stories were interesting, even dramatic. There were events in their lives, though not shunning, that would make for great reading, I thought. Grandmother's death by flu at an early age, the burning of the farmhouse, and so on. A few details would have to be changed, of course, or made up....

I had events that moved toward a plot. I had characters and, all along, I had the church, my memory of it, and I had the suffocation.

You hurt people when you try to take a breath. When you refuse to be suffocated any longer. What you don't always know is that they really do believe in how they live and that not everyone is suffocated by the same things you are.

Still, you have to breathe, even if it means lashing out. This is a beginning.

If you're lucky, you'll come to the day when you've not only gone past theology, but beyond atheism.

I have lashed out against judgement. And I have judged. I look in the mirror, and, often, I see what I reject.

*

The book was written quickly. In maybe two or three weeks. I had to decide to what degree I would use German, High or Low. I decided to minimize German words, but worked a lot in Germanic speech rhythms and, sometimes, word orders. Just enough to give the flavour, and to lead in interesting Germanic directions; not enough to be ridiculous. Low German is an earthy, humorous language not readily available to seriousness or tragedy.

Language, then, was specifically chosen, with Low German in mind, with the Bible and hymns in mind. It had to be a bare, evocative language. These were simple people in terms of life-style and theology. Their experiences, at best, were evocative, with no one language to speak them.

Visually, I remembered my grandfather's farm. I had spent many hours there. I had old photos of him, of his young wife who had died many years before I was born. I knew where on that farm everything happened. I choreographed the dance of "the shunning" on his farm, rather than in a church, or on the streets of a town. The places on his farm I used had spiritual value for me. I remembered what kind of boy I was when I stood on those places, when I fished in that creek. I had built-in values. These would be transferred to my characters. Inevitably I became part of the characters through this process. This was not intended, but was a corollary.

This book is set on a farm on the outskirts of the town where I was born. It's where my father was born. My mother was born in another town. This is significant only to me. I can't make anything bigger of it. It's my field.

And yet, I can find quotes from other writers that speak my experience better than my own words. How can this be?

Yet, how can this not be?

*

With the play I am writing I have a field; the field I am creating out of my personal experience and my place in Menno history. Yet, this is only partly right. There is another element, the storm field; where creation happens.

Hardy's novels have always resonated for me, especially *The Return of the Native*. Often life is being lived out dramatically, intensely, fatally in a field. What Hardy called a heath.

In my field I have Mennos, a small group in history, and I have a memory which I sometimes think I would like to be divested of. I'm not interested in writing a broad landscape. I want close-up. This must come first. Then, perhaps, there can be generalization.

I think I can get more personal on stage. At least, it looks that way at first. I can focus on interior lives in a more concrete way than I could in the book. It will still be characters talking, but they can

open up feelings in a more naked way than a book can. I'm not sure
of this. In fact, the opposite may be true.

The drama will be in the tension, the interplay of the personal,
even the melodramatic, with detachment. The individual will be seen
close-up, alone in his or her immediate world, circumscribed not
only by society, but also by individual self-consciousness. Sometimes these characters will reach out into history or, more likely,
the world will intrude on them.

Like Hardy, as a young man, was eating breakfast when he
remembered that someone was to be hanged that morning, at 8 a.m.,
in a town two or three miles distant. Hardy didn't know just what
the time was, but he knew it was near 8. He picked up an old
telescope from another room and ran up a rise from which he could
view the nearby town. Just at the moment he raised the telescope
to his eye and focussed, he saw the white-clad figure drop through
the trapdoor of the gallows. It shook him. He had been expecting
the hanging, but somehow, it took him by surprise, the way it
happened just at the instant he chose to look through his telescope.
Such a sudden and violent glimpse.

Shortly after The Shunning *came out, I read from it to a Menno*
audience. A middle-aged man came up later and told me that his
father had been banned when he, the son, was young. What he remem-
bered about the event was how his father stood in the doorway,
not letting the churchmen in, and not going out himself. Then, he
remembered, when the words had been spoken, the door slammed
shut. He wanted to know why I had written this shunning as taking
place with the screen door open. I couldn't really say. Just that it
seemed right. That I could see the men in various geometries around
the open door, that I could hear mosquitoes around their heads as
the event played out.

*

If people talked with the grace of feeling-thoughts, that would
be a talking play I would like. Not overly poetic, not naturalistic.

That's what I aim for. To some degree I worked this direction in the book. Now, I will take it further. String out the lines of poetry until they're talk. Not pub talk, but clear, conscious expression of what's inside a person. Some story, yes, but primarily, the slightly heightened language of an everyday personal poetry.

Peter, Helen and Johann will be subversive in language. It won't be their actions that will be radical, but their communicated feelings, or the fact that they communicate their feelings. These will stand, straight or subtle, in the midst of the religious lingo of the community; a lingo learned, and felt, only as on-going cliché. Their language will pierce through clichés and form, sometimes by playing off form, other times disregarding it entirely. They will give new meaning to old hymns. The initial, pre-cliché, poetry of the hymn, as song, must be retained.

Actors will carry the subversion even further. Who knows what they will do with the words given them. With their voices, their limbs, their faces. Who knows what the director will do, the set designer, costume designer, composer.

When I was younger, I wanted to be director, actor, the whole works. Now there is pleasure in giving something up to others to complete. Collaboration. Let them make of the words what they will. Whatever they do is right, whether or not it works.

A giving up.

My grandfather, on the day he died, said, from his hospital bed, "I guess this time I'm finished."

Recently, a Spanish bullfighter was gored in the heart. As he lay dying, he said, "That bull killed me."

I remember in high school, one of Shakespeare's characters said, as he died, "I am dying." I had to laugh.

What did I know? About dying; about words.

The play will be intimate, but not as immediate as the book. There will be the close-up, the actor alone on a bare stage with his grimaces or raised eyebrows, but the actor mediates between the words and audience. In the book there were only the words....

*

Today I went to the theatre. I was introduced to Maggie Nagle, the actress who would play Helen.

I shook her hand and looked in her face. I asked her if she was Helen. It was a strange feeling. Just then, having seen the set, the costumes, I knew this was Helen.

I wondered if she knew all her lines. If she did, she knew more of Helen than I did. I had finished the writing some weeks ago; Helen wasn't in me anymore. She was there, in this actress, in front of me.

What is it I want in a play? What can the stage, with its props and players, do? Henry Miller, in *Sexus*, has a line that partially answers my question.

"I want to see how I look in the mirror with my eyes closed."

For a moment this is what I felt as I met the actress. This is something I can't do with writing. There, whenever I look in the mirror, my eyes are open.

Avoidance and Confrontation: Excerpts from Notes on a Longpoem Poetics

Kristjana Gunnars

Even though the inspiration and influence of Charles Olson have been with me all along, newer names and fresher ideas have muted and qualified much of what I do in poetry. I was sidetracked by the "local colour" movement of the Prairies and by the surrealism of Borges and the poetry of Pablo Neruda, with its "objects touched by human hands." However muted, though, some basic tenets remain true. The basic assumption from which I work concerns the condition of estrangement; both as a human condition, and as a peculiar condition of the poem. Olson expresses this in *The Special View of History*: "Man is estranged from that with which he is most familiar."[1] Without that gap, there could, I still feel, hardly be any poetry. Olson has more to say on this:

> There are two estrangements, the permanent one, from that which is slipping by in the grass without moving a leaf of grass's top; but this other one, the contingent, of touch on all sides—of the company of the living, that they are distracted and dispersed. It is a lie of discourse to split this latter problem into the individual and society.[2]

I concerned myself with both kinds of estrangement in Olson's terms: the former, "permanent" alienation, where things pass, imperceptibly or not, and there is a continual state of Stevensian "flux" to contend with in existence (I depart from Stevens in the approach to transience; while he wants to accept it and swallow it entirely until the poem itself becomes so fluid that it is almost imperceptible, I want to make gestures of permanence, defiantly perhaps, by staking a claim or by using the language of statement); and the latter, perhaps temporary, isolation from other people, "the company of the living"; the social alienation which Camus developed so well. What prevents poetry from turning into philosophy for me (something that Jarrell criticizes strongly in Stevens, and which gives Eliot an elitist air), is this contention proposed by Olson: that "the falsest estrangement of all...is contemplation."[3] It would be a lie to try to bridge the gaps with "consolations of philosophy" — much as the Boethean lure remains a continual spell-binding attraction, in the end I think you have to treat it the way you treat your people or culture or background: by saying "you raised me and moulded me, but I have to leave your house."

I combined the Black Mountain ideas with my own form of "under-erasure," a term that always comes up with Eliot and Pound. This was, in the words of Daniel Hoffman in *Barbarous Knowledge*, to "commit" my "thought to such irrational sources as magic and superstition, folklore and myth."[4] The "defiance" of "staking a claim" in something that could, allowing for intellectual fallibility, possibly be permanent in a world of Existentialist nothingness, was an obeisance to the "need to root imagination in an *a priori* structure of experience, a frame of archetypes or myth,"[5] as Hoffman puts it. The need, in the case of poetry, was not merely a preferential or an ideological one: what I was doing concerned the nature of poetry itself. A poem has to start somewhere; it cannot begin in midair, and I have always been suspicious of Pound and Eliot, and even Gertrude Stein, for writing in a way that requires outside reading in order to establish some "centre that will hold" at least long enough to get through a passage or a canto.

I have the same quarrel with Black Mountain poetry: an appreciation of the poetry of Olson hinges on an understanding of his "special view" of things, which, while being genuinely innovative, still risks eventual irrelevance, if only because it is a "personal" view. I would say the same for Pound and Blake; they last only insofar as the community can find, in groping for new contexts, some sense of solidarity with their positions. In referring to "magic and superstition, folklore and myth" (which I did in *Settlement Poems, Moon Maps* and *Wake-Pick Poems*) I was also convinced that what Daniel Hoffman said about Yeats was true: that "he made the local legends of a remote country into the substance of great literature."[6] That, "in becoming more Irish...he became at the same time universal."[7] I could not then, and I still cannot, function with what is not "special" or specific; the more "remotely special," the better (that is, specific but strange).

Four specific points of post-modern poetics interest me in particular; not as applicable methods for a longpoem in Canada in the eighties, but rather as a "staircase" from which to carry on. These notions are: the "intertextuality" Pound develops, where an insertion of other texts (from any period or culture) becomes almost the utilization of innumerable "ghost writers"; the "undererasure" evident in Eliot, where the poem nullifies itself by undercutting statement and suggestion all along the line; the "evasiveness" of Stevens, where all is circumlocution and shift and the poem takes no direct stand; and the "continual present" Gertrude Stein relies on, where (in opposition to projective verse) no line leads out of any other, but practically every line or word-segment is a new start. All four ideas were necessary at the time of their appearance: the world was immersed in global conflict and scientists, philosophers and artists were finding ways of dispersing, dislocating, destroying "conventional" naive realism as a way out of an epidemic or a trap.

Those of us born as a direct consequence of (who exist *because* of) World War Two, have a peculiar burden unlike the pre-war generations: our perceptions are coloured by war. We are "war children" because our parents were still in horror-shock after the Second War when they raised us; because our upbringing was continually broken by cold-war crises; because we lived "at attention" through the Korean War and the Cuban missile crisis; because our schooling contained the *barbarous discovery* of the arms race and the possibilities inherent in atomic war; and finally, because the war in Vietnam acted as one long extended shock treatment. It seems impossible now not to be aware of the nuclear arms buildup in Europe, and with the doomsday machine in the background the very idea of "undererasing" your stance and "evading" it seems like deliberate deceit. The problem is that when a poem becomes "absolutist" in any way, especially if it turns political, it ceases to be a poem.

What we have to do, it seems to me, is to write poetry that will be unequivocally on the side of life (in no way support the destructiveness of modern life, which includes discrimination of all kinds), and to write poetry that will help rechannel the ingredients of the Nuclear Age. I believe that after our excursions into madness, into the subconscious, dreams, archetypes; after Cubism, Expressionism, Impressionism, Surrealism, and other avant-garde nomadisms, we are left with the necessity of relying on reason for purposes of survival. This is what I wanted my poetry to be about (as much as it should be "about" anything): I wanted it to be a groping for a basic (perhaps a "natural" as opposed to a "civilized") *reason* in the midst of our (often perfunctory) desire to act out our "craziness."

The need for reason is anti-poetic, and I see poetry now as going against itself. The conflict, or tension, is in the combining of harmony and disjuncture. My way of writing anything has always been to combine incongruities; to put things together that are not supposed to be combined. Anything harmonious, anything that goes well together, has almost become an unnatural act. Within the desire to create "unfitting" poetry, I have relied on a form of counterpoint harmony for a poetic pattern. The official definition of counterpoint is: "that of writing two or more melodies such as, whilst having interest and beauty in themselves, also *fit well together*" (Oxford). Putting open-ended pieces together contrapuntally does not have to mean that you assume control over your material. It seems more like a way of letting bulls into the arena, or releasing your pigeons. This is what I mean by Double Counterpoint: on the most obvious level, you may have poetry with either a "topmost voice" to which one listens, or poetry with no "topmost part," but all "lower parts" instead. In Double Counterpoint, you not only have two major "top voices," but they can easily be inverted, taking turns being primary and secondary. This occurs aside from all the "lower voices" which are inevitably there throughout. The lower parts should, theoretically, be without much tune in themselves, but should accompany the major parts.

It seems to me that poets should, in every work, try to depart from the influences that have made them and to break away from the influences that exert specifically new force. Part of what I mean here is to avoid aligning yourself with particular "schools of thought"; and constantly try to achieve a freedom of your own. If the influences I have been under in any way "made" me think the way I do about poetry, they are also voices I have tried to disallow. One of the initial motivations for any series of poems I begin is still this: if it is not supposed to be done, I want to try to do it; a kind of "poetry of belligerence." However, now that evasion, self-crippling, un-naming and lies are acceptable (more than acceptable: desirable) in poetry, I want to find another way of writing. The criticism of Deconstruction, Structuralism, and Semiotics interest me particularly as lines of thought I want to disown, and there are several points raised by these schools of criticism that are particularly involving.

I think it is true, as Harold Bloom says, that "the verbal mechanisms of crisis have come to dominate lyric poetry."[8] The point about belonging to a generation of "war-children" concerns the post-war language of crisis that comes with the nuclear age. We think in terms of absolutes and split-second timing, and we use words that are final and unequivocal. Evasive poets like Wallace Stevens, cultured poets like Robert Graves, and wordy poets like Gertrude Stein, have little to do with us. We are closer to Lawrence Ferlinghetti in point of departure, but there may be a tendency now towards the *constructive*, and away from the poetry of complaint. Most of what I have done so far has been in "crisis language," although I once wrote a cycle on the nuclear presence in Europe in contemplative conversational language, which I thought would be a good incongruity; and I do not really consider *Moon Maps* in this category either. Many of my poems still carry on with that language of desperation, but more and more of what I do is written with the idea of *entering into conversation*. This involves drastic shifts within the work, where you leap from crisis to crisis, but in between them there is abundant leisure to investigate the surroundings. There is no past, no future, no expectation; only an expanding present, dislodged from all possibility of holocaust.

What I am essentially looking for is a kind of freedom in poetry; freedom from constraint, tradition, regulations, preconceptions, clichés, borrowed attitudes, and so on. As with music, however, freedom is hardly achieved except through constraints of discipline and knowledge of the past; knowing what can be done in poetry because of what has been done before. And even though every poem is an escape *from* meaning, the attempt at meaning is continually begun again, for we are caught between discarding meaning as a hoax, and needing meaning to get by. Freedom in poetry for Harold Bloom is:

> ...freedom of meaning, the freedom to have a meaning of one's own. Such freedom is wholly illusory unless it is achieved through a prior plenitude of meaning, which is tradition, and so also against language.[9]

He also says:

> Freedom of meaning is wrested by combat, of meaning against meaning. But this combat consists in *a reading encounter*, and in an interpretive moment within that encounter.[10]

What is being said here is partly that the reader imparts some of the freedom that is in the poem, to the poem. Because the reader is going to "finish" writing the poem, the poet has to carry on a defensive struggle along with the "poetry of warfare" which the critical schools named above talk about (Jacques Derrida, Paul de Man, Harold Bloom et al.). The poem has to be vulnerable while it is strong; it has to show its weaknesses so as not to be taken for "positive and exploitative" language. To maintain such a precarious balance, it becomes necessary for the poem to break itself apart and "shatter the visionary gleam" it tries to impart. This is what Paul de Man calls "a systematic undoing...of understanding";[11] or as Harold Bloom says: "the authentic poem now achieves its dearth of meaning by strategies of exclusion, or what can be called litanies of evasion."[12]

The poem should be evasive and indirect, because directness kills a poem. I want to push the form around, because if form stiffens, the poem is constrained. I would rather have "dearth of meaning" than too much distinguished meaning, for the presence of too much meaning drains the force of the poem. Poetry should be hard to understand, impossible to cope with, and full of lies, but underneath, or above, such "barbed wire" communication, there should be a yielding and vulnerable, but distant, signal (such as the coded messages of the underground that slip into the public broadcasting system during periods of martial law) to the effect that we are in touch and have a strategy in mind. Because of the dangerous age we live in, we need to *seek* out a harmony of voices to bridge our estrangement.

---

1. Charles Olson, *The Special View of History* (Berkeley: Oyez, 1970), 25.

2. *Ibid.*

3. *Ibid.*

4. Daniel Hoffman, *Barbarous Knowledge* (London: Oxford, 1970), vii.

5. *Ibid*, viii.

6. *Ibid*, ix.

7. *Ibid*, x.

8. Harold Bloom, "The Breaking of Form," in *Deconstruction & Criticism* (New York: Continuum, 1979), 12.

9. *Ibid*, 3.

10. *Ibid*, 5

11. *Ibid*, 4.

12. *Ibid*, 15.

Essay Parcels from Andrew Suknaski

Kristjana Gunnars

You will paint a self portrait the rest of yer life…Sooknatski.
(Zelko Kudjundzic, Kootenay School of Art)

It was April when the parcels started arriving. The snow was melting.
Yellow grass could be seen by the fence. I went home after work one
evening. Opened the screen door. Two large thin parcels fell to my feet.
The postman hid them between doors.

I did not open the parcels. They went into the basement. Next day four
cards in the mailbox. Four more parcels at the St. Norbert post office.
I picked them up. Not because I wanted them, but because of the
Francophone clerk. He was so excited.

Those parcels went into the car trunk. There they stayed, unopened.
When the warm weather came a great perfumed smell arose from one
of the packages. When I got into the car it made me think of a field
of tulips in Amsterdam.

One Sunday I came home from a walk. Parcels were hanging from the mailbox, the doorknob, the fencepost. They deliver on Sundays. That was good to know. The new parcels also went into the basement.

Soon a corner of the basement had a pile of parcels. Some small, some very large. The trunk of my car was full. Opening them all would take a whole day. I put it off. I would prefer not to open them at all.

May began. Days were getting hot. The grass was turning green. I had procrastinated long enough. I must open them someday. I unlocked the trunk. It was Sunday. I began with the smelly one.

A perfumed candle melting in the May heat. Many pieces of paper. Markers and pens, envelopes. It was as I had feared. This was a happening. I was the victim.

The artist who sends me these things is laughing at me. The artist is forcing me to look. The artist is blocking my way into my own house, diverting my attention.

The artist is a poet. It was as I had feared. The artist was mad.

I opened parcels until sunset and I could see no more. Mostly pieces of paper. Poems, images, small gifts. Two treasures turned up: an original woodcut and a photograph from the private album of John Newlove's mother. Why does a pioneer woman in a long dress stand on top of a pile of firewood?

Next day yet another card. I opened the parcel in the post office, determined to take home no more. The Francophone clerk watched with interest. I pulled out a Juniper branch. A stone. A loaf of bread. "Gee," said the clerk. "You know who sent it?"

And a brief missive. "I have burned twenty two years of work. All my papers in the fire. The ashes took all night to cool. I raised this bread on the ashes. Poetry has turned to bread."

"Yes," I said to the clerk. "I know where this is from." This is the myth of the suffering artist. This is another anachronism. Romantic poets do not live in their own time.

Someone who always attempts the impossible. To do what cannot humanly be done. His prescription for "How to be a Poet":

> stay hungry
> razor/
> thin
> pure
> conden
> -sation
> of
> > spirit
> > /flesh
> > ethereal
> > un
> > -deviating
> > from
> > a single
> > dream...

"but i love beer/" he says, "i'm obsessed w/food/but i'd like to grow old lining my bottles up on a window-sill...one lamp shining bright through short days of long winter."

Because asceticism is impossible. To live in a dream. To exist ethereally. The gap between what is and what is dreamed. A sense of guilt. Imperfection. The self-destructive artist.

The Romantic cannot be heard, for he does not live in the same world. The one who calls himself a failed priest has only his own failure. His paper suicide is his own privilege.

My attention has been diverted. I have been raking up dead debris from the grass. Spring has its own chores. The parcels have been opened, cardboard thrown out. They have disclosed only one letter:

> ...what I like abt my critics is
> whenever they discover another version
> of me, i'm always somewhere else. One constant being
> ...for every star in the universe, there's one inside
> my head   they keep levitating between my cranium
> & my hands...

The one who cannot speak for himself will speak for himself anyway. Under the melted candle, the field of tulips in Amsterdam, lay his unintentional essay:

Barbed Wire

> & fences//
> taking down the fence
> *to the critics*
> if you wanna tell me who i am
> start by following some ole friend in wood mountain
> follow me
> following him
> who deadrings for GOD
> & forcrisake
> leave behind yer pencils
> pens   recorders   especially cameras
> there's so little fucking magic left
> an it takes an eternity to rebuild

an clean the barbed wire
every time you leave
an enough of rambling
back to the cornerpost
an me
comfortable with the ghost
crowbar
jis follow me
willy nilly
through rainsoaked sage
etherizing yer lungs
tell me of the simplest things last of all
the old reflexes
rolling barbed wire
it'll teach you more of west
GOD
A STILLPOINT
W/in THE
CIRCLE
        GOD
        THE DOTS
        THAT BLUR the CIRCUMFERENCE
        OF YER HEART
        MAPPING YER FOOTSTEPS
            or jist follow the ghost
            of yer marginalized self
            an what you once
            were
                before the mega-politic
                balkanized our soul...

It was Smaro Kamboureli who sat down beside me one day in March. "Laurie Ricou forgot to mention Andrew Suknaski," she said. "Suknaski is our William Blake."

I cannot reply to that. I only know that this Blake victimizes the post office. This Blake sends himself in pieces in parcels, and he will not write this essay.

It is May. The grass is green. The parcels have stopped.

When Fact Meets Fantasy

Caroline Heath

Is Prairie writing identifiable as such? Does it matter if it is? And is Prairie writing changing? It always puzzled me that *Grain* was considered a regional magazine, since only about a third of the writing in the magazine was by Prairie writers and many of them came from such places as Poland, India and New Zealand. Was it the name *Grain* (which never ceased to stimulate people's worst punning compulsions and invite misconceptions about the nature of the magazine) that made people jump to the conclusion that it was a regional magazine? Or was it simply the fact that it was published in Saskatoon?

When preparing submissions for circulation to my associate editors at *Grain*, I always put the editors' critique sheet at the end of the ms. and then tucked the covering letter under that. We wanted to approach the writing with as little extraneous information as possible. But as I read the submissions later I couldn't help trying to guess the geographical origin of the author and it was amazing how often one could tell.

It's obvious that Canada is comprised of regions and that they are quite distinct. It wasn't just reference to Niagara Falls or oil rigs that gave away the geographical identity of those *Grain* submissions. It was there in the obsessions, the stance, the tone, the language of the writer. Ontario became the easiest to spot. Always wordy, always taking a moral position.

Prairie writing most closely resembled Maritime writing—sparse, understated, ironic, flecked with black humour.

Certain things about Prairie writing have not changed in the last fifteen years. It is impossible to talk about Prairie writing (or Prairie art) without talking about landscape. It may be possible for a Torontonian, but not for a Prairie person, to be unaffected by sky and land and the elements, so this awareness continues to permeate our writing.

There may be, however, some change in the way landscape appears in the writing. We probably have fewer poems about gophers and grain elevators, generally less writing *about* the landscape, more internalization of the landscape and use of Prairie images as metaphor. But some of the best of this kind of writing was already being done ten years ago by Anne Szumigalski and Lorna Crozier, whose first book suggested this internalization with its title: *Inside is the Sky*.

Prairie writing continues to display an awesome reverence for historical fact. People are always asking the author: Is that a true story? And they don't mean true in an ontological sense, they mean *did it happen* and they don't care about the subtleties of fact being filtered through perception, etc.

Canada has earned an international reputation for documentary film. Documentary has become a Canadian fetish. It serves as a substitute for myth. I suspect this is the result of never having had a revolution, never having rejected our European antecedents.

Because Prairie society is so young, it only recently felt the need to document its history. The realization that its pioneers were dying set off a race to record the settlement of the West before they were all gone. This impulse to record and preserve, as seen in the rash of local histories that have been written in the last few years, has also motivated much of the creative writing done on the Prairies. The common form it took in the 70s was a quest for "roots." The *Best of Grain* anthology, published in 1980, opens with a spoof on this pursuit:

Roots

(This poem is not about Rudy Wiebe)
Rudy Wiebe, wiping the sweat from his brow,
calls a spade a spade.
He has a spade in his hands.
He is digging a hole near Winnipeg,
in the middle of a potato field.
He has blisters in his hands.
He has roots on the brain.
He is looking for his roots.

David Waltner-Toews

We're hearing a variation on the documentary theme now from women writers. "We need to tell our story," they say. These are often the stories of ordinary lives. Sandra Birdsell and Lois Simmie are both good writers, but I think they have been particularly warmly welcomed because they write with honesty and compassion about the ordinary lives of ordinary people, most frequently women. Sharon Butala and Merna Summers have been able to elevate ordinary, rural characters, despite their stark, routine existence, to heroic status.

The more traditional means of creating such larger-than-life characters has been to rely on historical figures, as Ken Mitchell has done with his plays on Davin and Bethune. The need for heroes, symbols and a mythology is legitimate; the danger lies in creating them artificially, either by borrowing the content from Native or European sources, or by forcing indigenous material into classical structures.

Eli Mandel's interest in mythology has provided an antidote to the documentary fixation, and Rudy Wiebe has tried to blend the two. But we are still working toward a true Prairie voice.

The man who has been talking most about voice in these last few years, of course, is Robert Kroetsch. Returning from New York, Kroetsch introduced young Prairie writers to structuralism and other stimulating ideas, and his influence as a teacher, like Rudy Wiebe's, has been profound.

It is in Kroetsch's poetry, however, that we can hear the Prairie voice most clearly. Kroetsch's poetry rings true because stone hammers and seed catalogues are powerful metaphors for the Prairies—of mythic proportion/significance. But the structure of his poetry also rings true. His use of silence/space within the poem recreates a key characteristic of Prairie speech. The loquacious storyteller is less typical here (at least among non-Natives) than the person who speaks quickly, in bits and phrases, often omitting the main point or not saying what he really thinks.

Some of our most recent writing seems less concerned with the search for an authentic Prairie language and form. Geoffrey Ursell's novel, *Perdue: Or How the West was Lost*, bears resemblance to the writing of Gabriel Garcia Marquez. Bizarre occurrences are not unknown on the Prairies; it is the way this story is told that is foreign. *Perdue* is a clumsy, wooden construct, but it won the 1984 *Books in Canada* Best First Novel Award and I think that tells us something. It is a novel which retains the Canadian/Prairie preoccupation with history and fact, but breaks out of the documentary frame and allows fantasy to play with the facts. There must have been a collective catching of breath among the judges at this daring. (Never mind if it worked or not.)

Two short stories that have particularly delighted readers in recent years are Gloria Sawai's "The Day I Sat with Jesus on the Sun Deck and a Wind Came Up and Blew My Kimono Open and He Saw My Breasts" and Carol Shields' "Various Miracles: A Roundup." Both these stories, like Geoff Ursell's novel, remind one of South American literature in their seriously playful rearrangement of our notions of historical event.

It is too early to tell what permanent effect this infusion of fantasy will have on Prairie writing. I don't like to see the link with reality severed in fiction, but we certainly needed to be shaken loose from a slavish devotion to fact, and Prairie writers in the future may have more freedom as a result of this infusion of fantasy.

Prairie poetry has been strong for a long time. Now fiction is catching up. In 1984, four out of five finalists for the *Books in Canada* Best First Novel Award were from the Prairies. In 1982 Guy Vanderhaeghe startled and pleased people by winning the Governor General's Award with his first book of short stories.

This is not to suggest that fiction blossomed overnight on the Prairies. Guy Vanderhaeghe's first story was published in *Grain* in 1974. He had been working in isolation for eight years, determined to develop his craft slowly and surely, when Macmillan accepted that first manuscript. But to the outsider it may look as if Prairie fiction has blossomed suddenly.

It's also noticeable that many of the new fiction writers are women and that most of them are writing short stories. For that reason, I responded to the suggestion that Fifth House should publish an anthology of Prairie women's fiction.

As I read the more than one hundred submissions for that collection, I noticed that most of the stories were about relationships (man/woman, mother/daughter, father/daughter, even the relationships between the laws of physics and human behaviour). Hence the title, *Double Bond*. It occurred to me then that women do tend to be obsessed with relationships, while men are more interested in action and its extension in time, namely history.

This would suggest that women write short stories not only for the practical reason that they don't have time to write novels when they're looking after children, but also because the short story lends itself more naturally to this often deep but narrow focus. Men, on the other hand, in order to show their characters' actions/effect on the world, need the scope of a novel. (I had thought of exceptions to this generalization before even finishing the sentence, but it may, nonetheless, provide a part of an explanation for the current explosion of short fiction by women.)

From my perspective, then, the most noticeable changes in Prairie writing in the last fifteen years (apart from the proliferation of writers, publishers, organizations and related activities) have been the coming to the fore of fiction, women writers and fantasy. Most Prairie writers are content to live and work here, and they continue to invite out-siders to teach and give workshops here. It is a healthy writing climate. The challenge for each writer, I think, will continue to be finding the voice and the form correct for him/herself and for this time and place.

The World as Theatre

Ken Mitchell

It's astonishing to me now to look back over the last few years, and observe how my writing has shifted away from fiction to a preoccupation with dramatic writing, in particular, for film and stage. This transformation feels involuntary, as though I am merely an interested bystander, and not at all representative of the free-willed artist. The fact is, I've been seduced by the theatre.

In the twenty years since my first short story was published, I've tried to develop skill in all genres of writing: poetry, short fiction, criticism, journalism, the novel, film, radio drama, and the stage. (It seems that pornography and children's literature are beyond me.) At the same time, I've had to be conscious of the dangers of spreading the effort too thin. Now, the track record seems to suggest that if I specialize it will be as a playwright.

The simple truth is that I *enjoy* writing drama above all else, and the sources of this pleasure prove intriguing. There are two elements of the theatre which make it different from other forms of communication. First, it is a social ritual, a form of communal celebration. Secondly, it is "live" and therefore unpredictable. A drama is above all initiation into an *experience*—a happening, an event.

The word *theatre* derives from the Greek for "viewing place." Even at its most boring (e.g. high school musicals) people go expecting to see something *happen*. Because it is live, and therefore unpredictable, everyone enjoys the uncertainty. At any moment, a scenery flat can fall on Hamlet. An untried novice can stun her audience with a brilliant performance.

In our post-industrial, post-literate age, people don't seek explanation or analysis of the mysterious forces behind the events of daily life: political crises, swings of the stock market, the complexities of a baseball game, or a movie or a poem. They want to make independent judgements, based on their own experience. Increasingly, people seem to want to *take part* in the action (even vicariously), not read about it. They want to be involved more than informed. This is essentially "theatrical" thinking.

Once the appeal of stage drama is fully appreciated, the whole world becomes a stage. Because, of course, there are many kinds of theatre, with functions far beyond mere "entertainment." The four theatres that interest me:

- The theatre of sport. "Sport"—from midget wrestling to the Olympic games—is far and away our most popular form of theatre, part of a global economy and culture. Perhaps it is the most "live," that is, unrehearsed and unpredictable. In any case, it is in the football stadia and hockey rinks that genuine tragic purgation still wrenches the guts of the masses.

- The theatre of politics. Though predominantly played on the low-brow medium of television, this is our most "serious" form of theatre. It ranges from the Watergate melodrama to Canadian leadership conventions and hostage crises.

- The theatre of education. The vestigial remnants of mediaeval European theatre (i.e., the rituals of the Roman Catholic church) can be found surviving in the modern classroom. The professor implants the doctrines of the prevailing morality, speaking from the raised altar of learning to the pews full of students.

• The theatre of entertainment. The playhouses and cinemas constitute the most recognizable "theatre," though these venues cater
primarily to a university-educated elite. Television sitcoms and soap
operas, of course, prove the more popular forms of creative story-
telling.

A playwright, then, might exploit any of these forms, or cross
over from one to another. As the word "playwright" suggests, the
function does not require a writer at all.

Like a shipwright or a wheelwright, s/he is one who "crafts" a
drama out of language, movement, music and magic. It's no fluke
that the great playwrights of history — like Shakespeare and Moliere —
were actors before they were writers. And the best advice I ever got
when I began writing for the stage was to go and work onstage
as an actor, to understand the dynamics of live performance, the use
of three-dimensional writing. A playwright must use the medium
instinctively, like an actor, without calculation. More than words, a
play consists of the movement of power among the performers, and
between the performers and the audience. Intellect helps, but the
theatre is governed by emotion. And to be even more provocative, I
have to admit that theatre thrives on fakery and mumbo-jumbo.
Drama doesn't analyse the contradictions of illusion and reality (as
fiction does) — but generates them. A good playwright will be a
successful magician/hypnotist before s/he is a thinker. The greatest
are both.

So I became an actor, then a playwright and director. I did so at
the time, it seems in retrospect, it has been most exciting to be wright-
ing in Canada — at the leading edge of the culture revolution initiated
by *The Ecstasy of Rita Joe* in 1967. The astonishing explosion of drama
(on stage and film) since The Centennial has been the most unanalysed
phenomenon of Canadian cultural history. No one knows yet if it
represents a benchmark of our political maturity, or a flash in the
pan caused by the Canada Council's generosity of the 1960s and 70s.

The euphoric sense of being in the vanguard is intensified by
the social nature of theatre. For anyone with a collective-thinking

bias (as opposed to the rugged individualist), theatre work can be exhilarating. The strongest ego must be subjected to the demands of the play—or it will fail. The playwright can't afford the indulgence of carving words in stone in the seclusion of his garret. The words must satisfy his collaborators: directors, actors, designer, composer, and producer. Ultimately, the audience itself becomes an integral element of this collaboration.

From the moment of conception, a play accumulates energy like an avalanche. As more and more craftsmen—actors, musicians, designers, technical personnel—are integrated into the project, the idea assumes an omnipotence beyond the control of any one person. It accelerates toward the magic point of no return: Opening Night. Changes, often radical and violent changes, are made as the hysteria swells. Rehearsals suddenly go into overtime—twelve-hour days—as the play's demands intensify. Time begins running out. Compromises are made. Tempers fray and masks crack open. Failures of confidence mount to epidemic proportions.

Through it all, there is a physical sensation like being swept toward the cataract of Opening Night—the moment of truth. Either the play will lift from the shoulders of the craftsmen and soar as a testimony to public imagination—or it will fall over dead in the orchestra-pit, stillborn. Nobody can predict the outcome. Only the audience decides. And the moment when (and if) the audience joins the collaboration is critical. When it works, the celebration is positively orgasmic.

The communal risk-taking that binds theatre people together is the source of the craft's social atmosphere. My first full-length play, the "country opera" *Cruel Tears*, was written with the Saskatoon musical group Humphrey and the Dumptrucks. The social and professional relationships formed among creators, cast and director Brian Richmond survive to this day.

Geoffrey Ursell, Barbara Sapergia and I were approached (as native Moose Javians) to write a Centennial musical for our home town in 1982, and we leaped at the chance to show that three playwrights were better than one. As novelists or poets, we would be mad to undertake anything so potentially divisive, but this three-part collaboration resulted in a play greater than the sum of our parts.

"Collective creations" have always left me cold, at least those that exclude the playwright. These shows are often entertaining, but rarely show any depth. Nonetheless, theatre work does encourage the exchange of roles and responsibilities. Actors are encouraged to write, writers to direct, directors to design, and so on. It's possible to become an all-round "theatrician," and not remain an isolated specialist. Imagine the chaos if poets, typesetters, publishers, compositors, press-men, and book sellers exchanged roles to produce a book. (But what a great idea in principle!)

Having become more committed to stagecraft over the years, I was pleased to observe my performing experience affect my work in the other genres of writing, too. Out of perceiving the powerful communication between actor and audience in a theatre, I've discovered something important about the nature of story-telling.

For years, I had been writing short stories that were really dramatic monologues. They usually feature a fictitious, nonauthorial narrator who speaks in a distinctive voice, and whose ironic viewpoint is essential to the theme of the story. Because I believed I was writing "literary" stories, I was trying with indifferent success to publish in the university quarterlies. Now I know that my task is to perfect sharp and credible dialects, and forget my efforts to develop an elevated or "experimental" literary style.

Similarly, my more occasional forays into poetry are conceived and written for performance, not publication. This sometimes feels like a rediscovery of the wheel—since most contemporary poetry bears little resemblance to any oral form of communication. I prefer poetry to be an *experience*, not a thing—especially a thing that requires obscure points of reference or elaborate footnotes before it can be understood. A published poem is to poetry what a printed score is to a symphony. Having abandoned the mainstream of Canadian poetry—the unread poetry mag, the subsidized chapbook—I sought less sophisticated audiences: students, bar-room patrons, radio listeners, astonished passersby in the street. When a poem is not written down, it becomes fluid and malleable, changing and improving with each performance. It's not good for poetry to be locked into concrete structures, without room to breathe. It *must* become more theatrical.

One performance piece I've called "Poem for a Reading" begins with conversational banality:

> If you've attended as many poetry readings as I have, you will have been struck by the fact that poets usually make long, introductory comments to their poems, which more often than not — are more interesting than the poem itself. A fascinating paradox, and one that may be true in this case, of a poem that I conceived when I first saw the castle above Astros
> like a Greek bird of prey
> squatting in the sun, grey stones
> crumbling down the cliffs like guano...

Most audiences never tumble to the fact that it *is* a poem — they're that interested — until the end, when it's too late for them to retreat into glassy-eyed "appreciation."

My faith in the aural dimension of poetry has had a reciprocal, and I think positive, effect on my playwrighting. The two most recent dramas, *Shipbuilder* and *Gone the Burning Sun*, are both lyrical — the former a drama for voices and percussion instruments, and the latter a monodrama with Chinese music, to be performed on a *pipa* (a classical lute-like instrument). The poetry is not blank verse or rhyming couplets, of course — but the organic rhythms of common speech.

Theatrical story-telling has become a fundamental element in my recent stage and screenplays. I've been working on a series of historical vignettes for the National Film Board with a number of Saskatchewan artists. Some are animated, some are dramatic, some are documentary—but each drama takes the form of a tall tale, or employs some other narrative trick from the folk culture which surrounds us.

The variety and combination of different genres of writing give rise to an interesting problem that I must face with each new subject: will it be a film, stage play, story, radio drama, poem or novel? In general, poems are shaped from personal experiences, and epic stories require the structure of a novel—but between these two poles a lot can happen. My task is to help the subject find its own form, and in the process I often end up wrenching material violently from one medium to another.

Shipbuilder, for example, is a drama based on the life of Tom Sukanen, a Finnish immigrant of the 1930s who built an oceangoing steamship on his farm near Outlook, Sask. He intended to haul it 17 miles overland to the Saskatchewan River and sail to Hudson Bay, and back to Finland—by himself. When I first encountered the story, I saw it as a film and scrambled to find a producer. Several filmmakers thought it a good story, but too expensive to make. Sukanen's epic had to be told, so I went to CBC radio with the research material. Because of the aural imagery demanded by radio drama, I introduced the element of percussion music. Into the script went rhythmic sound effects—anvils, clocks, heartbeat and so on—along with a musical score. This led to the development of rhythmic dialogue among the characters.

In the final event, the radio drama was not produced. The radio producer didn't see the need for music. The script was consigned to CBC limbo. With a sense of desperation, I rewrote it again—this time as a stage drama for a national competition. The plot had to be completely altered—from the movement of the ship to its construction. But in the process, the ship became a powerful theatrical metaphor— a physical symbol of work and the shipbuilder himself. The play won the competition and was successfully produced in universities and amateur theatres, though its size seemed to discourage Equity producers.

In the spring of 1980, however, Stewart Conn, a BBC radio producer, heard the drama in a playwrights' workshop in Edinburgh. It was produced on BBC, then rebroadcast a second time. The CBC finally showed a new interest, and a new radio version was done out of Vancouver—followed by its translation and broadcast in Finland and Sweden.

This outburst of interest renewed my faith in the drama, and a massive re-wright followed on the stage version—which had its première at Thunder Bay's Magnus Theatre in 1984. At the same time, ironically, I was completing a *Shipbuilder* screenplay for the National Film Board—based not on the new stage version, but on the life of Tom Sukanen. The story had progressed full circle back to the original material—in the form I had originally selected for it. And who knows what the final form of *Shipbuilder* will be?

Playwrighting teaches the value of revision. A play is constantly shaped and tested by the audience—until it often bears little resemblance to the original. *Gone the Burning Sun* was initially conceived in China as a one-man dramatic biography of Norman Bethune—because of a physical resemblance between the great doctor and myself that only the Chinese could have noticed. The first draft was written in the course of a three-week train journey through southern China. I intended to perform it myself as a vehicle for touring that vast country. Now, four years later, it has become a small prose opera for the actor David Fox and the virtuoso *pipa*-player, Pan Hui-zhu—an award-winning play and commercial success in Canada. But I am still here—having lost my ticket through the Middle Kingdom—working on a new radio drama about the Taiping Rebellion. You've never heard of it? Fantastic story—almost unknown in the West: the bloodiest civil war in human history, led by a man who claimed in 1851 to be the Younger Brother of Jesus Christ and went on to establish the Kingdom of Heavenly Peace on earth. Never mind. I'm incorporating it into my new novel. You can read about it then....

Small Town, Small World

Monty Reid

The truth is, I don't remember very much about it. About growing up in a small town, I mean. Until recently, I could have told you very little about my half-brothers and sisters. Their names, their ages, what they did. I didn't even know how many there were. Even now, I don't know when my father died, how old he was, how old I was. I can't recall the funeral—perhaps I didn't go. I possess one vivid image of him, sitting on the edge of the bed in his undershirt, leaning on a cane that had broken and was clamped together with two brass rings, then bound with tape. He is almost bald and his remaining hair, even the chest hair curling up from his unbuttoned, fleeced shirt, is white. That's all. Not a word, not a movement. And I have never tried to pursue it. I never ask.

The town itself was small, less than 500 people. It was named for the small east England city of Spalding, even though most of the local farmers were Scandinavian and French. The postmaster's wife was from Spalding. My father was a durable little Scot who ran, I'm told, a farm, a grain elevator, a pool hall. The land remains in the family, the grain elevator is torn down, and the pool hall is a drop-in centre for seniors.

I know this because I go back on occasion, to visit my mother and step-father. Every time I return my few surviving memories are shaken. Most recently, the bush around the town had been cut down. Looking down most of the streets you could see out over the fields, towards the horizon. Before, the town had seemed compact, rigorous, enclosed. Now, all 100 houses, it sprawled. Not the way I remembered it. Or my step-father recalls the time I fought another kid outside the café on mainstreet. I have no such memory; to the best of my knowledge it did not happen. The town, for me, becomes unstable.

And yet, is not this absence of memory something? It enables the town to persist, irremediably vague and fluctuating, there in my background. Perhaps one reason why I recall so little about it is that I do not want to peg it down, do not want to fix the instability. The town, it seems, has always lived with this uncertainty. And although it is the place where my roots inescapably go, perhaps I cannot follow them without digging them up and wringing the water out of them.

Nonetheless, I know some of them are grounded in religion. My family, at least my mother's family once my father had died, was devout. They were Seventh-Day Adventists, and this immediately set them apart. I think they were predisposed to this separateness. Their forebears were German peasants. They possibly did, and certainly thought they did, work harder and live more frugally than everyone else. Morally, they were more rigorous. And they wanted to be not only righteous, but also rich. They paid cash—my mother still cannot fathom the need for a mortgage.

In some ways, they may not have been so different. They wanted freedom to practise their religion and, certainly, freedom to make a private fortune. But this hardly distinguished them from their neighbours, who were all for making money and praying to whatever gods necessary. The neighbours, however, believed this was a public dream, that the necessary freedom could only be achieved by a community, a body politic capable of ensuring their rights. For the believers, the dream was private. They did not have to participate, they only needed to be left alone. For them the community could only be something that interceded between them and their ultimate salvation, and such intercession smacked of popery. The community, with its practical or even aesthetic considerations, was a distraction. Their puritanism could not stand such mediation and so they held back, apart. Religion just made their separateness feel better.

I did not feel better. I could not, for instance, play on the hockey team for many years because most of our games were on Saturday. Once I snuck away from home when our bantam team was invited to a tournament in Saskatoon. The first game was Saturday morning. I was checked into the boards in the first period and broke my arm. The hospital phoned my parents for permission to administer anaesthetic, so I couldn't try to tell them I had broken it after sundown, when the official day of rest was over. The break was, according to the church, divine retribution. My mother climbed up one side of the coach and down the other for letting me play.

Or I can remember standing in our back yard, watching the dust rise over mainstreet on Saturday evening as everyone congregated for late-night shopping, talk, drinks. I wanted to be there, but had to wait until sundown. The church office sent around a sunset calendar, with sundown times for different areas of North America marked on it. I had it tacked to my door, but it was never right. The sun always seemed to be down before the calendar said it was. Maybe we were too far north. But we went by the calendar anyway.

The feeling, though, of just being on the verge of community, of having it at your fingertips but not really being part of it, has remained with me. It's not lost, but not quite lived in either. Just a slightly longer reach would connect. It's there in *Karst Means Stone*, where Samuel Karst tries to write himself into a new world, in spite of his religion. And it is mapped in the more recent, more secular, poems of *The Alternate Guide*:

> your arms
> are like a
> greenbelt

proposed
to keep the air
constant...

...to ring that world
with residence, a
common air

(84B)

For me, small towns seem to capture the tension between
individual and community. They live it out day by day. It's no
accident that I have spent most of my life in them. At 15 I was sent to
a church school near Lacombe, Alberta. I attended university in
Edmonton, but then moved to Ryley, then Camrose, now Drumheller.
A movement around the perimeter of Alberta's major centres.

For the small communities I've lived in, proximity to a major
centre is a factor of huge significance. How long does it take, for
instance, to get into Calgary for parts, or for a good movie? Could you
make the drive every day if you had to commute? Camrose, for instance,
was less than an hour from Edmonton, while Drumheller is better than
an hour and a half from Calgary. It makes a difference. Casual trips
to the city from Drumheller are more rare. From Drumheller, the trip
must be planned, the city is still the desired object at the end of the
journey. Camrose felt more like the suburbs and, living there, you felt
subsumed by the journey. You were always part of it. It wasn't something you took, it took you.

Nonetheless, in Camrose or Drumheller, the country insists,
powerfully. It is just too close to be safely ignored. Four-wheel drive
tractors haul fold-up cultivators, metallic origami, through the streets;
the confusing town grid has been determined by the river; merchants
depend on farm incomes.

Here, talk about the weather is not small talk. The person you're
with may be ploughing his wheat under the next day. Still, the weather
is a mythical creature and is a clue to what I think is one of the definitive

features of small-town dwellers. The weather is beyond control, it cannot be organized, yet it is a determining factor in our lives. The small townsman, in other words, believes in power but knows he does not control it. Its source is always located somewhere else. They can attempt to go there and seize it, which is why so many rural people remember John Diefenbaker with nostalgia. Or they can create a mythology out of their own powerlessness. Hence the weather.

But I have never lived on a farm, and no one should mistake a small town for the west quarter. In some ways, the small town has a less restrictive mythology. The farmer, alone against the wilderness, subduing the land, enduring, living a kind of magnificent natural solitude, was a trickle-down version of the noble savage. The burghers sniggered at this a little, knowing their relation to the land and to the weather was a mediated, slightly better-protected one. The mediation came from community, and the burghers, dependent as they were on the farms, felt more sophisticated because they recognized this intercession.

Such community can be expressed in a local language, a language that designates something shared, in memory or in sight. It is precise and vital, simply because it is so close to the things it designates, whether it is the 'headframe' of Birk Sproxton's Flin Flon, or the 'crawlspace' and 'pitrun' of small towns like Ryley.

A friend, recently arrived in Drumheller from Edmonton, was amazed at the amount of language here. Not so much the sum total, but the total that was directed at her. On the street, everyone talked to her. She had become its address, it was not something that drifted around her like muzak and public relations. Similarly, city friends uncomfortable in a small town often cite the lack of privacy as an irritation. In a small town, they say, everybody knows your secrets, everybody talks. There is nowhere to be lost.

The small town insists on the primacy of community over privacy. The farm can be isolated, miles from the nearest neighbour. And the city, with its pace, its bustle, its consumer orientation, insists upon privacy as well. Too large to deal with its inhabitants as individuals, it sharply truncates any notion of the self. Although everyone is encouraged to acquire a personal space, with their own appliances and support systems, the individual is much reduced, defined not in relation to the community, the body politic, but in relation to consumer goods. The front yard, the public space of most single-family dwellings, is rarely used. Most activities take place out back, the vestigial farm.

The small town is an impure mix, with characteristics of city and country. Satellite dishes scoop American tv out of the air; retired farmers, who live in town for the summer, winter in Arizona trailer parks; the kids prefer heavy metal to country and western. But still, the local station plays Charlie Pride. By its very nature the small town is undogmatic, unable to define itself as rural or urban. And it is this very tentativeness, its determination to mediate between extremes, that gives it its quality of community.

While such tensions—between power and powerlessness, between isolation and community, between city and country—seem to me to be embodied in the small town, they are not resolved there. No one even dreams of resolution. This is one of the reasons I am attracted to them still. And it is for this reason that I think the small town may well be useful, both practically and conceptually, for prairie poetry.

Ambivalence about place is widespread in recent prairie writing. City and country are its rock and hard place. On the farm, writers needed the city. In the prairie city, uncomfortable and still provincial, they imagined another place. But no matter where they were, the need to imagine somewhere else didn't die. Eventually the prairie, once home, became the necessary other place. They returned, pervasively ambivalent about home and away. Where they came from was also where they had come to.

In *Out of Place*, Eli Mandel's book of return to small-town Saskatchewan, an "indescribable border" (14) is uncovered. The old Jewish colony evokes so many memories it is discomfiting; it makes "the journey in your bones/begin again." (48) The question nags: "Were we in the wrong place?" (37) Place itself is called into question and is constantly estranged. The book becomes a poetry of departures, a poetry in which the self is only a distant possibility.

But the self cannot be imagined out of the world. It is never disembodied. It is the subject of history, not of any single text. So if every place is ultimately somewhere else, the place of any potential subject is also deferred. It is infinitely delayed. And if the self is the site where meaning occurs, where code and practice articulate, then meaning is also postponed. And if meaning is communal, community itself has passed beyond reach.

Much prairie writing, just as it needs farm or city, opposing poles, needs a meaning guaranteed by providence or Oedipus, or meaninglessness. Eli Mandel looked at the petroglyphs at St. Victor and asked, "Do they mean anything?" The stone gods stand there with their mouths open but don't say a word. Caught between this silence and the strict rationality of demarcated farms, roadmaps and train schedules, Mandel felt out of place. Fair enough. But isn't there somewhere where world and subject articulate? Doesn't such articulation happen every day? Isn't there a middle ground?

All the townsman has is middle ground. He doesn't control meaning. The words that determine his life are, to use Bahktin's phrase, overpopulated with the intentions of others. And this is one of the pleasures of small-town living. Meaning circulates, linking farm and city, reader and text, social vision and subjectivity. A new idea, like new seed or new software picked up from the city, has to be tested against the practices of the country. It's neat, but what can it do? The process works in the other direction as well. And while meaning here is more unavoidably a practice than it is in most other places, the small town allows eccentric practice. It allows it, then cannot hide it. The tensions are enacted with a vengeance.

In poetry, it is in the formulation of such tensions that the subject, full of resistances and contradictions, is engaged. Subjectivity is the place of meaning, and is constituted by it. And it is in the engagement of tensions that the possibility of engaging the reader also resides. The tensions allow the possibility of identification.

Small towns, with their sheepish knowledge that they do not control everything, admit the tensions and thus re-create a place for the subject, perhaps articulate the subject in a new way, rifted by tensions it cannot control but dreaming nonetheless of meaning. Or they may provide a model for the subject as some other social context, marginalized but neither cynical nor indifferent. The subject's place must necessarily be created before the reader can again be engaged, can find a place for identification.

Such a place cannot be something as abstracted as 'prairie.' It is not a state of mind, or a statistical probability. It is a location with its own weather, its own history, and insisting on its own responsibilities. In fact, place itself does not exist, only places do.

To find such places is a problem within my work, and in the work of many contemporaries. Look at the anguished search for home in Andy Suknaski's recent poetry, the displacements in Claire Harris' books, the clearing—of plot, desk and mental space—that Lorne Daniel has been undertaking for the last several years, Bob Hilles' quiet and insistent probing.

We're not looking for paradise. But we want places that allow us, enable us, engage us—places with a past and a future. Without such places, there aren't any places at all.

A Statement of My Poetics

Brenda Riches

This is the eternal origin of art that a human being confronts a form that wants to become a work through him. Not a figment of his soul but something that appears to the soul and demands the soul's creative power. What is required is a deed that a man does with his whole being: if he commits it and speaks with his being the basic word* to the form that appears, then the creative power is released and the work comes into being.

The deed involves a sacrifice and a risk. The sacrifice: infinite possibility is surrendered on the altar of form; all that but a moment ago floated playfully through one's perspective has to be exterminated; none of it may penetrate into the work; the exclusiveness of such a confrontation demands this. The risk: the basic word can only be spoken with one's whole being; whoever commits himself may not hold back part of himself; and the work does not permit me, as a tree or man might, to seek relaxation in the It-world; it is imperious: if I do not serve it properly, it breaks, or it breaks me.

(Martin Buber, *I and Thou*)

When I first read these words, I recognized that they applied to my relationship with writing. After ten years, I have learned that my work best succeeds when I'm receptive to "a form that wants to become a work" through me. I don't succeed when I try to make my writing into something it doesn't want to be. In other words, I trust my subconscious and let what wants to come out, come out. I regard it as an I/You relationship. The activity is also more enjoyable than if I were to struggle with preconceptions. Someone once said to me that if you enjoy what you're writing, it won't be very good. For me, the opposite is true. If a piece is really difficult or sluggish, it's usually because I'm imposing my ideas of what it 'ought' to be. 'Ought' has no place in my work; it sets me on the wrong track. If I start a piece with ease, as long as it flows relatively unimpeded, I keep at it. When the breath runs out, I stop, leave it alone, and try again later, maybe even months later. It's not only no use flogging a dead horse; if you flog a live one too hard it'll wind up dead. Since this is the way my muse works, I have several pieces on the go at the same time. It's a distracting way to work, but I have three children and am used to distraction. In *A Room of One's Own*, Virginia Woolf said women have developed more as short-story writers than as novelists because their circumstances prevented them from devoting themselves to one long project with undivided attention. I find this is true of my life, but also it's my nature to get bored easily with what I write. I like intensity, and poetry and short fiction offer this. Sometimes I wish I could write a novel. Many of my short pieces eventually come together to form longer pieces. Perhaps I shall gather a patchwork novel in my dotage.

Instrumental

She plays her dulcimer in the dark in tune with a density of shadow where themes are veins of ore, waves breaking away from a night sea. Her song spreads like the skirt held in folds by the angle of her knees, sombre whorls of petal chains, links of sound binding the space of the corner where she cradles her instrument in the uncertain February room. Its painted wooden boards make a floor for her strumming, and a sturdy chair keeps her feet in place. Her hands are partners treading the simple strings, the dulcimer a platform for their measures. That hand lifts to arc and touch, this hand curves and plucks. If the opus were a garment it would clothe a nakedness: of branch, of flesh. It is a wallet of gravel flung to shatter thin glass and sting the upturned faces of children.

When people ask me what I write, I find it hard to say. I think for the most part I write poetry, but mainly in prose lines. I don't want to impose rhythm or pacing by breaking the lines. I want the words themselves to show how the pauses and phrasing should be. I do occasionally write poems in lines. And although I sometimes write stories that vaguely develop plot and character, I'm not truly a writer of stories, because nothing really happens in most of my fiction.

It doesn't matter what form the writing takes, the love of and obsession with language is what's important. "Obsession is all," as Shakespeare might have said. My interest in syntax has intensified over recent years. I like to play around with sentence structure, vary moods and tenses, try a question in place of a statement, a subjunctive in place of a question. I have become aware of tedious mannerisms, such as excessive use of relative pronouns, strings of prepositional phrases, linear progressions. This awareness has come to me thanks to the sharp eyes of a few friends who are also writers. I need my peers, and am grateful to those who have seen where my writing is, and where it wants to go. Writing has its own sense of direction, and sometimes the writer can be a real impediment by not seeing the signs. I once asked a writer friend where he thought I should go, now that my first book was published. "To the nearest bar," he suggested. Wine is a faithful inspirer, not only when I drink it, but also when I look at it in the glass, especially by candlelight.

Emily Dickinson said, "Tell all the Truth but tell it slant." That's what I want to tell—not so much the truth of factual events and people, but the truth of the imagination. I think metaphor is the most powerful vehicle of the imagination and the best way to slant the truth. Metaphor in its widest application, and influence, are my best literary allies.

There's a book called *The Anxiety of Influence*. I need influence to keep anxiety at bay—though I look forward to a time when I'll let go of influence to a greater extent that I can at present. My earliest conscious influences were Edna O'Brien, Virginia Woolf, Patrick White and Gabriel Garcia Marquez. There have been many unconscious influences too. Writers are like cows and wire fences—they rub off on each other. My recent influences are Samuel Richardson, John Cleland and Henry James. My writing was getting so sparse it was in danger of becoming bald, so I was glad to turn to the effusiveness of the 18th century style, and to James' late 19th century relative lack of restraint. I am at present trying to write a longer story in a style that to some extent catches that hurtle of language. My project could achieve aught. It could come to naught. It doesn't matter. Whatever needs to happen, will happen. The consoling thing is that it's ultimately out of my control.

In a television programme about the ballet choreographer Balanchine and the composer Stravinsky, one of them said, "We don't create, we assemble what's there." If we're to do that properly, we have to dump our baggage first. I'm frequently surprised by how much gets in the way of good expression: prejudices, uncertainties, clichés, fear of sounding stupid. It takes perseverance for the piece to shed all this and become itself. A writer friend said to me, "Live as if you're going to die tomorrow; work as if you're going to live forever." It's the point where these two meet that keeps the muse still, and the language spinning.

Northrop Frye said something similar to Martin Buber, but included the element of freedom in his statement. In *The Great Code*, Frye said:"...it is really language that uses man, and not man language... man is a child of the word as well as a child of nature...just as he is conditioned by nature and finds its conception of necessity in it, so the first thing he finds in the community of the word is the charter of his freedom." Strictly speaking, of course, this would imply an I/It relationship, where language exploits the writer, but the paradox is that it isn't until you commit yourself in servitude to language that you achieve this freedom. But paradox is the stuff of poetry.

*The basic word I/You is the expression of a relationship in which both parties are of equal, intrinsic value. They serve each other. Neither one treats the other as an object. The basic word I/It expresses a relationship where one party treats the other as a useful object. In this relationship, the service is one-sided, and therefore results in exploitation.

What the World was Saying When I Made It

Birk Sproxton

into the world

1. Bum shining

Another Yahoo joins the crew. What's going on here, he says. This place looks like the wreck of the Hesperus.

> night shift
> day shift

It took years before I began to hear the language my parents spoke. It was an exotic tongue, transplanted from the prairies to the rocks and bush of the Laurentian shield.

> afternoons
> grave-
> yard

What are you doing in there, my father would say, banging on the bathroom door, homesteading, and I knew it was time to get out. He spoke with fondness of the baldheaded prairie, and I never quite knew what he was talking about, but could hear the affection shining in his voice, especially at dusk when he liked to sing and tease.

He grew up in the parkland of Saskatchewan where he met my mother. She spent part of her girlhood in the drylands Mitchell writes about: "Here was the least common denominator of nature, the skeleton requirements simply, of land and sky...." For hours and years I listened to "Jake and the Kid," running my finger around the green light at the bottom of the radio or trying to read the curl and tuck of fabric on the speaker. I grew to like the Kid and Jake, but their language was not mine. They had nothing to say about underground, or headframes, or muskeg, the sudden dip of kneescraping elbowsmashing rock, and lake after lake after lake, from Athapapuskow to Schist to Beaver, the layering of languages, Amisk/lac aux castors/Beaver Lake, Cree/French/English, shifts in language and history.

Shift boss, I heard, not to be confused with shift, bossy, move yer ass, that tit squeezing kind of barnyard talk. I knew my world was not rural, not cowshit rural, not the snuffle of graindust down your shirt. Or chewing grainmush to gum gum gum gum. Smeltersmoke, we called that throat tickle, coughed it in the west wind, and on our horizon a highrise of smokestack and headframes and close to the earth

bumshining, an incessant sliding of the signifier under the signified, bumshining, the only way to travel, hook onto the tail of a car, or a bus, they're better, and squat down, ride on your boots, glide on the snow through the fingering cold to tennis ball street hockey with Carnation milk tins marking the goal, Birk Broda making the big save with a beat-up baseball glove, waiting to be a rink rat and boom the puck off the boards, drive a slapshot from blue line to short side....

And on the radio, voice of the north, other voices, the mailbag program, Reverend Horsefield telling stories in Cree, Joe Tobacco and Mary Custer sending greetings to friends at Pukatawagan or Beaver Lake or Sandy Bay or Big Eddy, voices of the north.

Chooque, they called me, after the toque I wore, *toque*, with lower jaw forward, after the Cree manner, Chooque. (In the city I met a woman called me Chuck.)

2. The Garden and the City

> Come down to Kew in lilac time
> in lilac time in lilac

We memorized and recited en masse. None of us had been to London, let alone Kew. I didn't know what a lilac was. Gardens had to be built before they could be planted and maybe grow something.

Here is what you've been waiting for, a recipe for building a garden.

1. Find a flat spot, if you can, and whack down the trees and rip out the stumps and roots and rocks, if you can.

2. You need lime, you know, the cementbag bags, muskeg, clay, sand, and black dirt hauled by the washtub full in the back of a 1954 Pontiac from the garden down by the lake, which is sort of a real garden, divided by a criss cross of ditches and stumps and the big fat boulder in the middle, the dry place.

3. Mix it all up and stir like crazy.

4. Throw in some horseshit too if you can get it.

> something to be said about moving
> earth   hauling dirt for fill

> lug an old washtub
> up and up the hill
>   one hill two hill

```
three hill down
                mix in muskeg
damp and brown
                stir in black dirt          .
clay and lime   mix in dry sand
take your time      turn it over in your mind


build a garden   mix in sand
haul the dirt there    all by hand
```

I delivered the *Star-Phoenix* by hand, brand spanking new every day, as a Phoenix should be. But there weren't a lot of takers. Saskatoon was Saskatoon.

The city was Winnipeg and Winnipeg was a street car ride to hospitals and surgeons, and the gut pain of being alone in a room with other people, alone, and wanting and not wanting to cry, and poking into my head with lights and sticks and knives, mining the ore, left a hole there big enough to land an airplane. (Pretended after that to be deaf. Got away with it, till an airplane stab of gravity sent me back to a specialist, ear in hand, says I'm not even hard of hearing, not officially. Convenient though to be deaf. Gave my family a new expression too. The one with the bad ear. Write poems to get even.)

That spring we moved the outhouse and Allen carved the inside of the door: "This hole dug by" and then my names and university degrees. The English professor finally does something useful.

That spring I chopped out stumps, hacking away with shovel and axe, the only tools a man can trust. Allen thought only a professor would be dumb enough to clear a stump by digging and chopping at the roots.

Here, get out of the way, he said, and backed his truck up to the stump. He spun his wheels. The truck jumped, the bumper landed on top of the stump. He jammed into forward, spun his wheels. The truck snuggled down, locking tight on the stump.

So we dug around the truck around the stump and chopped around the bottom around the truck and got the truck from around the stump and the stump from under the truck.

(And the bumper was bent and Al was mad and he carved a story on the shithouse door.)

3. Headframe

whump says the charge of dynamite. The jackhammers and mosquitoes snarl and rattle, snarl and rattle.

On the outskirts of town a sign says, Kelsey Trail, the end and the beginning of highway #10. The first Englishman in western Canada, Kelsey gave the place a name: "The Inland Country of Good Report." And since he was our first poet in English he hustled his ass to get here.

> The Inland country of Good report hath been
> By Indians but by English not yet seen
> Therefore I on my journey did not stay
> But making all the haste I could upon the way
> Gott on the border of the stone Indian country

A border country, Manitoba/Saskatchewan, full of bush and rocks, a marginal world. Not good for farming. Where the hell is everybody? The open pit? Underground? An abysmal place. Everybody swallowed right up, thrown into the pit.

Mise en abyme. A headframe marks the spot, an endless round of descent and ascent, the singing of the cables in the hoist room, an inner darkness, the singing of rocks and trees. *Mise en abyme.* The inner design, says J. Hillis Miller explaining the linguistic moment, repeats the overall pattern. Flin Flon: a descent and yes Orpheus and Eurydice, the life of the miner, day after day an entry into labyrinthine darkness where the rain never falls. A repetition (with variations), a doubling and a double going (doppelgangers), sound echoes (Flin Flon), envelopes (a headframe, sign of coming and going, marks the spot), a sense of vertigo (the open pit). "The *mise en abyme* must constantly begin again."

The railroad begins (and ends) at the headframe. And the town dangles there on the edge of the shield at the end of the line, an infant.

At the mother end of this infant town, the navel, is a novel. Flin Flon was born in a novel. The novel is called *The Sunless City* and tells an underground story. Flin dives in his man-made fish (this is a subtext) down to the bottom of the bottomless lake, spiralling down to the city where the streets are paved with gold and women take charge, keep men in line. This underground city is the matrix of story: not urban or rural or suburban, but a sub world. Sub rural sub real   sur real   a world spinning at the end of the line reaaaling   you can reel it in   it's all there on the line   reaally an open pit   the novel   headframes   as the whirled is saying/
      unreeling   un   real   ing

      I can hear my mother whisper Horsefeathers
      That's just horsefeathers and you know it
          whispering

Fill with Words the Distant Places

Merna Summers

The impulse to write, where does it come from? From just about anywhere, it seems. Even contempt can trigger it.

Let us say that a young person of literary bent encounters the work of a writer he knows to be highly thought of, but discovers that the work is not much good. *I could do that*, the young person thinks. And so the desire to write is born.

Or it is born in some other way; almost anything will serve. Writers are self-elected and they do not have to account for their voting patterns.

Once having decided to be a writer, the young person must think of something to write about. He must somehow discover the story or stories for which he—the one individual writer—is the proper spokesman.

The writer hopes, of course, to produce something "new," and his desire to do this can cause him to be either too receptive to the ideas that come to him, or not receptive enough. He may think that every idea is brilliant just because he has been so fortunate as to have had it, or he may hold every idea up to scrutiny, asking himself if it is "new" or if somebody else has already "done it," and discount it for that reason. He knows that the world is his subject, but how is he to get a handle on that world?

I once took part in a seminar at which writing students and writers were brought together, the idea being that the former would be able to learn something from the latter. I am not sure that things worked out that way. The reason they did not had to do with a question that the students showed a stubborn tendency to ask each time one of the "real" writers read a story. The question was: *"Did this really happen?"* and the writers reacted to it with considerable crossness.

They should not have. What the students wanted to know, I believe, was: *What is the relationship between reality and fiction? How do you turn one into the other?*

These are important questions, and there are others related to them. *What parts of reality are worth turning into fiction? Where does the writer get his reality? What do you start out with? If what life provides you with isn't good enough, how do you go about acquiring a better kind?*

A writer's working life is determined by the answers he thinks up for such questions.

Writers write for many reasons. For some, writing is a thing asked of them by the place they come from. Margaret Laurence has said that, "Any writer who can put this country down on paper has a sacred duty to do so."[1]

Pablo Neruda, the great Chilean poet, was of similar mind. He once said that we, the writers of the Americas, "listen unceasingly to the call to fill this mighty void with beings of flesh and blood. We must fill with words the distant places in a dumb continent, and we are intoxicated by this task of making fables and giving names."[2]

Fill with words the distant places: a wonderful description for the task of a writer. The writer takes something out of his own place on earth and then puts something back, something different, something that was not there before, but that was, he hopes, needed.

"Fiction depends for its life on place," Eudora Welty has said. "Every story would be another story...if it took up its characters and plot and happened somewhere else."[3]

One reason this is so is that it is not the *first* job of fiction to present ideas, but to create a reality, a world out of which ideas may emerge. Fiction, if it is to stand firm, needs the support of a real world, and this is true even of fantasy, of the surreal novel. Robert Kroetsch's card players may play on for 151 obsessed days, but they speak in the accents of Heisler, Alberta. Indoors they keep score on ripped-off calendar pages; outdoors they use wooden shingles.[4] As someone from the same country as Kroetsch, I can testify that this is exactly what they *would* do. The pleasure of this book, part of it anyway, is in the juxtaposition of wild fancy and homely detail. As Welty says, "Fantasy itself must touch ground with at least one toe."[5]

Welty feels that the reason fiction is "all bound up in the local is that *feelings* are bound up in place." "Place," she says, "has a more lasting identity than we have, and we unswervingly tend to attach ourselves to identity."[6]

What writers choose to write about is influenced not only by place but by other works of writing. Our writing comes not only out of the life we know, but also out of the life we have learned to recognize by reading what other writers have written.

Is this "being influenced," that menace that so worries young writers? Of course it is, and a good thing too. It is the writer's business to grow in any way he can. The broader his sympathies, the greater his chance of having something worthwhile to say. The young writer needs to realize that no one expects him to write as if no one had ever written before he took up the craft. Every writer is the spiritual child of at least one other writer; many of us are multi-parented. And generally speaking, originality is a thing that can be counted on to take care of itself, to creep in when the writer is paying attention to what he has to say.

How do you turn reality into fiction? What should the writer write about? Of all the things he might write about, what is worth his time, his life? And who is to be the judge of that?

The writer, you would say, and you would be right, and the writer's salvation depends upon his also saying it strongly and firmly. There are, nevertheless, pressures on a writer, and I would like for a moment to consider some of them.

The writer does not write into a vacuum, but into a world of readers, of critics, of writers for the daily press. And if he listens to the sounds coming from that world he realizes that certain subjects, subjects which he may have thought important, have become unfashionable. Certain places and certain times may be ruled out.

"Our rural past has been written out," we sometimes hear, and as a writer currently at work on a novel set in the rural Alberta of the 1920s, I find this conclusion of more than passing interest.

Voices are raised on both sides of the question. Mario Vargas Llosa says: "In general, I think that literature is apt to nourish itself more from remote or extinct realities, from past experiences, than from immediate actuality. Often writing is done to recover the illusion of what is already dead. The living, that which is here, is less stimulating and, basically, less malleable as literary material."[7]

Equally distinguished voices are raised on the other side.

"Fuck the past," Robert Kroetsch says.[8]

But with all due respect, with all admiration for the wild and wonderful things that Kroetsch is doing in his fiction, I would cast my vote on this with Vargas Llosa. I note that Kroetsch said "Fuck the past" only *after* he had written *The Words of My Roaring.* And if that book were still unwritten, I believe that it would still be necessary for Kroetsch to write it, because it is an absolutely necessary book for us to have. There may be other necessary books about our rural past as yet unwritten; a necessary book is not a thing you can predict in advance.

In fairness to Kroetsch, I should note that he has since clarified what he meant to suggest. "As for my 'Fuck the past' stance," he has written in personal correspondence, "it is of course the official version of history that I dislike so intensely. Good fiction is what I call 'archaeological' in that it unearths the history that has been concealed from us."

There are, nevertheless, some critics who would still declare certain subjects off limits for literature. Alberto Manguel, who reviews books on the CBC program, *Morningside*, is given to referring dismissively to "novels about growing up in Halifax." Once, speaking of a novel he liked, he said that here was a book that would henceforth make it impossible to write novels "about growing up in Halifax."

But is this true? And would it be a good thing if it were? There is trendiness in literature as in all things, but I wonder if it is the proper business of critics to rule out whole categories of literature. Whether it is or not, those of us who are not critics but writers need to be wary when we hear this kind of thing. We need to keep our attention on what can be done, not on what can not. The writer has limitations enough of his own without accepting any that other people would impose upon him.

How does a writer know what to write about? Sometimes beginning writers want to talk about their writing before it exists. They have an idea for a story, and they want to know if it is a good idea before they go ahead.

Such discussions are rarely profitable. What the young writer needs to know is that an idea is good if it involves something vitally important to him: there is no other test. (Please note that here I am talking about *ideas*. The resulting work is another matter.)

The whole world is there to be written about, the world of "reality" and the world of imagination. Carlos Fuentes has said that it is the task of modern literature "to reclaim the plural sources of man's humanity and inhumanity."[9] That is to say, anything that is human is there to be explored. The only thing that matters is that the reality (in all the meanings of that word) be important to the writer who is trying to depict it. What the writer needs to ask himself is not *Would this idea make a good story?* but *Do I care enough about it to try?* A novel may take ten years to produce or it may take two; either way it's a lot of time to spend on an idea that doesn't preoccupy you, seduce you into thinking that it is important.

What if the writer can't decide about these things? What if he is afraid that he is not the right person to decide what is important and what is not?

He has to make that assumption. He cannot write well unless he can at least convince himself that he is a person who knows what is worth writing about.

Nor should the young writer worry if he finds that his sense of what is important leads him into literary territory that has been explored before. It is not his business to produce novelties, but— perhaps—to seek revelations.

"Whatever our theme in writing," Eudora Welty says, "it is old and tried. Whatever our place, it has been visited by the stranger, it will never be new again. It is only the vision that can be new; but that is enough."[10]

----

1. Margaret Laurence, cited by Marian Engel in "The Woman As Storyteller," *Communique*, May, 1975, 6.

2. Pablo Neruda, in his Nobel Prize lecture, published as *Toward The Splendid City* (New York: Farrar, Strauss and Giroux, 1977), 27.

3. Eudora Welty, *The Eye of the Story* (New York: Vintage Paperback, Random House, 1977), 118, 122.

4. Robert Kroetsch, in *What The Crow Said* (Toronto: General Publishing, PaperJacks, 1979).

5. Welty, *The Eye of the Story*, 126.

6. Welty, *The Eye of the Story*, 119.

7. Mario Vargas Llosa, in an interview with Carlo Meneses, *Latin-American Literature Today*, ed. Anne Fremantle (New York: Mentor, 1977), 327.

8. Robert Kroetsch, cited in promotional material for *Driving Home*, a conference on Canadian writing held at the University of Calgary in 1982.

9. Carlos Fuentes, *Central and Eccentric Writing, Latin American Literature Today,* ed. Anne Fremantle (New York: Mentor, 1977), 140, 142.

10. Welty, *The Eye of the Story,* 133.

Poetics of Tension and Encounter

Anne Szumigalski

Apologia

Thus far I have managed to avoid making any public statement of my poetics, choosing instead to answer all questions by directing the enquirer towards my poems. "Judge for yourself," I have said. "Here are my poems. Read them. They themselves are my statement. If you are interested in my poetics, deduce them from my work and then come back and tell *me* what they are."

This I have done not from laziness, muddleheadedness, or fear of explanation or exposition, but simply from fear of death. I am not of course speaking of personal death but of the death of my work, or rather the death of the current phase of my work. For expressed poetics must, I feel, be nothing less than an epitaph. "From these and these insights and positions I have written. Heaven only knows what stand I shall take tomorrow." Amen, amen.

And so in hope of a new phase in my work I lay me down to sleep with these statements of my poetics folded beneath my pillow. May these words enter my head and then fly out again making room for better poems than I have ever written before.

For the poet, that absurd combination of naiveté and sophistication, can never be satisfied with her work, must find a new tune and saw away at the broken fiddle forever.

Our Sullen Art

the language of poetry has something to do
with the open mouth the tongue that jumps
up and down like a child on a shed roof calling
ha ha and who's the dirty rascal now?
the same boy sent to his room for punishment
leans from his window listening for animals
far away in the woods strains his ears to catch
even the slightest sound of rage but nothing howls
even the hoot of owls in the dusk is gentle

he hears the tiny snarl of the shrew
the rasp of the snail's foot on the leaf
the too-high squeaking of bats which comes
to his head as the vibration
of distant hacksaws   he hum humms
with his lips tight shut he stands there
listening and humming almost through the short night
then   falls into the tangle of sheets and blankets
where fitfully he sleeps while slowly
the window greys to four panes of bleak light

the day's first traffic travels carefully
past the windows and doors of the shut house

so as not to awaken in the child
those savage cries our violent
our pathetic language of poems

Elements of the Poem

self
other
insight
the interpretive role
the imaginative vision
tension and struggle: that is person against poet, reader against writer
language first and always
the physical landscape
the landscape of the mind

The Poetics of Tension and Encounter

Poetry is great passion under great restraint.

is imagination struggling against form.

is an overriding idea in conflict with an assertive language.

is great risk set against great certainty.

is insight arguing with logic.

is vision in contention with knowledge.

Poetry is the energy of the body (expressed in rhythm, sound, repetition, and so on) wrestling with the energy of the intellect (expressed in theories, ideas, logic).

The Influence of Place — The External Landscape

This prairie, this place to which we have come, or from which we have emerged, has never so far failed in its overriding influence on those who write in it and of it. We have so often expressed the struggle of poetry by the struggle of man against the violence and oppression of the elements. Other landscapes, other poems. From gentler places may have come pieces that glorified Nature and her motherly beauty. Not from the prairie. Her beauty is spacious and unrestrained, as well as pitiless and ruthless. Drought, fire, heat, cold, privation and loneliness, these have been recurring images and themes in our prairie writing: Man against nature, Natural Man against the civilized interloper, the land itself against those who would tame her.

For our prairie writers are first of all riders. They have ridden their ponies on and off the pages of our history and literature, trampling the grass, marking the land with the hooves of their steeds. Somewhere out there beside a grid road is an abandoned and roofless farmhouse. A flock of birds flies up as we pass in our racketing vehicles (not horses any more, but we like to give them horsey names, Pinto, Mustang, and so on).

The birds then, which rise up so readily into the huge skies of our reality and our imagination, are screeching out prairie poems, not so much songs as anecdotes of our foremothers and forefathers. Grandma is fighting the dust and loneliness for the sake of the family. Or perhaps Grandpa is withering out there on the prairie, refusing in his old age to leave the place which is rightfully his own. Meanwhile he is relating those stories and incidents which are to become myths for his descendants.

from THE QUESTION

behind the woman a window is open   a breeze pushes
against the back of her head causing her voice to empty

itself into the room   the wind gives her words the
twang of an out-of-tune harp   they shape themselves

into a question she's been asking about the scheme
of things   *it all seems to be rushing away from us* she
remarks *as from an abhorred centre*

beside a small table a naked man sits with his legs
crossed   where skin touches skin his body hairs lock
each one tangling with another   the light enters the
glassy cones of his eyes which glint like the eyes
of a dog wandering on a road at night

with one hand he fondles the brass stem of the lamp
on the table beside him with the other he reaches
for the woman's hand counting her fingers with his
own   why can't he remember how many fingers this
woman has

The Influence of Space—The Internal Landscape

Then what of those poets to whom the prairie is apparently more or
less incidental—who seldom write of the external prairie, wilderness
or forest? There are more and more of us lately whose prospect is an
urban one; that is, whose external landscape is an urban one. The
internal landscape is quite another thing.

For a prairie poet is a prairie poet. The amazing place of his birth or his
choice cannot easily be forgotten or set aside. What happens I think is
that the physical place, the place which he has lived in, or driven
through, or heard of, or seen, becomes his internal landscape. And
this landscape of the mind, of the poetic imagination and vision, has
become part of the writer's thought, part of the poet's poetic. It may
never be expressed as an image, a symbol or an anecdote; it will almost
certainly be expressed as a contention, an argument, a struggle. Perhaps
it is in this sense of conflict, this urge towards conquest that the prairie
is best described by our non-landscape poets, of whom perhaps I am one.

Current Prairie Fiction: Openings/Beginnings

Wayne Tefs

Fifteen years ago I spent six months trying to read John Updike's *The Centaur*. I'd get about ten or fifteen pages into the book before closing it in a mood of frustration fast warping into rage. This perplexed me since I'd read with great pleasure a number of Updike's other works. And I prided myself on being an eclectic reader. Several weeks would pass. I'd try again. Perhaps a few pages further in than on the previous occasion I'd have the same experience. Eventually I did finish *The Centaur*, but that hasn't prevented the same thing happening with other books: I'm currently going through a similar struggle with a Rosamund Lehman.

I record these experiences not to demonstrate my persistence as a reader but to raise an issue about current "prairie" fiction. Fiction, particularly the novel, invites its readers into a world. That invitation occurs within the opening pages of every novel where the writer gives voice and shape to experience. (It is within those critical opening thirty pages that most novels are embraced or abandoned by readers; very few readers, I suspect, put novels aside after reading a hundred or so pages.)

The experience of rage and frustration that all readers have with fiction arises from our inability to enter certain worlds—particularly those shaped by new and unconventional voices. When we hear the voice of a narrator who imposes on our sensibility, who makes new demands on us, who proffers an unfamiliar vision, we draw back. For complex social and psychological reasons we reject the invitations of some writers—and even, as my own experience with *The Centaur* indicates—some books by writers already known and loved.

Such rejections occur in all places and periods since serious novelists are continually exploring the limits of their craft—and inviting readers into uncharted and often troubled worlds. In the period following the Great War the upset was perhaps more pronounced than usual. In the nineteenth-century novel, and its naturalistic/realistic foster child that survived into the twentieth, the world (or more accurately, worlds) into which readers were invited was both known and comfortable. This does not mean that world was simplistically predictable or homogeneous. In fact it was both greatly varied and profoundly complex, particularly in terms of morality. But it was usually comfortable because it reflected a set of assumptions, values, and perceptions about society and individuals which had been honed through the nineteenth century and carried into the twentieth. It was this "set" that was shaken in the aftermath of the Great War. (Think of the difference between Hardy's *Return of the Native* and Céline's *Journey to the End of Night*.)

The novel that sprang up on the Canadian prairie had its roots in that late nineteenth-century ethos. Hence its earliest flavour was realistic in the manner made popular on this continent by writers such as William Dean Howells, Stephen Crane, and Frank Norris. The Canadian prairie novel typically depicted day-to-day life in a naturalistic setting, its writers relishing the lyric evocation of the particulars of place. One of these, Robert J. C. Stead's *Grain*, illustrates well such writers' enthusiasms:

With an unreasoning disregard for the fitness of things, the early settlers always made use of shingle nails half an inch too long for the boards into which they were driven. It was the only shingle nail they knew, and that every nail should protrude through the board, splintering off a fragment at its end, they accepted as inevitable, very much as they accepted early sunrise in summer and late sunrise in winter. In frosty weather each of these nail-ends became a condensing point for the household vapours, and a thousand little globules of ice formed in rows between the poplar rafters, dripping a little when the heat from the stove overpowered the cold at the other end of the nail.

The details are, of course, charming. But they are cast in a remarkable way. Notice particularly how the passage is defined by acceptance, the settlers described in it accepting both the anomalies of hardware and the exigencies of climate as "inevitable." (Metaphysically given, so to speak, and beyond the reach of human revision.)

Up until very recently the invitation proffered by prairie novels was to this world: a narrow world of harsh climate, hard work, and simple morality. Over it all brooded the severe countenance of the landscape. Here is the opening of one such novel:

On the road leading north from the little prairie town Minor two men were fighting their way through the gathering dusk.

Both were recent immigrants; one, Lars Nelson, a giant, of three years' standing in the country; the other Niels Lindstedt, slightly above medium size, but compactly built, of only three months'. Both were Swedes; and they had struck up a friendship which had led to a partnership for the winter that was coming. They had been working on a threshing gang between Minor and Balfour and were now on their way into the bush settlement to the north-east where scattered homesteads reached out into the wilderness.

It was the beginning of the month of November.

The voice here is not necessarily comforting—and what occurs in Grove's *Settlers of the Marsh* is not either—but the voice here is busy developing a comfortable situation for the reader: colouring in setting, for example, details relating to character, a basic plot. Very quickly the reader is located in space and time, adjusted to mindscape as well as landscape.

Hand in hand goes something else: the essentials of the typical prairie fictional experience are here in place. A harsh—predictably rural—environment stands over and against the aspirations and desires of men and women bound to each other by the tenets of faith and bound to the land by the need to eke out a subsistence. Two things can be safely predicted: that human aspirations will be thwarted by a landscape described at once as a lover and a tyrant; that various human betrayals will occur on the way to growth in the sustaining virtue of loving-kindness.

The most striking dramatization of these themes occurs in Sinclair Ross' *As for Me and My House* where Mrs. Bentley continually symbolizes her plight in images that reflect the Lilliputian stature of humans in the prairie landscape. Here she is at one typical moment: "It was as if there were a lantern hung above you in a darkened and enormous room; or as if the day had turned out all its other lights, waiting for the actors to appear, and you by accident had found your way into the spotlight, like a little ant or beetle on the stage." This can perhaps be called the prairie version of "unaccommodated man." Such vulnerability and helplessness lead to the other "inevitable" of the prairie novel, despair.

Until quite recently these have been the benchmarks of the prairie novel. W. O. Mitchell, Sinclair Ross, Rudy Wiebe, even Margaret Laurence have contributed not only to a prairie sense of place—a sense that this is a place and that it deserves fictional treatment—but to a rootedness in a prairie ethos that has at times come perilously close to reverse snobbism: pride in this instance arising not from privilege and achievement, but from hardship and defeat. Some of this ethos has carried over into contemporary fictions, particularly when the protagonists have been involved in a struggle to overthrow one or another version of oppression. Terrence Heath's *Last Hiding Place*, dealing with a native's spiritual conflict, is one example. In another, Margaret Clarke's *The Cutting Season*, we are introduced to the typical prairie version of anti-pastoral:

> The stillness of the lake was absolute in the weak autumn sun as the mother and daughter walked beside the shore. The water was so undisturbed that the gray rock of the shoreline was reflected perfectly in the cold clear surface. The world was divided into two sharp images; the clarity of each was startling in the northern air. When the mother glanced at the water, the rock, there was a moment when she was unsure as to which was the real earth and which its watery reflection. The world turned itself upside down and she righted it only by a mental effort. The daughter did not look at the lake or the land. She followed her mother doggedly, like a shadow, and occasionally she spoke.

Again there is that very clearly defined sense of place: rocks, water, trees, the contours of a space at once absence and imposing presence. The people are dwarfed by landscape—dwarfed in the psychological as well as in the physical sense. Geography imposes a new variation of the Immanent Will. Though a long way from Mitchell's folksy depiction of the encompassing plain or Ross' landscape as nullity, there is nevertheless the brooding presence of an environment hostile to human habitation. In the early years of this century that attitude was appropriate, life on the prairies until the conclusion of World War Two being little more than the history of rural peasants attempting various forms of survival and flight.

The predominant mood of such writing was irony; humans were depicted as ant-like creatures struggling for survival, inevitably doomed. The heroic achievement of such novels amounted to little more than endurance, the defining features of life being suffering in the face of insurmountable odds and acceptance of the limitations of human experience. An appropriate epitaph for all the novels written under that banner might be: Death By Landscape.

This oppressive mood of irony hanging over the "prairie" novel is challenged (as are readers) with the arrival of a new and, at first, startling voice:

> People, years later, blamed everything on the bees; it was the bees, they said, seducing Vera Lang, that started everything. How the town came to prosper, and then to decline, and how the road never got built, the highway that would have joined the town and the municipality to the world beyond, and how the sky itself, finally, took umbrage: it was all because one afternoon in April the swarming bees found Vera Lang asleep, there in a patch of wild flowers on the edge of the valley.

Vera Lang is the central character in Robert Kroetsch's *What the Crow Said*. The depiction of Vera in the opening paragraph of that novel is instructive, for the sweep of events in which she becomes an integral actor is as breathtaking for its vitality as it is stunning for its vision. What marks the voice of Kroetsch as different from his predecessors and, more important, from contemporaries such as Wiebe, is not his striking narrative pyrotechnics, or his celebrated "magic realism." True, those elements of his work set him apart from other prairie novelists in obvious stylistic ways: there is an energy in Kroetsch so fresh and so demanding that reading him requires a loosening of restraints not unlike that which Falstaff forces on Shakespeare's audience. But the pyrotechnics and magic are secondary to (subsumed under) a radical shift in vision.

With Kroetsch the prairie novel begins to transform the landscape rather than to be moulded by it. Instead of the typical realistic treatment in which humans are oppressed and defeated by climate, work, and sexual relations, in Kroetsch it is human eroticism and human vision which triumph over environment. The tables have been turned. Where in the typical early prairie novel landscape dominated people, it is now shaped by the (usually erotic and irreverent) human imagination. The predominant mood is comedy rather than irony; those typical shrugged shoulders of the "defeated" in the naturalistic novel have been replaced by the manic laugh and the impudent erection.

Perhaps the most striking element emerging in the new equation is play. The defining feature of the early models was a kind of tragic endurance fortified, often, with piety. Here is Martha Ostenso in *Wild Geese* commenting definitively, if not entirely beautifully, on that: "The austerity of nature reduces the outward expression in life, simply, I think, because there is not such an abundance of natural objects for the spirit to react to." The new prairie fiction focusses precisely on that quality of spirit, not in its manifestation as spiritual, but as spiritedness. Now elements such as fantasy, dream, and carnival are central on the fictional stage. Ridicule replaces angst, sympathy, oppression, and sexual energy, helplessness. Emotion is boiled in the open pot of comic burlesque rather than in the sealed furnace of heroic suffering.

The more ambitious of the rising generation of prairie novelists have taken up the challenge. Two among them, Guy Vanderhaeghe and Geoffrey Ursell, open their recent works as follows:

> The Beast destroyed my brief peace. Before him I could live without guilt, unwatched; for the first time in my life I found myself in the unfamiliar situation of having no one to disappoint. My wife Victoria had walked out on me months before, and although I wished she hadn't, her departure meant I could do more or less as I liked. My father, recently retired, had removed himself and my mother to a mobile-home park near Brownsville, Texas, a sprawling anthill of pensioned worker ants, thousands of miles away. That meant Pop no longer had his eye on me. There was no one left to offend, no one to despair of me and my misdemeanors. After a fashion, I was free.

> More than two hundred years later, Perdue, standing on the very spot, would remember how the cavalcade, with his father in the lead on a stallion, finally came out of the forest and reached the top of the last ridge of hills.

Such openings mark an important departure for the "prairie" novel—a new beginning, in a way. Here landscape is secondary to human aspiration and desire. To human intelligence. Vanderhaeghe's central character, Ed, has about him the unprincipled, clever, but nonetheless likeable faults of the conventional picaro. And Ursell's Perdue is an innocent visionary. Each of the speakers assumes a role that defines him not as the anguished hero who must learn first to suffer and then to accept his narrow role in the cosmic scheme, but as the controlling consciousness of a vibrant human civilization. The intelligence in charge is not the daemon who inhabits the sinister garden of the naturalistic narrative which twentieth-century writers inherited from the nineteenth, but the formative human mind.

I like to think that those of us writing novels and living on the prairie—writing about the prairie in one way or another—are on the cusp of this development. Recognizing our enormous debt to those who have gone before. But also finding, in a sense, new ways to begin, ways which sustain the radical vision introduced by Kroetsch: of man civilizing nature through acts of vision and imagination. Sweeping away something oppressive about the naturalistic view of things, and giving a wider sweep to the powers and potentials of the human intelligence. Each opening that risks such imaginative scope takes the prairie novel one step further away from the ironic vision of the realistic landscape novel toward a more triumphant human perspective—of men and women celebrating life and giving it human energy and shape.

The Making of a Docudrama

W. D. Valgardson

When John Juliani called me—he's a CBC producer who has encouraged me to write a half-dozen radio plays during the past four years—to say he wanted an hour-long docudrama, my first response was that I could not do it. Before our conversation was over, I'd agreed to write the script. However, my insecurity was so great that I placed the cheque for the initial payment in an envelope ready to send back. It sat there for three months.

By asking me to write the story of Flight 314, Juliani started me off on six months of research and writing. To get me going, he sent a file which contained an accident report and a lot of newspaper clippings. Naively, I believed that everything I needed would be there. Even a quick first reading of the newspaper reports proved that idea wrong. The newspaper material was both highly unreliable and repetitive. The major accident report was better. It gave, in clear, precise detail, a lot of factual information. Unfortunately, it also left a lot of gaps. As well, this was to be a docudrama and that meant that the centre of interest was not solely around what happened but what happened to someone—with the emphasis on the someone.

What did come out of the initial reading of the file was a focus for the play. When Flight 314 tried to land at Cranbrook, there had been a snowplough on the runway. The pilot had touched down, then taken off again. After climbing to 400 feet, he crashed. The newspaper clippings told a poignant story about the snowplough operator. He had quickly been blamed by the local people. Daily life had been made so difficult for him and his family that they'd had to move out of their home. The investigation proved that the snowplough operator was completely innocent. He must, I thought, have been the loneliest man in the world from the moment he saw the plane's lights in his rearview mirror until a newspaper article was printed pointing out what an injustice had been done to him.

A first reading also made me realize that because the crash was only six years old, I would be faced with particular problems which would not exist for the writers of the historical episodes. First, there were obvious legal problems. Legally, you can say what you want about the dead but there were six survivors. Also, PWA, the pilot's union, etc., could be sensitive to any unfair allegations or implications. The legal problems, though, concerned me less than the feelings of the relatives and friends of the victims. The trick was going to be to find some way to be as honest and authentic as possible, without unnecessarily opening recently healed wounds. There was also the problem of being factual. If I got anything wrong, there were plenty of people around to contradict me.

My first thought was to begin by interviewing the survivors and some key airport personnel. There was no budget for travel. I didn't care for the idea of phone interviews. Instead, I turned to the Coroner's Office. To my relief, the Chief Coroner made the files available to me. Although I could not take any material out of the office, I was free to take all the notes I needed.

The Coroner's report filled many books. As well, there were diagrams—of where people sat, of the airplane's path, of where the victims' bodies were found, of the airport—which were critical in helping me get absolutely clear the basic outline of the tragedy.

My research done, I returned to Victoria. However, it still was not time to write. Instead, using the computer, I began a file for each individual involved. This did not just include passengers and crew, but RCMP officers, airport personnel, rescue workers, Calgary air control, airport visitors, the Coroner's Office. Into each file, I placed every reference to that individual. When this was finally completed, I began a time line starting in Calgary before take-off and lasting until rescue operations were well underway.

At first, the time line was quite simple but, gradually, as the plane moved closer and closer to Cranbrook, it became more and more complex. For weeks, the time line lay like a white spine across my office floor. As I cut material from the printouts, I taped it to the appropriate place. Who was where. Who said what. Who did what. The nearer I got to the actual crash, the more material there was to attach. When all the pieces were in place, the paper formed a massive cross twice as long as my office. I then marked every major individual with his own colour so that I could see, at a glance, where he or she appeared. With that material assembled and digested, I finally began to write.

Because I could not know what was said or done by the people who were killed, I created six characters to represent all the victims. Radio drama is an intimate medium and works best in close-up so a focus had to be created. Other than these fictional characters, I concentrated on using actual material.

A lot of scenes fell into place. All I had to do was recreate them from the transcripts. But I had to decide how to begin. I tried starting in Calgary but there was too much empty space. I tried starting with the crash and working back but that created terrible confusion. A focus was needed. To get that focus, I started after the crash, in the kitchen of the snowplough driver. He is talking to his daughter.

DAUGHTER: Did you kill those people, Daddy?

SOUND: TEA SOUNDS STOP. A PAUSE AS TOM TRIES
                 TO DEAL WITH WHAT HAS BEEN SAID.

TOM:	Of course, I didn't, honey.
DAUGHTER:	They said you did it and you'll go to jail.
TOM:	I'm staying right here with you. Don't you worry.
DAUGHTER:	Even Jimmy's mother said.
TOM:	She's wrong. She doesn't understand what really happened.

Obviously, the play was going to explain what really did happen.

As I wrote the various scenes, I made a number of critical decisions. For example, I did not want a narrator. I wanted the play to stand on its own. Too often the term *documentary* is used as an excuse to avoid the effort required to write a coherent, unified drama. I also did not want to try to recreate reality in all its details. I did want, in some way, to speak for both the dead and those they left behind. Each of these decisions created problems. It was my creative task to find suitable solutions.

Radio drama is a wonderful medium because it does allow creative solutions. For example, it allows the writer a free hand to change location on an instant. All a character has to say is, "Now we're on Mars" and, boom, you're on Mars. In film or TV, because of cost, the writer can't do that. Or, you can write, "There's the Roman army" and a sound tech creates that army by shaking a box of charcoal. On the other hand, the lack of visual images means that you have to keep focussed on a small number of people. A conversation with ten people is chaos. Also, transitions are buggers. In film, it's easy. The scenes change and the audience sees it change. On radio you can't constantly have characters saying, "Now we're on the parking lot at the airport. Now we're leaving the parking lot." Every scene change has to be communicated with sound. But those sounds have to be prepared for. On page 7 of the script, Tom says to the Cranbrook radio operator, "I'm going onto the runway now." We hear the snowplough. That sets us up for the next scene in the snowplough. There must be no other sounds like those from this machine so that from then on every time the audience hears the snowplough it knows where the scene is taking place.

A more difficult problem, but one which was also solved by the medium, was my desire to speak for the dead. Because I've been involved in tragedy, I'm acutely aware that corporations/institutions/the law, all treat the bereaved with indifference and callousness. Executives don't worry about emotional loss or shattered lives. They worry about lawsuits, bad publicity, how the accident is going to affect their next promotion, whether or not they're going to get home on time for supper. They are aided and abetted in this because we live in a society which thinks a man is a fool if he does not go to a doctor when he breaks his leg but holds him in contempt for going to a doctor if he breaks his heart.

To begin this sub-theme, I wrote this:

SOUND:	WE HEAR POUNDING OF METAL STAKES INTO FROZEN GROUND, BUT SOME DISTANCE AWAY. WE DON'T KNOW WHAT IT IS. THEN, CLOSE UP, FOOTSTEPS IN SNOW APPROACHING US. THEY STOP.
MOUNTIE:	(TO COMPANION) Put markers in beside these bodies.
SOUND:	THE SAME SOUND WE HEARD BEFORE BUT NOW CLOSE UP. THE SOUND SHOULD BE MEASURED. IT CONTINUES UNDER THE NEXT FOUR SPEECHES.
PASSENGER 1:	(THESE PEOPLE ARE ALL DEAD BUT IT IS LIKE THEY ARE PROTESTING AGAINST BEING IDENTIFIED AS DEAD. THEY ARE TRYING TO CLING TO LIFE.) Not me. My wife's waiting at the terminal. We're going to see our son play basketball tonight.
PASSENGER 2:	Not me. I'm getting married next month.
PASSENGER 3:	My purse. Where's my purse? All my pictures of Hawaii are in it.
PASSENGER 4:	Not me. Not yet.

This scene shifts to a scene at the Coroner's inquest. The Regional Pathologist who did 30 autopsies is testifying. A list of the dead is read to him. To each name and address, he repeats *yes*. The voices of the dead protest. With this scene, I feel I've established the dramatic strategy of the play. The scenes will be quite short. There will be abrupt shifts in location. There will be a lot of characters. The play will not try to be literal.

One of the six created characters is a young woman. She is on a ski trip and will be getting married in a month. Through bits and pieces of dialogue, she reveals herself. Also, in shifting time, I present her boyfriend. In scenes in Calgary before she leaves, their wedding song, "We've Only Just Begun," is playing.

Later, after the crash but before he knows about it, her boyfriend has a monologue in which I try to capture the shock experienced by those who lose someone unexpectedly.

> BOYFRIEND: I was at the library studying when her Mom came in. I didn't recognize her at first. Out of place. You know, someone in a place where you've never seen them before. I looked up from my books and thought, "That woman's been crying."

His monologue is half a page long. In it, he does not describe his reaction so much as that of his fiancée's mother and father. Later, there is his reaction to her loss.

When the final draft of the manuscript was accepted, I thought that would be the end of it. Fortunately, it was not. I flew to Calgary to join Juliani and his co-Producer, Greg Rogers. The first morning, the cast assembled and did a read-through. Then Greg announced that we had a very special visitor. It was one of the survivors. She was asked a lot of questions about the crash but, after that was over, she made my six months' work worthwhile when she came to me and said, "Thank you for the integrity of the script."

The production itself was amazing. There were 24 characters. That meant everything had to be tightly organized. As in a film, because it is cost-efficient, scenes were done out of sequence. Some producers are hurried, satisfied with anything, but in this production there were as many as nine or ten takes. I had already acted in my play "The Cave" but was pleased, this time, to play the Coroner. Acting in one's own work I recommend to every writer. It is the ultimate humbling but educational experience. There can't be any excuses about the lines being badly written.

Being involved in the pre-production, the production and then the initial post-production is emotionally difficult but, I feel, absolutely necessary for me to grow as a writer. It allows first-hand experience plus a chance to write under pressure during production. Recently, because of budget cuts, the CBC has moved away from producing radio drama and even further away from providing training opportunities for Canadian writers. However, my experience as a writer is that "An Unacceptable Standard" and the way it was produced is precisely what the CBC should be doing. I can think of nothing more valuable the CBC could do for the culture of this country. This task which I had taken on so reluctantly proved, in the end, to do more for my development as a writer than anything else I have ever done.

A Gentle Circumcision

Aritha van Herk

I come from the west, kingdom of the male virgin. I live and write in the kingdom of the male virgin. To be a female and not-virgin, making stories in the kingdom of the male virgin, is dangerous. You think this kingdom is imaginary? Try being a writer there. Try being a woman there.

This west is a kingdom of discontent. This, the promised land, still regrets Eden, and in that regret edges toward Apocalypse, denying the pastoral fiction that has been imposed upon it from outside. This west is a fiction disintegrating: a kingdom of male virgins who have never forgiven Eve for seducing them.

Genesis: In the beginning, God made Adam and Eve. God said to Adam, "Do not eat of the fruit of the tree of the knowledge of good and evil." Eve wasn't around yet, according to the story. When the serpent beguiled Eve, and Eve, being a curious woman, ate of said fruit and gave some to Adam, he didn't resist, although it was to *him* that God had given the explicit instructions. Look it up. I could enter into a protracted discussion of the intelligence of the curious person, but that would interrupt the story. The long and short is, when God started asking difficult questions, Adam said, *"She* gave it to me. Not *my* fault."* This displacement of blame is a key to the large question of virgins and kingdoms and gardens, but I would like to deal with it specifically in relation to the west and its fiction.

Regret for Eden is peculiar to the fiction of the west, and for good reason. Johnny Backstrom, in Robert Kroetsch's *The Words of My Roaring*, says,

> Christ, you have to dream out here. You've got to be half goofy
> —just to stay sane.
>
>   I'm a great one for paradox. My reading of the Bible, I
> suppose; dying to be born and all that. But really, it isn't an easy
> place to live. Like when the wind blows black, when it's dry, you
> drive all day with your lights on. Great electioneering weather.
> The fish lose their gills in this country. The gophers come up for
> a bite to eat, and they crawl right into the air.[1]

Almost all male tales (tall) attest to drought and death, the quixotic viciousness of the weather, as a counterpoint to the lost garden.[2] And to compound the difficulties of such dyslexia come the definitions imposed on us from outside. We are referred to as the frontier, the wide open spaces, the glorious wilderness, the *region* of the west, labels always breathed in a properly worshipful tone, this incantation of difference anointing and cursing us at one and the same time. The result is an image of "contemporary primitivism, a world of romance that sorts oddly with our seasonally-adjusted social order."[3] And this contradiction has aggravated the kingdom of the male virgin.

There they go, those men of the west, riding horses into the wind, praying to the first rays of dawn, going nobly forward to be hanged: courtly, bashful, foot-shuffling, plowing, plowing, suffering, suffering, yearning, yearning for Eden. The only way to regain Eden is through innocence, abstinence, purity. Just try getting one of them by the belt buckle, let alone getting him off his horse. He's laced up into the chaps of his own myth so tightly that he could just as well be a cowboy who hasn't undressed all summer. And if you think you'll get that oil-rigger's hard hat off his head, you're wrong. Even if you do, he'll consummate the business with his eyes clenched shut and his face averted; afterwards he'll go out into a thirty-below snowstorm and pray to the spirits to cleanse his soul. This is the kingdom of the male virgin. I did not make this up. It was first defined by Robert Kroetsch in a review of *Petrigo's Calgary*, a book that attempted to delineate the innate character of that city of male virgins, my home:

> Petrigo captures magnificently the failure of sexuality in this new-created city; as if it came into being without anything so gross as a good fuck. Success and money don't get you laid in Calgary, they get you a big new car. Petrigo is obsessed with the circle, but only at the farthest remove of metaphor is it ever the great vagina that lets us into or out of true being. The world phallus is the city-centre, the world vagina, at its worst, has in its iron centre a huge machine, at its best, a pair of skyscraper teeth or a forest of fern. For Calgary is ultimately Christian in its sexual posture: women are the source only of man's fall.[4]

Try being female and living in the kingdom of the male virgin; try being female and writing in the kingdom of the male virgin. Women must come to a place in this kingdom themselves but until now it has been dominated by a romantic fiction that is disintegrating like a paper cowboy put into water. This kingdom boasts adventure and chivalry; it proudly displays all the characteristics of romanticism: innovation, spontaneity, sensuous nuance, limitless aspiration. This is big sky country; both the fiction and its criticism have relied on endless landscape as a metaphor. But it is also a kingdom which practises a kind of perverse courtly love: don't touch the lady. She'll sully your purity.

Of course, male virgins take many shapes. Cowboys and Indians, politicians and martyrs, preachers and farmers and studhorse men. In my search for a female place within western fiction, I uncovered the Protean shapes of the male virgin, the grandfathers of this literature.

Virgin Frederick Philip Grove. Necessarily the first one who comes to mind in our quest for origins and ends. He says in his note to the fourth edition of *A Search for America*:

> Imaginative literature is not primarily concerned with facts; it is concerned with truth....In its highest flights, imaginative literature, which is one and indivisible, places within a single fact the history of the universe from its inception as well as the history of its future to the moment of its final extinction.[5]

This is prettily put, except we know that for Grove "the imaginative process is not a mirroring of experience...but the creation of a self or an identity."[6] Grove created his own personal fiction:

> E. P. Grove is a writer of great moral intensity because he is himself a sham, a liar, a criminal, a fraud. Out of the terrible pressure within himself, he creates moral predicaments and explores in violent and new ways the connections between auto- biography and the novel, between fiction and reality.[7]

Here is the virgin imposter, virgin because he re-creates himself pure and chaste, his life created by his fiction. And look at Niels Lindstedt, in Grove's novel, *Settlers of the Marsh*. Virgin incarnate, Niels is a character completely pure, "chaste to the very core of his being."[8] His innocence is more burden than attribute because it prevents him from seeing clearly. He is easily shocked and his fear of passion or desire is underlined by his dedication to an ascetic ideal: work, a homestead, and yes, a wife, but a wife in the genre of the Virgin Mary, a mother who conceives without the messy business of sex. Every aspect of his life is devoted to this ideal. He rises to work at three-thirty in the morning and he works with stolid passion, all the passion he otherwise subverts. He yokes desire with sin and guilt. When he does, finally, give in to desire, he does so unwillingly; in literal and figurative darkness he is enveloped by the arms of a woman and he yields. Of course, the male virgin pays dearly for the loss of his virginity. He marries his seductress because he is so innocent he cannot "bear the thought of having gone to bed with a woman who was not [his] wife,"[9] not knowing — or more likely refusing to recognize — that this woman is the local whore. Their marriage is nothing less than macabre. "Niels felt as if he must purge himself of an infection, of things unimaginable, horrors unspeakable, the more horrible as they were vague, vague...."[10] And he does purge himself, finally, by murdering the woman, his wife, and paying for that murder in jail. Only then can he return to his beloved land pure, re-virgin, and set about realizing his chaste ideal. In the canon of western Canadian literature, *Settlers of the Marsh* is considered to be of germinal importance, indeed, almost sacred. In Grove, we find the implacable prairie imposing on its men the implacable demand of purity. Grove has been foisted on us when in reality he is a virgin imposter, renewing his innocence with every fictional lie.

Virgin Sinclair Ross. In *As for Me and My House*, the failed artist virgin, virgin because he has never and will never consummate his desire to be an artist. He is artist impotent and thus virgin, isolated from his wife, who is the narrator of the novel and whose protective nurturing of her husband has been critically derided as predatory. This novel, too, is regarded as a benchmark in western Canadian literature, but not as an articulation of the silenced woman; rather, it is lauded as a eulogy to the hero as thwarted artist.

Philip Bentley is a preacher, a small-town, down-home preacher, not by choice but by necessity, fortune's implacable hand turning him into a solid wall of restraint, restraint, white-lipped frozen restraint. Most of what we see of this would-be artist, failed preacher, is a closed study door, metaphor of a cloistered monk. Virgin — this character is not only virgin but bloodless. The closest he comes to expressing emotion is a wince, and the most usual physical image of him is one of a man solitary, hunched over a table drawing impotent pencil sketches of the dust-driven world of prairie he lives in.[11] He and his wife are childless; in the whole novel they make love only a few times. That the seed of Philip's one outbreak becomes the consolidation of his pitiful position as a failure only underscores his innately virgin soul. This man ought to be a monk, totally removed from secular life, especially the wild and unpredictable life of the prairie. The garden that the silenced Mrs. Bentley plants withers and dies. There will be no return to Eden for either her or her husband. In his implacable solitude and restraint, Philip Bentley remains very much a male virgin; his bastard son only serves to emphasize his virginity by representing dead love. Ross' writing fits all the preconceptions of the prairie as arid dust-bowl, dead garden; he is a virgin refusing to be seduced by the wild artistry of the prairie.

Virgin W. O. Mitchell. The virgin as hired man. The eternal prairie becomes a Wordsworthian pastoral of innocence and experience in *Who Has Seen the Wind* and *Jake and the Kid*. The presence of the hired man acts as a counterpart to the disappearing father that Harrison has identified in *Unnamed Country*.[12] The father is always gone, dead or away. Instead of hanging around and displaying the progression of age, he vanishes, leaving behind his youthful, romantic image. He is never going to be caught sucking his gums, incontinent; he remains virgin unviolated by age. And in his place, the hired man: story-maker, myth-maker, infallible forecaster. 'Jake says...'is the kid's most common refrain. Jake has knowledge beyond all ordinary men and the source of that knowledge is his priest-like celibacy: *he don't have nothin' to do with wimmin*. The hired man may be selling his services for remuneration, but he is the surrogate of the disappeared father and as such he is omnipotent, historian and soothsayer rolled into one. He is the real interpreter of the prairie and thus represents the romance associated with the "feeling of the prairie":

> The feeling has something to do with simple natural beauty, with the basics of life embodied in the prairie rhythms and with the sense of man's insignificance and responsibility in the

midst of vastness. 'You do a lot of wonderin' on prairie,' says
Jake.[13]

Jake's purity enables him to interpret the mystery; only a virgin
shaman can preside over the kid's coming of age.

Virgin Rudy Wiebe. Wiebe rejecting history, implicated by history, writing visionary virgins. The protagonist as rebel: hero, villain,
outlaw. The glory of imperfection; the epic failure that attests to the
grandeur of the visionary, the prophet's aim. Visionary virgin Big
Bear foretelling the future, refusing to be seduced by treaty or white
man or fine words, wives only to keep him warm at night, no swerving
from vision. Recreated virgin pacifist riding through the changing
prairie without swerving from his vision/version until at last, a long
cold virgin ride into death and Big Bear returns to the earth naked,
pure:

> ...what he saw was the red shoulder of Sun at the rim of Earth,
> and he closed his eyes.
>
> He felt the granular sand joined by snow running together,
> against and over him in delicate streams. It sifted over the
> crevices of his lips and eyes, between the folds of his face and
> hair and hands, legs; gradually rounded him over until there
> was a tiny mound on the sand hill almost imperceptible on the
> level horizon. Slowly, slowly, all changed continually into in-
> distinguishable, as it seemed, and everlasting, unchanging rock.[14]

Virgin prairie, before the white man.

And Riel, trained to be a priest, become an outlaw, refusing to
sully the purity of the Metis vision, the Metis cause. Praying through
a hail of bullets, never firing a gun himself, finally led to the scaffold
a sacrificial virgin to appease a nation. Clenched against women,
Catholic celibacy despite wife and children, recipient of God's word,
divine disciple, the holy fool of Wiebe's Canadian west crucified for

his virginal naiveté. Both Big Bear and Riel are imposed by Wiebe on the west as historical, archaeological, archetypal virgins in not lie but schism, the wrenching of art into actuality. No wonder Toronto sent out troops.

Virgin Robert Kroetsch. The male virgin with the perpetual hard-on, screwing himself into oblivion. Philandering virgins who are re-created virgins each time they succumb, their reluctant acquiescence always beyond their control. "I was framed," he says, unzipping his fly, his pants around his ankles. In *The Studhorse Man* the male virgin carries the grail of his calling, to "get hold of a mare."[15] That Poseidon, the horse, never does, is ironically reflected by the promiscuity of his owner, Hazard Lepage. Hazard plays the reluctant virgin again and again seduced by lustful and devouring women. Because every human capitulation is for the sake of his virgin stallion, he is over and over again resanctified, free to resume his quest for the perfect mare. "There are virgins and there are virgins," says the narrator.[16] Hazard's fiancée, Martha, is an inaccessible virgin; Demeter (the mad narrator) is a virgin too, who, when he feels Hazard has abandoned his sacred destiny, takes it over. Hazard's capitulation (when he and Martha unite) is of course the cause of his death; he has remained intact (!) only through profligacy, and when he betrays that celibate calling, he must die. By death re-virginized, his memory is preserved by his virgin biographer. This is the ultimate example of the kingdom of the male virgin, virginity coupled with the male world in a baroque overstatement of Edenic homesickness.

This kingdom, like most chaste and idealistic worlds, needs some re-evaluation. Those male virgins need to be ravished. Only too readily has literary criticism accepted the facile geneology of Grove, Ross, Mitchell, Wiebe and Kroetsch. Perhaps there is a lesson to be distilled from one ravishment that is not the west as a fiction but this fiction as a west: *The Double Hook*.

In Sheila Watson's *The Double Hook* there are no male virgins, in disguise or otherwise. This is the kingdom of coyote, the trickster, a true (not Hollywood) western figure, seldom seen but often heard as a shivering song across an expanse of prairie bluff and slough.

James Potter, at the beginning of the novel, having murdered his mother and impregnated Lenchen, is man fallen, already not-virgin. He tries the old virgin trick of running, but is robbed (by a woman) of the money that will buy him a train ticket out, and is thus "freed from freedom."[17] He returns to his levelled home to accept the world he is part of and to accept woman and child. "I ran away, he said, but I circled and ended here the way a man does when he's lost."[18] This is not a case of the disappearing father (although he tries) and the male virgin that we have seen before. This is the kingdom of coyote, the trickster, who forces the reader beyond the personal into the universal, who shoves our noses up against art as more than a tease. It is only too easy to deal with the west as the kingdom of the male virgin, but that kingdom is insufficient. It leaves characters awkward and foot-shuffling, holding their pants up with both hands—or holding something else. Caught in the act. It's too easy to fall into: we're the west, that strangely regional region of storytellers manqué. When it would be better to take the following advice from, ironically, one of the virgins:

> the artist him/her self

> in the long run, given the choice of being God or Coyote, will, most mornings, choose to be Coyote:

> he lets in the irrational along with the rational, the pre-moral along with the moral. He is a shape-shifter, at least in the limited way of old lady Potter. He is the charlatan-healer, like Felix Prosper, the low-down Buddha-bellied fiddler midwife (him/her) rather than Joyce's high priest of art. Sometimes he is hogging the show instead of paring his fingernails. Like all tricksters, like Kip, like Traff, he runs the risk of himself being tricked.[19]

Only coyote can seduce the male virgin, give him experience, sight. Make an honest man of him.

Still, there is something charming about the clumsy maneuvers of the honest male virgin, the one who does not pretend to be something else, for whom virginity is no ficelle but a real and unfortunate condition which is difficult to cure. Compared to the male virgins created by the senior fictioneers of the west, his voice quivers authenticity.

Calgary Lover

and me,
I shoot roses.

Holding the barrel to each blossom,
I touch the trigger
as if it might be a thorn.

The petals take flight at the whispered
blast.

I protect myself from the tongues
of outraged women

:by wearing a parka
:by growing pineapples
in Pincher Creek
:by hanging a black cape
over the canary's cage
:by sleeping in a highrise
:by eating peanut butter

> (It must contain
> no words. It must be pure.
> I must allow
>
> nothing.)

I carry a gun
on the rack
in the cab of my pickup.

I shoot roses
on sight.[20]

I recognize this one. He comes from Calgary; he's authentic. I am an outraged woman. I like him. I'll take him.

---

1. Robert Kroetsch, *The Words of My Roaring* (Toronto: Macmillan, 1966), 53.

2. See Dick Harrison, "Eden, Surveyed and Fenced," in *Unnamed Country: the Struggle for a Canadian Prairie Fiction* (Edmonton: The University of Alberta Press, 1977), 72-99.

3. Eli Mandel, "Romance and Realism in Western Canadian Fiction," in *Prairie Perspectives: Selected Papers of the Western Canadian Studies Conferences, 1970, 1971*, edited by A. W. Rasporich and H. C. Klassen (Toronto: Holt, Rinehart and Winston, 1973), 198.

4. Robert Kroetsch, "Kingdom of the Male Virgin," *NeWest Review*, Vol. 1, No. 4 (November 1975), 1.

5. Frederick Philip Grove, "Author's Note to the Fourth Edition," *A Search For America* (Toronto: McClelland and Stewart, 1971).

6. Eli Mandel, "Romance and Realism in Western Canadian Fiction," 201.

7. Robert Kroetsch, "Contemporary Standards in the Canadian Novel," in *Essays, Open Letter*, Vol. V, No. 4 (Spring 1983), 38.

8. Frederick Philip Grove, *Settlers of the Marsh* (Toronto: McClelland and Stewart, NCL, 1965), 40.

9. *Settlers of the Marsh*, 154.

10. *Settlers of the Marsh*, 149.

11. Sinclair Ross, *As for Me and My House* (Toronto: McClelland and Stewart, NCL, 1970), 25.

12. Dick Harrison, 187-189.

13. Laurence Ricou, *Vertical Man/Horizontal World* (Vancouver: University of British Columbia Press, 1973), 109.

14. Rudy Wiebe, *The Temptations of Big Bear* (Toronto: McClelland and Stewart, 1973), 415.

15. Robert Kroetsch, *The Studhorse Man* (Richmond Hill, Ontario: Simon and Schuster, 1971), 7.

16. *The Studhorse Man*, 21.

17. Sheila Watson, *The Double Hook* (Toronto: McClelland and Stewart, 1959), 115.

18. *The Double Hook*, 126.

19. Robert Kroetsch and Diane Bessai, "Death is a Happy Ending," in *Figures in a Ground*, edited by Diane Bessai and David Jackel (Saskatoon, Saskatchewan: Western Producer Prairie Books, 1978), 209.

20. Robert Kroetsch, "On Being an Alberta Writer," in *Essays, Open Letter*, Vol. V, No. 4 (Spring 1983), 69.

The pun of virgin on version is deliberate. This essay stems from my position as a woman writing in the west, the need for alternate readings of our texts. Before I can write, I have to re-write the male virgins.

Cosmos: Order and Turning

Jon Whyte

Order and turning: the limits of my poetics; the extremes of cosmos, essence of structure.

Orders of things enchant me: geological columns, the relationship of compositae, chains of being, order-genus-species, order's superiority to priorizing, ordinals, ordinates, coordinates, right words in the right order, the hope a poem can show its ordonnance, abscissa making the heart a function of "x", order in dominions—if an emperor have not order about him, he shall lack order in his dominion—order in the restaurant, order in ranks, measure, mapping, metre, Mendeleev's periodic table, order of seasons, orders of knighthood, order of the ordinary, taking orders—whatever that may mean—and finding order, and disordering. Poetry is—can be, should be, ought to be— order, and "these two things are one." The search for the essential aspect of hominids, the meaning of the appendix, the index, the opposable thumb, the meaning of the sonnet, Huttonian uniformitarianism, accumulatio, the development of the "yoke" in the Indo-European language.

Those orders suggest their corollaries inevitably: anarchy, chance, coincidence, freak occurrences, centripetalism, erosion, decay, rot, the loss of essence, irreproducible phenomena, the never-repeating dance of molecules: all that is science in opposition to the orderly construction of art.

Turning likewise fascinates me: boustrophedon, versifying, cycles, wheels, spokes, metaphor, metamorphosis, becoming, changing, process, turning phrases, turning puns, turning a round, turning around, turning over (a new leaf?), turning back, the Darwinian exultation of order turning and turning ordering. Take your turn, and then it's mine. Tide and milk both turn, worms and wheelwrights and potters and poets and languages and trilobites turn and turn about and in turn-about turn about as "the world turns," days become days, and poetry is—can be, should be, ought to be—turning, and this one thing is not one but everything.

Turning is as complex as I wish it to be, involving (and it's in there too) from the Latin word for it, verse and version and versification, versus, converse and conversion, diverse and diversion and diversification and diversity, convergence, reverse and reversal, adverse and adversity, subvert and subverse and subversion, inverse and inversion, animadversion, transverse, and, likely, many other stems from the root that you'll wish to think of—like universe.

From the Greek for turn we obtain trope and tropism, and a passel of tropisms, like geo- and hydro- and rheo- and helio-, all manner of turning toward the sources of force, energy, and nature.

In English we add prepositions to generate meanings. Consider, for example:

turn on	turn off	turn back
in	out	toward
over	upon	from
against	into	by
up	down	beside

(and the innumerable transitive and intransitive variations upon those possibilities).

None of them precisely opposite, not when we pause to wonder what the relationship is between a person turning on a light and a dog turning on its master; between a couple turning in after *The Journal*, a student turning in a paper late, and a faithful citizen of the state turning in a spy; between a maid turning down the bedcovers and a woman turning down a job because her husband won't turn over a new leaf.

Turning is metaphor—into; a turn is a verse; in this game of life we play we each get a turn, ballerina, poet, or spelling bee expert; milk turns; cars and bicycles turn; the world turns; day turns into night; we all turn into adults and death turns us off.

A turn is a verse? Ancient agriculturalists, whose oxen ploughed their fields, turned at the end of each row, each furrow becoming a versus. In the earliest forms of written Latin, writers turned their words about and wrote back towards where they had come from, ploughing words in boustrophedon as the Greeks had done before them. So—in my poetry—the poem turns upon each verse end, turns into a modifying part of all that has preceded it, all imagination lying fallow before it. A poem is a shuttle of words weaving a thought into a warp of syntax—warp and warping being kinds of turns, too, once I've stopped to think about it—and as the weaver turns out his fitte, a length of cloth suitable for a suit of apparel, likewise do poets their fittes turn out.

Metaphor and turning, the shimmer of hummingbirds' iridescence is—while the Rufous inspects the red shirt I'm wearing today—so much the process of being both matter and light, the transformation of the sucrose in the feeder into his embodiment of spirit and dance in the air about a bold and glowing golden red at his gorget, the green sheen of her brown feathers against the light so near, so far from all the dragons' lizard-like, light-scattering skin, spirit of life in everything from radiolaria to sea slug, radial and biaxial differences.

Still point? Narrative orders turning and becoming, the slice we return (of course) to, and "in the beginning" set day and night (by a nice turning of this old sphere) and the seasons (by a nice turning of the old sphere about the big orb in the sky) and—oh so orderly.

Henry Kelsey, whom I wrote about once, a genteel Canadian figure and apt, too, orphan and dictionary maker (dictionaries, among the highest orders of all orders), interested me because he is a turner, a verisifier, a diplomat, peacemaker, metaphor-maker, seeker of silence; so I turned him into a point on a map, a locus, a wandering line, a lens, a circle of observation created by the intersection of two spheres, and let his mathematical propriety beseem concept, rigour, vigour, vitality, and telling narrative, let him become Adam in a peopled Eden, take upon himself the taxonomic task—to recognize things and name them, find order, get lost, find himself, be found, and he—bewildering for a Canadian hero—got to return.

Our prologue, he talks to us all, foresees us. We people his dream; he becomes our dream—to become primal, sincere, innocent, wandering, amiable and—important for me—be first English speaker to confront grizzly bear, musk ox, bison, and penetrate wilderness until it permeates him.

So—there in Eden (which turns out to be Canada it's no surprise, even with the Tories in rule)—Henry Kelsey stands as archetypal western Canadian—takes Indian woman to wive (or at least swive) with him, discovers how riverine the country, rivers being part of the return, and becomes poem. Becoming, as Sheila Watson pointed out in one of her classes once, being the existential mood of the verb "to be".

After he has played Prologue, chorically and cosmically Canadian, coming on the stage to say the curtain has risen on a new act, Kelsey disappears into the landscape and becomes what all Canadians secretly yearn to be: a tree. I take it as a fact we all wish to vanish and turn into part of the land: some of us to become drumlins and eskers, others to become sloughs and bogs, yet others to become mountain ranges and forests and arctic barrens. Americans rarely understand this, I believe.

My poems declare their epic intent. Epic? A cosmological word that, in my wordhoard, means something akin to "the narrative that

defines the universe at a time." After that I become quite loose, allowing all the things I like into it: works like *The Canterbury Tales*,
Richard II-Henry IV-Henry V, *Finnegans Wake*, and *The Anathemata*.
I don't care how big the universe becomes so long as its mythical
richness allows frivolity and joy amid the gloom of such a portentous
word. Bigness is part of it—a grand theme, lots of language to roll
around in, so we can shake ourselves like a dog standing up after a
roll in a manure heap and say, gosh that felt good. Ain't no room for
simple language in an epic. If you like your language full, robust,
redolent, vibrating, full of echoes in the vault of myth and mind,
you'll like the type of epic I like.

Epics contain humanity. Joy, pain, reward, and despair contain
the human universe.

Few of us in Canada write with the awareness of E.J. Pratt's
being one of our ancestors. Long before I read Hugh MacDiarmid's
"On a Raised Beach" and David Jones' *Anathemata*, two poems which
probably had more influence on me than e. e. cummings' always
dazzling wordplay, I read and liked "Newfoundland" and "The
Titanic" and *Toward the Last Spike*, and I even wrote a part of a long
poem in a sort of tetrameter I had picked up from a vile translation
of *Beowulf* I read in highschool, a poem about the Frank Slide, the
only disaster I knew anything about. As I look back, 25 years on, I
am more than dimly aware I knew then, though could never have
enunciated it, my bent was toward epic (Pound's definition of epic as
"a long poem containing history" will suffice here), and a Canadian
topic, a Rocky Mountain subject, and a poem full of tropes, majestical
language, hyperbole, mystery, celebration, and the despair, horror,
and threat of landscape. All I recall of it now—oh those tetrameters!
—is the mountain waiting "like a puma perched upon a pine."

A post-post-modernist, I believe post-modern reductionism
reached a just conclusion in the writings of Samuel Beckett and
Robert Creeley; replenishment, as John Barth adequately pointed out
years ago, compensates the Age of Exhaustion. Occasionally I write
poems so brief some people have difficulty believing they're poems

or literature. (I occasionally use one brief poem in classrooms as an exercise: answers to how many letters it contains range from four through five and six to fourteen and eighteen.) Usually I write them in circular form; like sea urchins, they turn in upon themselves in closure. The big poems turn in upon themselves, too, but it's more difficult to believe the galaxy turns than that the Earth turns.

My poetics: neither within nor opposed to the mainstream. Most poetry has been metric, measured, and in closed forms, so I feel kinship with all the writers of tropistic verse of the generations of song.

My cosmology? I like the ideas of beauty in the hummingbird and the exquisite move in a game of chess. I like the sense of order in the new geomorphology of J. Tuzo Wilson, but I admire Sir William Logan's order too. I don't have much time for Eastern—or Western—philosophy, and feel it can really mess up a poem. What was good enough for John Milton—i.e., the cosmology of the age; in his age the Ptolemaic Universe—is good enough for me—i.e., the cosmology of the age; Big Bang creation physics and the charm of quarks—so long as there's room for mythology. My religion? I believe Earth should be capitalized.

After Post-Modernism

David Williams

Canadian literature has evolved directly from Victorian into Post-Modern.... The country that invented Marshall McLuhan and Northrop Frye did so by not ever being Modern.

(Robert Kroetsch, *Boundary 2*)

No set of critical standards derived from only one mode can ever assimilate the whole truth about poetry. There may be noticed a general tendency to react most strongly against the mode immediately preceding, and, to a lesser extent, to return to some of the standards of the modal grandfather.

(Northrop Frye, *Anatomy of Criticism*)

An example in criticism is the neglect of the immediately preceding New Criticism by post-modern critics, who have jumped back to Wilde, the New Criticism's 'grandfather,' to re-erect their theories of non-representative art.

(Paul Fussell, *The Great War and Modern Memory*)

In the interlude between swathing and combining in the fall of 1962, my grandfather, David Edward Williams, called a meeting of the clan to delay my proposed entrance to journalism at the University of Western Ontario. It was decided that I should attend Bible School for three years where I would be inoculated against atheism, agnosticism, and secular humanism.

In the same autumn, my grandfather and parents stopped at the Bible School outside Moose Jaw on their way to a reunion with Mom's father, Jacob Dahl, whom she had not seen since her childhood. I could not be excused from classes, so I was left to imagine this meeting of grandfathers who had kept worlds apart — the one Welsh-Irish, well-to-do, and well-spoken in all his genial moral judgements, the other Norwegian, penniless, illiterate, and utterly immoral, even in his exuberant telling of tales on himself. Though his deathbed conversion would make him "respectable" at last, Jack Dahl would leave me to occupy a troubling middle ground.

As with natural grandfathers, so too with modal grandfathers. Born between V-E Day and V-J Day and educated in a two-room school, I literally didn't hear of Faulkner or Hemingway until after they were dead. Joyce was only a girl's name. By the time I did get away to university in Saskatoon, *Giles Goat-Boy* was proposing a *Revised New Syllabus*, and my graduate professors at the University of Massachusetts were beginning to define what was wrong with the old one. Modernism, it turned out, had erred on the side of aestheticism — in the idea that a work of art could be self-contained, free of mess and contingency, a verbal icon transcending the human muddle. The artist was convicted of taking refuge in tradition, Eliot the self-appointed hero with his finger in the dyke. Post-modernism took forceful aim at this kind of wall between art and life, tried to let chaos in again, get the reader in on the act. And yet all these dazzling reminders that our fictions were really fictions did not return us to life, only to the making of fictions. The new aestheticism, it turned out, was too occupied with its own resources to see us out of the fun house. We were invited to quest through labyrinths of voice, searching for absence, not presence.

At its best, the aesthetics of absence has proved to be a liberation movement against the dead hand of the past, designed to free us to be modern in a way that traditional modernism failed to do. Its definitive tool has been the new semiotics of French criticism, not surprisingly taken up most enthusiastically in America where revolutionary tradition has likewise hardened into authoritarianism. This new semiotics has challenged our oldest literary authorities, beginning with Aristotle and his doctrine of imitation, on grounds of an irrevocable split between signifier and signified, between word and world. If the correspondence between signs and things is purely arbitrary, then mimesis is an empty doctrine, pointing only to an absence of reality in language. Freed into speech, narrative can now avoid the tyranny of temporal progression (story as history) and the rigid control of myth (story as universal pattern). It offers only itself in the act of telling, free of any other inheritance, resisting both determination and interpretation.

The relevance of post-modern theory for Western Canadian writing is fairly obvious. It refuses the political authority of the centre; it rejects the binary oppositions of two founding cultures in favour of the whole spectrum of excluded middles. In Bob Kroetsch's terms, we have resisted the temptation of the single for the allure of multiplicity. But what one finds in popular versions of our ethnic mosaic (the metaphor is the message) is a curiously static reification of "central Canada." At least as it is institutionalized in Folklorama or its equivalent "festival of nations." Island pavilions, really, where we go to share new foods and drink, and to watch the other guy's song and dance. What is more likely shared is an entrenched form of the old modernism: fragments we have shored against our ruin. The old folk art defending against the new way of life. Québec/Canada; East/West; Wasp/Ethnic; David Edward Williams/Jacob Dahl: our inability to overcome the binary oppositions of structuralism, that ruling philosophy of the modernist era, declares at the deepest level of culture our secret allegiance to the Moderns.

The abyss which separates us from the past first opened at the feet of those same Moderns. They, like us, felt pulled two ways, were driven to reconcile their divided allegiances. Eliot's "mythical method" gives a clue to what the age demanded: in "using the myth, in man-ipulating a continuous parallel between contemporaneity and anti-quity, Mr. Joyce is pursuing a method which others must pursue after him." Contemporaneity and antiquity: they are more than counters for a dead age of faith and a new age of uncertainty. They are binary terms in the artistic process of reconciling past and present in a "timeless" world of myth. Though Wallace Stevens would put more faith in the imaginative act itself, his "poem of the mind in the act of finding/What will suffice" makes art, like myth, into a self-sufficient object transcending time. The function of such useful objects is more cunningly explained by Joyce's Stephen Dedalus in terms of what happens to his soul in the moment of aesthetic "arrest": "Glimmering and trembling, trembling and unfolding, an open flower, it spread in endless succession to itself." The soul of this self-named "priest of eternal imagination" is writ large upon the world; world is subsumed in the Word; the eternal Self is All. Only trouble is, Joyce exploded the solipsism of autonomous form long before the priests of New Criticism came along to put Humpty together again.

Post-modernism has now shattered this poor, patched Humpty once and for all by shoving the "modernist" Self off the wall. The "author" vanishes in the new aesthetics of absence as authority is decentred or relocated in a plurality of readers. (Irony is a reader-oriented aesthetics too, but it smacks of Socratic privilege, the very possibility of knowledge.) The post-modern reader who shares in the imaginative process no longer has to find identification on the level of character or plot but in the "position" of the inferred author. For author and world, like the Word, are equally fictions; even history and physics are forms of saying, all subject to the contexts of dis-course. What language now refers to is language, signs endlessly mirroring other signs, until fiction comes to represent itself. If this sounds like Babel revisited, well and good. The New Jerusalem was four-square anyway, self-contained. Language is where it's now at.

Even if it's language which is now self-sufficient.

At its worst, post-modernism's refusal of referential language is a denial of anything but the imaginative process spreading in endless succession to itself. Even where it is shared with the reader, this process is not the same thing as the shared dreaming of older literature. The "absent" character and author who are to be inferred or co-produced by the reader do not make up for the presence and force of life speaking directly from the unconscious. Word-games now threaten no one with possession, it is true; the authorial reader is in no danger of losing control. But language can also turn solipsistic in another way. The post-modernist's distrust of history as a coercive form of narrative makes him resist the historical meaning of words. Barthes' *l'écriture blanche* describes the post-modern writer's need to strip words of their past associations. But it is an old phenomenon by now. The calendar of the French Republic changed all the names to destroy the Christian associations of the Gregorian system. A significant number of Americans were surprised that the Revolutionary War had not done away with the English language.

The road to Babel in recent Canadian writing seems hardly so revolutionary in its ongoing pursuit of lines of ancestry. But because "our genealogies are the narratives of a discontent with a history that lied to us," says Robert Kroetsch, our literature "comes compulsively to a genealogy that refuses origin." It is the delusory myth of American Adam, freed of history, inheritance, and the whole burden of the past, to which he does not quite refer. It has always been one way — the refused way — of overcoming our cultural stasis, our traditional fear of upsetting the balance.

Our refusal to become American leaves us nonetheless to drift into becoming, like Eliot, ersatz Europeans. *The Waste Land* turns into another version of "mosaic," a blueprint for our own uneasy national existence between past and present:

> I can connect
> Nothing with nothing.

The broken fingernails of dirty hands.
My people humble people who expect
Nothing.

Of course, Eliot's manipulation of myth here discloses a more fundamental motive: his fear of life as the source of his rage for order. The
myths of Western tradition turn out to be about destructive passion;
they have to be exchanged for a few Eastern words of wisdom. Shoring
up the self becomes the only "tradition." In contrast to this fear of
life, the Canadian post-modernist at least appears as Trickster, carting
his outsize penis in a box on his back. Freeing us from the whiteman's
burden. Returning us to archaic sources of energy. Promising us a more
primordial America.

Trickster, in post-modern terms, is meant to keep us free of the
intolerable choice of whom we are going to be. But Trickster is forced to
grow up in Indian myth, and he undergoes a seachange in Sheila
Watson's *The Double Hook*, the one modernist text in Western
Canadian literature which sees him as the figure who might really contain our opposites and so raze the walls of our ethnic isolation. Here,
Thompson Indian, Métis, and European immigrant all live under the
eye of this bilingual citizen who speaks the language of Indian myth and
Old Testament Jeremiad. At least until his people see how he oppresses
them, or rather how they are divided by their own fear and self-interest.
Then Trickster delivers the Word of the Psalmist's messianic prophecy.
But Watson has publicly doubted that she would use Coyote if she were
to rewrite the novel. Evidently he speaks the most artificial language of
all in a novel about dead language. And the birth of the wordless child,
the coming of the Word, makes him positively evangelized. Coyote
High-Churched. This is put for that. Metonymy, when the life of the
novel is metaphor. Words made one with things again, the community
rejoined, by the fact of Lenchen's pregnancy. Metaphor as sexual
fusion. But that fusion has not happened at the level of myth. Splendid
narrative risks end in the service of tradition.

The more wily post-modernist knows that his borrowed myths

can only define him in terms of the alien culture, unless he un-invents them. And so he parodies, deconstructs, unnames inherited versions. Holding to his own authority, he tells his way out of the labyrinth, turning it to child's play, unmasking the demon for a Rumpelstiltskin. Convinced of his own innocence, he will see no evil, do no evil, repeat no evil. Especially repeat no evil. For the myth threatens always to repeat itself. He must therefore stop short of naming a new version, of putting himself back inside any labyrinth save the maze of his own telling. And yet there are only two alternatives to repetition. Silence is one — an ultimate surrender to absence. The other is the deferment of "meaning and other finalities," an escape from closure, from a fatal surrender to myth. But if the post-modernist avoids entrapment, he is also avoiding ruin. Fear of life/fear of death. Modernism and post-modernism make the next binary opposition.

My own way out of this cultural labyrinth has been maddeningly slow, and mostly a failure. It's pretty clear that I surrendered to the temptation of myth in *The Burning Wood*. I wanted to find a myth, like Faulkner's second Eden in *The Bear*, that would put an end to the perverse sense of our own cultural innocence (a remarkable flying in the face of our Calvinist inheritance). But most of all I wanted a unifying myth. Grandfathers again. But also the local Chagoness Reserve and Stony Lake Bible Camp. During three weeks every summer our church held Bible Camp, then two weeks of Indian Camp. The names are straight from social use — lived binaries (I was a counsellor at both camps). But the more I tried to tell it, the less I could write it straight. Too much subversive fun in names like Joshua, in the business of letting out flats in Jericho. I knew nothing yet of theories of deconstruction, but my instincts said nothing much was sacred if it wouldn't let you laugh. So the Sun Dance turned into another form of carnival, though comedy taken literally could also turn into tragedy. The only way back to comedy, it seemed to me, was in the renewal of the myth. What I failed to see in Coming-day's death (though I kept revising it right down through the galleys) was that I had surrendered to the old myth of sin and redemption. Newly naturalized, of course. But even an open-ended subversion of Ovid couldn't change the Christ myth.

The River Horsemen was understandably iconoclastic. According to some critics a modernist work, it marks my own fall from myths of transcendence. That could be why it was so hard to write (or to read, I'm told by most). For each of the men in the novel loses his faith in some sustaining myth of his culture, at least as he defines it. The old shaman Fine-day has given up believing in the spirit world; Many-birds blasphemes a powerless Thunder Bird; Nick Sobchuk falls with his "mad" mother out of grace into a version of her Ukrainian myth of the fallen angels humanized by grief. Even the faith-healer Jack Cann is shattered by his vision of a god who needs to be saved by man. The breaking of each myth leads, however, to new points of contact, if not to a new "mosaic." The technique, blamed by some on Faulkner's *As I Lay Dying*, points in opposite directions to a shifting series of doubles by which each man glimpses his unacknowledged self. The fragmenting of narrative leaves gaps across which sparks are meant to fly, but the reader has to make such jumps for himself. Much difficult work, with little guarantee of illumination. And sometimes the leap is into silence, albeit a charged silence, latent (I hope) with new energies. Silence can even point to new namings of a myth. But the story of a man who "becomes" god to die for the sins of godhead does not lead to an ordinary form of closure. Nor do the metaphors allow for an easy return to the fathers. They concern artists of differing types who must make their own answers to death and so free themselves to live.

Entrapment in myth was always quite immediate for me, given my parents' Biblical literalism. If any man shall add unto these things, God shall add unto him the plagues that are written in this book. And if any man shall take away from the words of the book of this prophecy, God shall take away his part out of the book of life, and out of the holy city, and from the things which are written in this book. End of book, end of my world. Unless I could tell another story, violate myself back into life. As it happens, the story of the end of the world is also mine by ethnic inheritance. Othin, the god of Norse myth, father of magic, the shapechanger, Trickster, could not by all his knowledge and riddling art defer the meaning of the sibyl's prophecy. I was persuaded of the necessity of endings.

Eye of the Father turns on succeeding versions of the story of a father who absents himself from endings. The flight from Europe to America, from the States to Canada, ends somewhere all the same. Apocalypse here. But the problem of defining apocalypse now becomes the problem of art and life together.

Wagner's *Ring* first proposes the terms which prevent any others: the world is to be overcome through art. The "sin" of existence is to be atoned for in the death of men and gods alike, if in repeated performances at the Bayreuth festival. Wagner, in this sense, is the prototypical modernist, vouchsafing the world's continuance in his art. But the art that makes life does not want more than itself, and will not allow for its own succession. Even the majestic cataclysm of *Völuspá* in old Norse myth had Baldr coming back to a new throne after the end of the world. World trees and family trees continue. Only the authority of patriarchs has been ended.

Eye of the Father is thus about fathers who resist succession and so hold their families hostage to the past. Wayne Goodman evades any confrontation with his dying grandfather so that he might be free to write about him in the novel the reader is reading. But his passage in several voices through the dead centre of Wagner's "negation of the will of life" proves to be his refusal to expose himself; the act of writing is for him an assumption of false identities. Only when he is stripped of his last mask can he be overtaken by his grandfather's story, in an act of surrender, a willed succession. The world renewed, as it always was, in the next generation, the next telling. So long as it is lived.

Nietzsche contra Wagner. We escape the bondage of the past not by refusing or resenting it but by choosing it. Wagner made the mistake of swallowing Schopenhauer's Platonism, the idea that will was the source of all suffering. But the will's secret sorrow, said Nietzsche, was its inability to will backwards. And so Zarathustra's "post-modern" fear of recurrence had to become his laugh of joy, his learning to will the past into the future.

Becoming one's own ancestor: the heart of the story. Not to enclose the world inside the self, but to recreate the whole work of time. Making our own connections in the writing and the reading. The family tree branching into the world tree.

Post-apocalypse. What follows the deconstruction of every world of myth.

Ideology, Obscurity, and the Health of Poetry

Christopher Wiseman

13 Ways of Looking at a Credo

1. The primary function of poetry is to give pleasure—a pleasure different in kind from any other.

2. Poetry should be accessible to an intelligent adult reader.

3. Good poetry is written out of necessity, not out of any technical, critical or intellectual ideology.

4. A complex surface is not necessary for the generation of complex feeling.

5. Poetry is not working if it doesn't diagram and shape deep feeling and thereby help to give meaning to previously inarticulated feeling in writer and reader.

6. The transmission of meaning is more important than what kind of surface technique is used, though the two are obviously inter-related.

7. It is not helpful to talk about old and new, relevant and irrelevant styles of poetry—though I shall do something close to that in this paper for the sake of argument. It only makes sense to talk about poetry which succeeds or does not succeed.

8. Formal experimentalism must be fully understood and at the service of content if it is to work. When it becomes habit or ideology, it becomes a denial of creativity. To take over another poet's experimentalism makes it less, rather than more likely that a poet will find his/her real voice. Not understanding this, or ignoring it, has probably weakened Canadian poetry more than the poetry of other English-speaking nations. (In this paper I refer only to verse in English.)

9. Dismissiveness—of forms, techniques, subject-matter, approach —by any poetic faction is the enemy of fruitful growth.

10. Poetry without metaphor is a body without blood.

11. Whatever the landscape, the history, the mythology or lack of mythology, the writing of poetry in Western Canada is in no essential way different from writing it anywhere else. It is no easier, no more difficult.

12. Poetry is a mixture of sound, sense and suggestiveness, in which mind and feeling play against rhythm and syntax in a creative way. The visual aspect of poetry is much less important. Poetry is a serious art, helping us to understand better what it is like to be human. It is not a game, a critical process, an illustration or justification of an ideology. It deals primarily with the things which touch us most—love, time, death, joy, wonder, grief, loss. It gives shape, form and order to the urgent disorder of our feelings.

13. The more violent the dislocation of syntax, diction and space, the less likely the poem is to be able to create order, make sense of life, transmit deep feeling, be understood by others, shape the unshapeliness of experience.

Problems

Three examples of things which worry me.

1. The poetry section of one of Calgary's best bookstores consists, almost exclusively, of American "Beat" poetry from the 50s and 60s. There are only a few random Canadian books. This may be seen as quaint, but it is more serious than that. Stocking a Calgary bookstore with these poets in 1986 is suggesting that they are still important, central, of top quality; more worthy to be read than the leading poets in Canada, the States or elsewhere.

2. The "Prairies" reporter of a national poetry journal, straying from the assigned job of simply reporting literary news, commented on a recent and quite eclectic poetry anthology by asking: "Will future collections feature more poetry by women and some experimental writing?" I would hope that the editors have told her in no uncertain terms that it will feature the best poetry they receive, whatever its style, whatever the sex of the writer. Do we now have to have affirmative action for experimentalism, for God's sake?

3. A reviewer, in a journal from Central Canada, spent three pages trying to prove that the poetry he was reviewing was really English and not Canadian. Why was it English? Because the language was "rich and connotative," which, he claimed, is something Canadian poets grow out of and "abandon for starkness." Astonishing, that a reviewer would be so knotted up over nationality rather than quality, and, more, that "rich and connotative" language is foreign, immature, something to break away from. I hope I can always find something rich and connotative for my own poetry and in the poetry I read.

Three small things, perhaps, but they bear upon central concerns of mine which might perhaps be loosely lumped together under the ideas of obscurity and ideology. I am, to get right to it, increasingly depressed by the seeming need of many Canadian poets, reviewers and critics to ape certain American styles in poetry, and especially experimental and avant-garde styles. Why? Are we afraid to seem dull and square? The battle-cry is let's embrace it—the Beat, projective verse, structuralism, post-structuralism, deconstruction, postmodernism—whatever the name might be. Let us, frighteningly, bring in sexual politics and experimental bias to the judging of an anthology. Never mind the quality, feel the width. Implied, of course, is that experimental poetry is better than...than what? Than rich, connotative language, I suppose. Sound-poetry, open-form, the long collage poem, the anti-metaphoric, anti-linear progression, anti-left-hand margin, magic realism—oh yes, we're with it. We're at the cutting edge of poetry and poetic theory, right? Wrong. We imitate too uncritically. Our avant-gardism is usually out of date; much of our poetry seems to be ideologically inspired, written not for a general, intelligent audience, but for fellow ideologues, academics, and a few tattered groupies. And the subservience to the United States would have Canadian writers out on the streets with placards in a minute if it were in any area but "progressive" poetics.

Perhaps I overstate to make a point. But my concerns are genuine and deep. When I find myself moved and affected by more poets from Britain, Australia, the United States (yes, of course they have fine poets—why don't we locate them better?) than by Canadian poets, then I worry. Of course there are Canadian poets I respond to deeply. Don Coles, Patrick Friesen, Ralph Gustafson, Florence McNeil, Richard Outram, for example—all very different—reject surface frenzy and complexity and communicate powerfully and directly, create strong feeling, speak as one feeling and thinking person to another, have their own distinctive voices, base their work on the organization of sound, image and syntax, are fine craftsmen, are willing and able to expose personal feelings honestly, even painfully, will use, if necessary, traditional rhythmical devices against which to play the wounded or joyful human voice, employ powerful metaphors, know exactly what they're doing when they break a free-verse line, reject the poetically political, don't have the arrogance to believe that techniques and approaches developed by poets over thousands of years are suddenly irrelevant and out of date. They know what the magic realists don't care to know—that it is more valuable to make the ordinary magical than to make the magical ordinary. And so with other poets from outside Canada who have meant the most to me over the past twenty years—Philip Larkin, Seamus Heaney, Donald Justice, John Berryman, Robert Lowell, Elizabeth Bishop, Vincent Buckley, Stevie Smith, Ted Hughes and many others. Let two of them talk for me.

Words from the Wise

Philip Larkin's *Required Writing* (1983) should be required reading for all poets writing in English:

> I write poems to preserve things I have seen/thought/felt...both for myself and for others, though I feel that my prime responsibility is to the experience itself, which I am trying to keep from oblivion for its own sake....I think the impulse to preserve lies at the bottom of all art.

Preservation of human experience. And Larkin having some fun, but ultimately serious:

> The term 'modern'...denotes a quality of irresponsibility peculiar to this century...the artist has become over-concerned with his material (hence an age of technical experiment), and...has busied himself with the two principle themes of modernism, mystification and outrage....He has written poems resembling the kind of pictures typists make with their machines during the coffee-break, or a novel in gibberish, or a play in which the characters sit in dustbins....if painting is to be a blank canvas, if a play is to be two hours of sexual intercourse...then let's get it over, the sooner the better, in the hope that human values will then be free to reassert themselves.

Extreme, but perhaps a starting point for a debate which some Canadian poets don't seem to realize has two sides.

Donald Justice, American poet and Pulitzer Prize winner, from *Platonic Scripts* (1984):

> One motive for much if not all art...is to keep memorable what deserves to be remembered....The age of experiment is exhausted and moribund, temporarily at least....Meanwhile, much of poetry is awash in a great ruck and welter of sentimentality. In most universities, most journals, the attitudes prevailing are attitudes left over from the sixties; but the sixties are dead....A tradition could be put back together...not forgetting rhythm; not forgetting truth.

And, on clarity and technique, the things which interest me greatly as a poet:

> I would like as much sense out of things as possible. And not to go through art, even if I may be obliged to go through life, confused. I would like to make efforts towards clarity and per- ceptions truly registered....I think a vice that's arisen...is so great a loss of formal awareness or concern that an unattractive, an actively unpleasant, chaos results, a total abandonment of what I would call, very simply, organization. Order, to be more high-toned. And this, then, is not only absent but prized for being absent, which I cannot go along with.

And neither can I. Poetry is organized sound—it derives, after all, from tribal drums and chants—and the vast amount of chopped prose in Canadian poetry, in which the poet clearly breaks the line at random, or loosely open-form poetry, which again, if you ask, often cannot be explained by the writer, is no adequate substitute for the order which Justice calls for. And finally, Justice says, "We seem to be producing a new kind of bad poetry, not the old kind that tries to move the reader and fails, but one that does not even try." And that's the tragedy. Much of our poetry is using techniques which, unintentionally mostly, are working against a poetry of feeling. As a poetry editor, I see hundreds of such poems, looking, on first glance, to be interesting, but ultimately, like Swift's horses, a skin stretched over a void.

Conclusions

1. If we accept that two main streams of poetry diverged—the Whitman stream and the Dickinson stream; or, if you like, the Pound stream and the Hardy stream— I am firmly from taste and instinct in the Dickinson/Hardy stream. I would guess that at least 80% of my fellow Western Canadian poets—those who have published widely—are in the other stream, the one which has led to postmodernism. It is a clash between restrained, organized power on the one hand, and wildness, the shout of power, on the other. Both have produced fine poets and fine poems; both have their techniques. But the Dickinson/Hardy stream seems less vulnerable to misuse, to damaging excess, to riding roughshod over the quiet places in us, to the determined neophiliacs and ideologues, to the acceptance of the trendy, the fashionable. When the poetic mainstream seems to be largely experimental, then content suffers, audiences dwindle, the avant-garde is celebrated and over-rated, not for what it is *per se*, but for how far it goes, how impressive the surface, how great the shock value.

2. The self-congratulatory tone of Canadians writing about Canadian poetry—in our tiny poetic world, usually fellow-poet about fellow-poet—disturbs me. There are many talented and original poets here, but, let's be truthful, we have no Seamus Heaney, Philip Larkin, or anyone to touch the very best Americans. Many will disagree with this, but it is an honest, considered judgement. Nor will we have, either, until we stop imitating, read more widely, see more possibilities for a new poetry than those piped in from the latest avant-garde American journal. We must stop imitating the passé, and, if we must fill our shelves with American poetry, let it be with the work of Donald Justice, Philip Levine, Anthony Hecht, Henry Taylor, Marvin Bell, Mark Strand and others.

3. I insist that our poetry needs more clarity, more serious exploration of personal feeling, less ideology. When young Alberta poets tell me they're trying to write like Olson or Bukowski or Ginsberg I become enraged (quietly, of course, as befits a good Dickinsonian!) and see there the sickness I worry about. Why these poets? Because they're somehow seen as trendy, anti-establishment? What can their work say to an 18-year-old Albertan, I wonder? Of course, the young seek excitement, and should. But the middle-aged and old seem to, as well, and that's the problem. If I knew that for every poem by Bukowski, Olson or Ginsberg, they would read a poem from *The New Yorker, Atlantic, Encounter* or the *Times Literary Supplement,* I'd be less concerned. At least then they would see, however much it is fashionable to sneer at the work in these magazines, that poetry of grace and style and feeling is still possible and still being written, and that it is a possible alternative. We must have more alternatives. There's an audience out there for poems of clarity and honesty and authenticity of feeling; an audience which has been short-changed for too long.

4. "It must give pleasure"—Wallace Stevens. Mystification and outrage, wrenching and twisting of word and line, will never give enough pleasure to enough people. Myself included.

Part Three

Notes on the Authors

GEORGE AMABILE

George Amabile has published five books of poetry, and has appeared in a dozen anthologies and more than fifty periodicals in Canada, the United States, Great Britain and South America. His most recent volume, *The Presence of Fire* (McClelland & Stewart, 1982) won the CAA Silver Medal for Poetry.

His poetry has appeared in recent issues of *Dandelion, Canadian Literature, Grain, Border Crossings* (formerly *Arts Manitoba*), *NeWest Review, Poetry Canada Review, Uncle, Pivot, Prism, Open Spaces, Ariel, CVII*, and *The New Yorker*.

Further Reading:

Writers at Work, The Paris Review Interviews

Erza Pound, *Literary Essays*

The League of Canadian Poets, *New Poet's Handbook*

Susan Ioannou, *The Crafted Poem*

Josue V. Harari (ed.), *Textual Strategies: Perspectives in Post-Structuralist Criticism*

Robin Skelton, *The Poet's Calling*

Curtis B. Bradford, *Yeats at Work*

Pat Kubis and Bob Howland, *The Complete Guide to Writing Fiction, Nonfiction and Publishing*

DAVID ARNASON

David Arnason was born in Gimli, Manitoba, in 1940, "on May 23, at 10 o'clock in the evening. There was a thunderstorm and it was a forceps delivery. I objected to coming into the world." He went to school in Gimli, and received his M.A. at the University of Manitoba and Ph.D. at the University of New Brunswick (thesis on the Development of Prairie Realism). Currently, he is a professor at the University of Manitoba, and the author of poetry, short stories, plays, film and radio scripts, and a critic and editor.

Arnason was a founding editor of the *Journal of Canadian Fiction*, and has edited *19th Century Canadian stories* (Macmillan, 1975), Dorothy Livesay's *Right Hand, Left Hand* (Porcépic, 1977), and was general editor of the 18-volume *Themes in Canadian Literature Series* (Macmillan). As well, he has edited several books for Turnstone Press, of whom he is a Member of the Board. He is the author of *Marsh Burning* (Turnstone, 1980), *50 Stories and a Piece of Advice* (Turnstone, 1982), *The Circus Performers Bar* (Talonbooks, 1984) and co-author of *The Icelanders* (Turnstone, 1981). He has written two plays *(Section 23: The French Language Revue*, and *Welcome to Hard Times: The Canadian Cultural Cabaret)*, produced by Prairie Theatre Exchange, and co-wrote and narrated the NFB film, "The Lake."

For Further Reading:

Henry Adams, *The Education of Henry Adams*

Michael Foucault, *The Archaeology of Knowledge*

Julio Cortázar, *Cronopios and Famas*

Bruno Schultz, *Sanitorium under the Sign of the Hourglass*

Robert Kroetsch, *The Words of My Roaring*

Jorges Amado, *Gabriella, Clove and Cinnamon*

PAMELA BANTING

Pamela Banting was born in 1955 in Birch River, Manitoba, where she lived until the age of eighteen. In 1976 she graduated from the University of Manitoba with a B.A. in English and philosophy. In 1977 she obtained her teaching certificate and then taught in the Interlake for two years. Pamela moved to Calgary where she worked as a technical editor for Burroughs/Carswell Law Publishers and reviewed books for the *Calgary Albertan*. In the summer of 1980 she attended the poetry writing workshop at Fort San, Saskatchewan, instructed by Patrick Lane. Pamela attended the International Summer Institute for Semiotic and Structural Studies in Toronto in 1984. In 1985 she worked as a Research Associate in Archives and Special Collections, Elizabeth Dafoe Library, University of Manitoba, organizing the Dorothy Livesay Papers and writing a series of essays on Livesay's short stories, poetry, autobiographical fictions, and correspondence.

Banting has earned writing grants from Alberta Culture and the Manitoba Arts Council as well as scholarships and fellowships from the University of Manitoba.

Her first book was a work of poetry, *Running Into the Open* (Turnstone, 1982). She has a prose manuscript in progress called *Pamela: Or, I Took Piano Lessons from the Virgin Mary*.

For Further Reading:

Roland Barthes, *The Pleasure of the Text*

Elaine Marks and Isabelle de Courtivron, eds, *New French Feminisms: An Anthology*

Luce Irigaray, *This Sex Which is Not One*

Shirley Neuman and Robert Wilson, *Labyrinths of Voice: Conversations with Robert Kroetsch*

John Sturrock, ed., *Structuralism and Since: From Lévi-Strauss to Derrida*

*In the Feminine: Women and Words/Les Femmes et Les Mots/Confer-
ence Proceedings, 1983*

DOUGLAS BARBOUR

Douglas Barbour was born in Winnipeg in 1940 and spent his first
14 years in that city. He has since lived in Montreal, Wolfville, Halifax,
Kingston, Toronto, and, for the past 17 years, Edmonton, Alberta.
He teaches Canadian Literature and Creative Writing at the University
of Alberta.

Douglas Barbour has published more than ten books of poetry,
has edited various anthologies, and written many articles and reviews.
Recent publications include *Canadian Poetry Chronicle (1984)* (Quarry,
1985), and *Visible Visions: The Selected Poems of Douglas Barbour*
(edited by Smaro Kamboureli and Robert Kroetsch, NeWest, 1984).
Visible Visions won the Stephan Stephannson Award for Excellence
in Poetry as well as the Alcuin Citation for excellence in book design.

For Further Reading:

George Bowering, *Craft Slices*

Guy Davenport, *The Geography of the Imagination*

The *Open Letter* issues on *No Tay Shun*, especially the essays by Frank
Davey & bp Nichol codifying the notational discoveries of open form
verse.

"Leaf through *The Poetics of the New American Poetry*, eds. Donald
Allen and Warren Tallman, for there's much of value in there."

SANDRA BIRDSELL

Sandra Birdsell was born in Morris, Manitoba in 1942. Besides her
two collections of stories, *Night Travellers* (Turnstone, 1982) and

Ladies of the House (Turnstone, 1984), her work has appeared in numerous journals and anthologies. Ms. Birdsell is co-writer of a play, *A Prairie Boy's Winter,* which has toured Manitoba extensively the past two years. She is currently at work on a play commissioned by Prairie Theatre Exchange to be produced in their 1986-87 season. The play is based on the lives of several characters who appeared in *Night Travellers.* Ms. Birdsell, who lives in Winnipeg, is a founding member and past president of the Manitoba Writers Guild. She is among the ten writers selected in 1986 by the Canadian Book Information Centre as part of "Forty-Five Below," the "new generation" of Canada's quality writers. Her first book won the Gerald Lampert Award.

For Further Reading:

Tillie Olsen, *Silences*

Graeme Gibson, *Eleven Canadian Novelists*

Graham Greene, *Ways of Escape*

DENNIS COOLEY

Dennis Cooley was born in Estevan, Saskatchewan in 1944 and was raised on a farm until he was 14. He received his B.Ed., B.A., and M.A. at the University of Saskatchewan and a Ph.D. from Rochester, NY (thesis on Robert Duncan). He has received a Canada Council Award and the Olive Beatrice Stanton Award for teaching.

Dennis Cooley is the editor of *Draft: An Anthology of Prairie Poetry* (Turnstone/ECW, 1981) and *RePlacing: Essays on Prairie Poetry* (ECW, 1981), and the author of *Leaving* (Turnstone, 1980), *Fielding* (Thistledown, 1983) and *Bloody Jack* (Turnstone, 1984). His *Soul Searching* (Red Deer College) and *The Vernacular Muse* (Turnstone) appeared in 1987.

For Further Reading:

Walter Ong, *Orality and Literature*

Mikhail Bahktin, *Rabelais and His World*

Jonathan Culler, *Structuralist Poetics*

Frank Davey, *From There to Here*

Donald M. Allen, *The New American Poetry*

LORNA CROZIER

Lorna Crozier, who has previously published under the name Uher, was born in Swift Current in 1948. She studied English literature at universities in Saskatoon, Regina and Edmonton, receiving her Master of Arts degree in 1980 from the University of Alberta. For several years, Crozier taught in high schools and at the Saskatchewan Summer School of the Arts. She has also been a guest instructor at the Banff School of Fine Arts and the Cypress Hills Community College's summer writing workshop. In 1980-81, she held the position of writer-in-residence in Swift Current and in 1985 at the Regina Public Library. Prior to her residency at the library, she was the Director of Communications at the Saskatchewan Department of Culture and Recreation. After years of moving from city to city across Western Canada, and after living in Montreal and Ottawa, Lorna Crozier and Patrick Lane, who have been together since 1979, now make their permanent home in Regina. Presently the recipient of a Canada Council grant, Crozier also does freelance work for CBC. Her poems have appeared in magazines and anthologies across the country.

She is the author of six books, including *No Longer Two People* (co-authored with Patrick Lane; Turnstone, 1979), *Humans and Other Beasts* (Turnstone, 1980), *The Weather* (Coteau, 1983). Her latest book, *The Garden Going On Without Us* (McClelland and Stewart, 1985), received a nomination for the Governor General's Award for poetry.

For Further Reading:

Mary Daly, *Gyn/Ecology*

Joanna Russ, *How to Suppress Women's Writing*

John Berger, *And our faces, my heart, brief as photos*

Italo Calvino, *Marco Valdo*

Adrienne Rich, *On Lies, Secrets and Silence: Selected Prose*

Virginia Woolf, *Three Guineas* and *A Room of One's Own*

Raymond Carver, *Fires: Essays, Poems, Stories*

Doris Hilles, *Voices and Visions*

E. F. DYCK

Born in Turnhill, Saskatchewan, 1939, Dyck studied mathematics in Saskatoon, Munich, and Minneapolis, and taught the same in Minnesota, Missouri, and Saskatchewan. He began to write in the seventies and now writes (poetry and criticism), edits (e.g., *Grain*, 1980-83), teaches (occasionally, English), and reads (literature and rhetoric). He lives in Saskatoon with Gloria and her daughter Lara. Dyck was awarded a SSHRCC Doctoral Fellowship 1984-86; and a SWG Poetry Manuscript Prize 1983.

Ed Dyck's poetry titles include *Odpoems &* (Coteau, 1978), *The Mossbank Canon* (Turnstone, 1982), *Pisscat Songs* (Brick, 1983). He is editing an anthology of essays on Saskatchewan writing.

For Further Reading:

"I'd say read everything (that applies)!"

PATRICK FRIESEN

Patrick Friesen was born in rural Manitoba in 1945. He left his home town to attend the University of Manitoba, where he studied history and English literature.

Pat is currently employed as a television producer for the Manitoba Department of Education. He has produced films on artists Esther Warkov and Don Proch and on poet Patrick Lane. He also directed the last two of those films.

As a writer, Pat has published essays, reviews, stories and poems. The CBC recently produced his radio play *Amanda*, and the Prairie Theatre Exchange produced his stage play, *The Shunning*, based on his long poem of the same name (Turnstone, 1980). Patrick Friesen's most recent book is *Unearthly Horses* (Turnstone, 1984). He has won Manitoba Arts Council awards.

Further Reading:

Nadezha Mandelstam, *Hope Abandoned*

Henry Miller, *The Rosy Crucifixion*

Oriana Fallaci, *Letter to a Child Never Born*

Gwendolyn MacEwan, *The T. E. Lawrence Poems*

John Berger, *About Looking*

Richard & Lynda Thompson, *Shoot out the Lights* (LP album)

KRISTJANA GUNNARS

Kristjana Gunnars was born in 1948, Reykjavik, Iceland, and studied at Oregon State University 1966-1969. She immigrated to Canada in 1969. She has lived and worked in Squamish, B.C., Vancouver, Toronto, Regina, Winnipeg. She studied at the University of Regina

(M.A. 1978) and lived in Iceland '75-76, working as teacher, and '80-81, as journalist. She studied for her Ph.D. at the University of Manitoba, 1981 to date. Gunnars is editor of *Freelance* (Sask. Writers' Guild) and editor of *Prairie Fire*. She is a literary agent for Writers' Union of Iceland for North American markets, which developed into ownership of a publishing firm in Winnipeg that concentrates on the publication of translations into English of European writing. She sits on a membership committee for the League of Canadian Poets. Currently, with help from the Alberta Foundation for the Literary Arts, Kristjana Gunnars is translating the work of Stephan G. Stephansson for a book of selected poetry.

She has published five books of poetry, including *Settlement Poems* Vol. I and II (Turnstone 1980), *One-Eyed Moon Maps* (Porcépic, 1980), *Wake-Pick Poems* (Anansi, 1981), and *The Night Workers of Ragnarök* (Porcépic, 1985). She has also published a collection of short fiction, *The Axe's Edge* (Porcépic, 1983), and has translated a collection of essays, *In Retrospect, Stephan G. Stephansson, Seven Essays* (Reykjavik).

For Further Reading:

"These are not strictly on writing, but have been inspiring for me as far as writing goes":

Franz Kafka's *Diaries*

The essays of Adrienne Rich

Leslie Fiedler's essay, "No, in Thunder"

Julia Kristeva's essay, "How Do We Speak to Literature?"

Conversations with Isaac Bashevis Singer

CAROLINE HEATH

Caroline Heath was born in Oregon in 1941, and received a B.A. in German Literature and journalism from the University of Oregon in

1962. She lived in England and Germany before settling in Saskatoon, Saskatchewan in 1966. She was married to Terrence Heath, 1962-82, and has three sons.

Heath was a member of Saskatoon Poets Group, 1970-78, editor of *Grain*, 1973-79, freelance editor, 1980-83. She has served as juror for the Canada Council, Alberta Foundation for the Literary Arts, Manitoba Arts Council and Saskatchewan Arts Board. In 1980-82, she chaired a Saskatchewan Arts Board literary committee. She has conducted numerous writing workshops, held short-term editor-in-residencies, and adjudicated competitions, including a CBC short story competition.

In 1983, she founded Fifth House publishing company. Twelve titles have been edited for Fifth House, including: *Achimoona* (stories and art by Native artists, 1985); *Doctrine of Signatures* by Anne Szumigalski, nominated for Governor General's Award for English Language Poetry, 1983; and *Country of the Heart* by Sharon Butala, nominated for *Books in Canada* Best First Novel 1984.

Caroline Heath reviews theatre for CBC and *NeWest Review*.

HENRY KREISEL

Henry Kreisel is the author of two novels, *The Rich Man* (1948) and *The Betrayal* (McClelland and Stewart, 1964), and of a collection of short stories, *The Almost Meeting* (NeWest, 1981), which was awarded the J. I. Segal Foundation Prize in 1983. His story "The Travelling Nude" won the President's Medal of the University of Western Ontario in 1960. A major collection of his work is *Another Country: Writings by and about Henry Kreisel*, ed. Shirley Neuman (NeWest, 1985).

Henry Kreisel was born in Vienna, 1922, and escaped to England during the Nazi occupation. He came to Canada in 1940 where he has had a very distinguished academic career. He has served at the University of Alberta for thirty years, including five years as Academic Vice-President. He is currently a University Professor.

Henry Kreisel has written widely on literature and his essay "The Prairie: A State of Mind" is a seminal essay on prairie literature. Critic Neil Besner says Kreisel has explored in his writing "the raptures, discontinuities, and 'almost meetings' between Old World characters and visions." Henry Kreisel's major contribution to Canadian literature has been to bridge two worlds—the European and the Canadian.

Further Reading:

"I always tell students to read as much imaginative literature as possible. Most highly recommended: novels by Laurence, Richler, Wiebe, van Herk, Atwood; short stories by Gallant and Munro."

ROBERT KROETSCH

Robert Kroetsch was born in Heisler, Alberta, in 1927. He did his undergraduate work at the University of Alberta. After six years of working in the Canadian North he entered graduate school, first at Middlebury College, Vermont, then at the University of Iowa, where he earned his Ph.D. in 1961. After teaching for seventeen years at the State University of New York at Binghamton, he moved to the University of Manitoba. He has published seven novels, numerous volumes of poetry, and a considerable amount of critical and theoretical speculations.

Robert Kroetsch won the Governor General's Award for fiction for *The Studhorse Man* (Macmillan, 1969), and a Killam Award, 1986, to study the characteristics of Canadian narrative.

Robert Kroetsch's recent publications include a novel, *Alibi* (General, 1983), a collection, *Essays (Open Letter,* Spring 1983), a volume of poetry, *Advice to My Friends* (General, 1985). He edited with Reingard Nischik a collection of criticism: *Gaining Ground* (NeWest, 1985). Forthcoming are *Excerpts From the Real World* and a re-issue of *Seed Catalogue.*

For Further Reading:

"I can't decide!"

MARGARET LAURENCE

Margaret Laurence was born in 1926 in Neepawa, Manitoba. She graduated with a B.A. from United College (now the University of Winnipeg) and lived in England, Somaliland, Ghana and Vancouver before settling in Lakefield in 1974, where she lived until her death in 1987. She is the author of fifteen books, including her major series of novels based on characters in and from the fictional town of Manawaka. The Manawaka series comprises *The Stone Angel* (McClelland and Stewart, 1964), *A Jest of God* (McClelland and Stewart, 1966; winner of the Governor General's award), *The Fire-Dwellers* (McClelland and Stewart, 1969), *A Bird in the House* (McClelland and Stewart, 1970), and *The Diviners* (McClelland and Stewart, 1974; Governor General's award). Margaret Laurence published, in addition, translations of Somali folktales and poetry (*A Tree for Poverty*, Nairobi, Eagle Press, 1954; Dublin, Irish University Press and Hamilton, McMaster University Library Press, 1970), essays on Nigerian literature (*Long Drums and Cannons*, London, Macmillan and New York, Praeger, 1968), several children's books and a collection of personal essays (*Heart of a Stranger*, McClelland and Stewart, 1976). Her novel, *A Jest of God*, has been made into a feature film, *Rachel, Rachel*, starring Joanne Woodward and directed by Paul Newman.

Margaret Laurence was the recipient of many honours and awards. She received the Molson Award and was named a Companion, Order of Canada. She has been conferred with more than a dozen honorary degrees, the most recent by the University of Manitoba in 1986. Margaret Laurence served as Chancellor of Trent University for 1981 to 1983. She was also active in peace and disarmament groups. *First Lady of Manawaka* is a National Film Board documentary based on the life and work of Margaret Laurence.

DOROTHY LIVESAY

Born in Winnipeg in 1909, Dorothy Livesay started early as a poet but later became, as well, a journalist, social worker, teacher, editor, broadcaster, and university professor. She studied at the University of Toronto, the Sorbonne, University of British Columbia and Waterloo. She is an Honorary Fellow of St. John's College, University of Manitoba and Trinity College, University of Toronto and has been conferred honorary degrees from Athabasca and McGill.

Dorothy Livesay is the author of many books of poetry; her first, *Green Pitcher* (Macmillan), was published in 1928. Her most recent books include *Collected Poems: Two Seasons* (McGraw Hill Ryerson, 1972), *Ice Age* (Porcépic, 1975), *The Raw Edges* (Turnstone, 1981), *The Phases of Love* (Coach House, 1983),and *Feeling the Worlds* (Fiddlehead, 1984). Two prose books are *A Winnipeg Childhood* (Peguis, 1973) and *Right Hand, Left Hand* (Porcépic, 1977), a collage of unpublished poems, stories and articles from the Thirties. Her essay, "The Documentary Poem: A Canadian Genre," stands as a major contribution to Canadian criticism.

Dorothy Livesay was a founding member of the League of Canadian Poets, Amnesty International (Canada) and the Committee for an Independent Canada. She won the Governor General's Award for poetry in 1944 and 1947, and the Queen's Canada medal in 1977. In 1984 she was awarded the Person's Case Medal.

Now a free-lance writer, poet, and lecturer, Dorothy Livesay lives on Galiano Island, B.C.

For Further Reading:

Gaile McGregor, *The Wacousta Syndrome*

Robert Lecker and Jack David, eds., *The Penguin Book of Canadian Literature*

Canadian Literature, No. 99 (Winter 1983), No. 100 (Spring 1984), No. 106 (Fall 1985)

Sandra Gilbert and Susan Gubar, eds., *The Norton Anthology of Literature by Women*

No Feather, No Ink, (Thistledown, 1985)

Dennis Cooley, ed., *Draft: An Anthology of Prairie Poetry*

All issues of *CV/II*

ELI MANDEL

Eli Mandel was born in Estevan in 1922. He served in the medical corps in World War II and returned to study at the University of Saskatchewan and subsequently at the University of Toronto. He has taught at the University of Alberta and at York University where he is Professor of English and Humanities. He won the Governor General's Award for Poetry in 1967 with *An Idiot Joy* (Hurtig). His other books of poetry include *Stony Plain* (Porcépic, 1973), *Crusoe* (Anansi, 1973), *Out of Place* (Porcépic, 1977), *Dreaming Backwards* (General, 1981), and *Life Sentence: Poems and Journals, 1976-1980* (Porcépic, 1981). In 1979 Eli Mandel served as Writer-in-Residence at the Regina Public Library. In 1982 he was named Fellow of the Royal Society of Canada.

Eli Mandel is an important editor and critic. He has written critical books on Irving Layton, edited *Contexts of Canadian Criticism* (University of Chicago, 1971), and published a collection of critical articles, *Another Time* (Porcépic, 1977). *Criticism: The Silent Speaking Words* was originally broadcast on CBC radio (1966). Another collection of essays, *Family Romance*, is available from Turnstone Press.

KEN MITCHELL

Ken Mitchell was born and raised in Moose Jaw, studied at the University of Saskatchewan, and now teaches Canadian Literature and creative writing at the University of Regina. He is well-known as playwright, novelist, poet and editor. His works include *Cruel Tears*, (Talon, 1977) *The Great Cultural Revolution* (Playwrights Canada, 1980), *Wandering Rafferty* (Macmillan, 1972), *Everybody Gets Something Here* (Macmillan, 1977), *Sinclair Ross: A Reader's Guide* (Coteau, 1981). Coteau Books has published a collection of his shorter works, *Ken Mitchell Country* (1984). His drama, *Gone the Burning Sun*, won the Canadian Authors Association prize for Best Play and was nominated for the Governor General's Award.

Ken Mitchell has a number of works forthcoming: a volume of poems, *Through the Nan Da Gate* from Thistledown, a new play, *All Our Yesterdays*, opens in Regina (July 1986), and a film, *The Medicine Line*, is scheduled for release by the N.F.B.

In 1985 Ken Mitchell was appointed Honorary Professor, Centre of Canadian Studies, Chongqing, China. In the fall of 1986 he will be teaching Western literature in Beijing.

Further Reading:

Peter Brook, *The Empty Space*

Diane Bessai (ed.), *Prairie Performance*

Robert Wallace and Cynthia Zimmerman (ed.), *The Work: Conversations with Canadian Playwrights*

MONTY REID

Monty Reid was born in Saskatchewan in 1952. He moved to Alberta in 1967 and has lived in the latter province ever since. He has received a B.A. and M.A in English from the University of Alberta. His M.A. Thesis became his first major publication—*Karst Means Stone* (NeWest)—in 1979. He has lived in Ryley, Camrose, and currently resides in Drumheller, where he heads the Public Programs Department at the Tyrrell Museum of Palaeontology. Reid has been active in the literary community since 1976. He edited *NeWest Review* for one year, and was a founding editor of *The Camrose Review* and its offspring, *The Dinosaur Review.* He has served on the Executive of the Writer's Guild of Alberta since 1984, and is married, with two children.

Monty Reid has published five books of poetry, including *The Life of Ryley* (Thistledown, 1981), *The Dream of Snowy Owls* (Longspoon, 1983), *The Alternate Guide* (rdc press, 1985).

He has received writing awards from the University of Alberta and the Canada Council. *The Alternate Guide* won the Stephan G. Stephansson award for Poetry.

Books that have been Important for Me:

bp Nichol, *The Martyrology*

Robert Hass, *Praise*

George Bowering, *Kerrisdale Elegies*

Sinclair Ross, *As For Me and My House*

William Carlos Williams, *The Desert Music*

Robert Kroetsch, *Seed Catalogue*

"I've also been moved and provoked by the work of Atwood, Audrey Thomas, Roo Borson, Siv Fox, among others. But when I get to my bookshelf, I never have to hunt for these six books—I know exactly where they are."

BRENDA RICHES

Brenda Riches was born in India and moved to England at age four. She was educated at Taunton, Somerset and the University of Cambridge. In 1974 she moved to Saskatchewan and began writing seriously. She currently lives in Regina where she writes prose and verse and is editor of *Grain.* Her first book, *Dry Media*, was published by Turnstone Press in 1981. She is a past president of the Saskatchewan Writers' Guild. Brenda Riches has won writing awards from the Saskatchewan Arts Board and the Canada Council.

For Further Reading:

"One learns best from reading the best of the genre one writes oneself. Recommended: Patrick White, Virginia Woolf, Gabriel Garcia Marquez."

Rust Hill, *Writing in General and the Short Story in Particular*

John Gardner, *The Art of Fiction*

William Gass, *On Being Blue*

BIRK SPROXTON

Birk Sproxton was born in Flin Flon, Manitoba in 1943 and grew up chasing hockey pucks and listening to tall tales of the north. He graduated from United College (now the University of Winnipeg) with a B.A. in English and taught high school for a year before beginning an M.A. at the University of Manitoba. He taught at the University of Regina for four years and then returned to Manitoba for a Ph.D., where he won university and Canada Council awards. He is a founding editor of *The Sphinx: A Magazine of Literature and Society*, published at the University of Regina. He edited *Sounds Assembling: The Poetry of Bertram Brooker* (Turnstone, 1980). His *Headframe:* (Turnstone, 1985), a longpoem in the menippean tradition of mixed prose and verse, is now in its second printing. At present he teaches Canadian literature and creative writing at Red Deer College and is writing a prose work on the political activist Mabel Marlowe.

For Further Reading:

Paul Fussell, *The Great War and Modern Memory*

Susan Stewart, *Nonsense: Aspects of Intertextuality in Folklore and Literature*

Barbara Herrnstein Smith, *Poetic Closure: A Study of How Poems End*

A Great Big Ugly Man Came Up and Tied His Horse to Me: A Book of Nonsense Verse, illustrated by Wallace Tripp

Anthony Easthope, *Poetry As Discourse*

Angus Fletcher, *Allegory: The Theory of a Symbolic Mode*

ANDREW SUKNASKI

Andrew Suknaski is well-known for his wonderfully complicated jokes. He was born in 1942 near Wood Mountain, Saskatchewan to a Ukrainian father and a Polish mother. In his poetry he continues to explore the linguistic and ethnic heritage he grew up with. He studied at Simon Fraser and UBC, the Kootenay School of Art and the Montreal Museum of Fine Arts School. In 1977-78 he was Writer-in-Residence at St. John's College, University of Manitoba.

Andrew Suknaski's books of poetry include *Wood Mountain Poems* (Macmillan, 1976), *Octomi* (Thistledown, 1976), *The Ghosts Call You Poor* (Macmillan, 1978), *East of Myloona* (Thistledown, 1979), *In the Name of Narid* (Porcupine's Quill, 1981), and *Montage for an Interstellar Cry* (Turnstone, 1982). In 1982 NeWest Press published *The Land They Gave Away: New and Selected Poems*. Andrew Suknaski and his work are the subject of a Harvey Spak NFB documentary, *Wood Mountain Poems*.

MERNA SUMMERS

When Merna Summers' first collection of stories, *The Skating Party* (Oberon, 1974), was published, Margaret Laurence described the new author as "extremely talented." When her second collection, *Calling Home* (Oberon, 1982), appeared, Marian Engel called Summers "one of our best." Merna Summers has won the Katherine Anne Porter Prize for Fiction, given by the University of Tulsa and *Nimrod* magazine, and an Ohio State award. She was born in Mannville, Alberta and lives in Edmonton.

Reading List:

V. S. Pritchett, *The Living Novel and Later Appreciations*

Flannery O'Connor, *Mystery and Manners*

Joyce Cary, *Art and Reality*

Reginald Gibbons, *The Poet's Work*

William H. Gass, *Fiction and the Figures of Life*

Eudora Welty, *The Eye of the Story*

E. M. Forster, *Aspects of the Novel*

John Updike, *Picked-up Pieces*

ANNE SZUMIGALSKI

Anne Szumigalski was born in London, England and brought up in the country with six brothers and sisters. She came to Canada in 1951, and has lived in Saskatoon since 1956. She is the mother of four grown children and is a founding member of: the Saskatchewan Writers Guild, Sask. Writers' and Artists' Colonies, AKA Artist-run Centre, and Saskatoon Moving Collective. She taught poetry-writing at SSSA 1969-1979, was associate editor of *Grain* for eight years, and for the past three years has been poetry editor of *NeWest Review.*

Anne has read her work in all parts of Canada, and some parts of the USA and UK. She is the author of six books, and two others in collaboration with Terrence Heath, with whom she has also collaborated on four poems for voices produced by CBC.

Her recent books include *A Game of Angels* (Turnstone, 1980), *Doctrine of Signatures* (Fifth House, 1983), *Risks* (rdc press, 1983) and *Instar* (rdc press, 1985). *Doctrine* and *Instar* were both nominated for Governor General's Awards.

WAYNE TEFS

Wayne Tefs was born in Winnipeg in 1947. He was educated at the University of Manitoba and the University of Toronto. He is a Woodrow Wilson Fellow and has been an instructor at several universities. Since 1978 he has taught at St. John's-Ravenscourt School. He has contributed articles to a number of literary journals and is a Contributing Editor of *Border Crossings*. Currently, he lives in Winnipeg where he divides his time equally among teaching, writing, and playing hockey.

Wayne Tefs is the author of two novels, *Figures on a Wharf* (Turnstone 1983) which was a finalist for the *Books in Canada* First Novel Award, and *The Cartier Street Contract* (Turnstone 1985).

Suggestions for Further Reading:

Leslie Fiedler, *What Was Literature?*

Benjamin Nelson (ed.), *Freud on Creativity*

John Updike, *Hugging the Shore*

E. H. Gombrich, *Art and Illusion*

Wolfgang Iser, *The Implied Reader*

Italo Calvino, *If on a Winter's Night a Traveller*

W. D. VALGARDSON

Bill Valgardson taught high-school English and Art for seven years in Manitoba. After teaching at a private college in the United States, he moved to Victoria in 1974. Currently, he is Professor and Chairman of the Creative Writing department at the U. of Victoria. He has published three books of short stories (*Bloodflowers*, Oberon, 1973; *God is Not A Fish Inspector*, Oberon, 1975; *Red Dust*, Oberon, 1978), a book of poems (*In The Gutting Shed*, Turnstone, 1976), and a novel (*Gentle Sinners*, Oberon, 1980). A number of his short stories have been made into films and TV shows. The film adaptation of his novel was released on CBC last year. Since then it has been widely distributed abroad. He frequently adapts his own fiction for other media but particularly, for radio. He has received a number of awards, including the University of Western Ontario President's Medal (1971) for "Bloodflowers," the *Books in Canada* Best First Novel award (1981) for *Gentle Sinners* and the CAA medal for *Granite Point* as best drama produced in 1983.

The Carpenter of Dreams, a book of poems, is available from Skaldhus Press, Victoria.

Further Reading:

"I'm afraid that I don't recommend books on writing for beginning writers. To do so leads people astray for it confirms to them that if only they knew the tricks they would be rich and famous or at least published. Instead, since fiction is not about what happens but about what happens to SOMEONE, I recommend that they buy books on abnormal psychology, or normal psychology, on psychiatric case studies, on body language, on dream analysis. Plus as many books as they can afford on the world around them (e.g., books on plants, animals, fish, local histories). The basic problem isn't lack of writing skills, it is lack of knowledge about a specific world."

ARITHA VAN HERK

Aritha van Herk was born in 1954 in central Alberta. She grew up on a farm near the village of Edburg, just a few miles from the Battle River, an area that she still writes about. She published her first poem when she was twelve, and her first published story won the *Miss Chatelaine* Short Fiction Award in 1976. In 1978 she won the Seal First Novel Award for *Judith*, and in 1981 she published her second novel, *The Tent Peg*. Her third novel, *No Fixed Address*, was released in the spring of 1986. (All novels have been published by McClelland and Stewart.)

She has been a secretary, a hired hand, a bush cook, an editor and teacher; her most recent editorial work is *West of Fiction* (with Leah Flater and Rudy Wiebe), published by NeWest. As a child of immigrant parents, she has always inhabited multiple worlds; she is interested in the unexplored landscapes of Canada, as well as the unexplored areas of human myth and possibility. A regionalist and feminist, she works through her fiction to rediscover lost stories and myths within contemporary time and space.

Ms. van Herk received her M.A. in English from the University of Alberta in 1978. She is currently Associate Professor of English and Creative Writing at the University of Calgary. She is married to Robert Sharp, who is an exploration geologist.

For Further Reading:

Christa Wolf, *Cassandra*

William Gass, *The World within the Word*

William Faulkner, *Absalom, Absalom*

Rachel Blau DuPlessis, *Writing Beyond the Ending*

MIRIAM WADDINGTON

Miriam Waddington was born in Winnipeg in 1917. She studied at Toronto and Pennsylvania, specializing in Social Work, before turning to advanced study in literature. Miriam Waddington has been a social worker and teacher, and is now Professor of English literature, York University. She was writer-in-residence at the University of Ottawa in 1974, and has been invited to be writer-in-residence at the Toronto Metropolitan Library, June-December, 1986.

She published her first book of poetry, *Green World* (First Statement), in 1945 and numerous books since. She wrote a critical study of *A.M. Klein* (Copp Clark, 1970) and has edited *John Sutherland: Essays, Controversies and Poems* (McClelland and Stewart, 1972) and the *Collected Poems of A.M. Klein* (McGraw-Hill Ryerson, 1974). Her recent books also include *Driving Home: Poems New and Selected* (Oxford, 1972), *Mister Never* (Turnstone, 1978), *The Visitants* (Oxford, 1981), and *Summer at Lonely Beach* (Mosaic, 1982). She has published many critical articles, reviews, and short stories as well as translations of prose and poetry from German and Yiddish. *Driving Home* won the J.I. Segal award in 1972. In 1980 Miriam Waddington was Canada Council exchange poet to Wales. Her *Collected Poems* has recently been published by Oxford.

For Further Reading:

Virginia Woolf, *A Writer's Diary*

Louise Bogan, letters and essays

George Gissing, *New Grub Street*

Bernard Malamud, *The Tenants*

JON WHYTE

Jon Whyte was born and raised in Banff, Canadian Rockies, and received his education in Banff, Medicine Hat, Edmonton, Stanford, and in the world at large. He is influenced by geography, geology, geomorphology, weaving, pottery, and Geoffry Chaucer, Earle Birney and the *Penguin Anthology of Longer Contemporary Poems* and is "one who believes we may not learn how to be post-modern until we get over being Victorian." A superlative reader of his own and others' poetry. Curator of the Heritage Collection, Whyte Museum of the Canadian Rockies; secretary of the Alberta Museums Association, 1983-1986. Active conservationist.

Jon Whyte's *Homage, Henry Kelsey* (Turnstone) won the Stephan Stephansson Award for Poetry in 1984. His other recent publications include *Carl Rungius, Painter of the Western Wilderness* (with E. J. Hart; Douglas & McIntyre, 1985), *Indians in the Rockies* (Altitude, 1985), *Fells of Brightness*, Volume I, *Some Fittes and Starts* (Longspoon, 1983) and Volume II, *Wenkchemna* (Longspoon, 1985).

For Further Reading:

Lewis Carrol, *Alice in Wonderland* and *Through the Looking Glass*. Two great books.

Eric Partridge, *Origins*. The most fun dictionary of etymology; indispensable for rooting around in English.

Octavio Paz, *The Bow and the Lyre*. The book on poetics so far as I'm concerned.

Eric Partridge, *Usage and Abusage*. Idiosyncratic like Fowler, and British, which helps fight the U.S. hegemony.

Brewer's Dictionary. I cannot imagine being without it for its quirky knowledge.

E. B. White, anything except *The Elements of Style* (e.g. *Points of my Compass*) for elegance, humour, wit.

RUDY WIEBE

Rudy Wiebe was born in 1934 into a small Mennonite community near Fairholme, Saskatchewan. He now lives in Edmonton and teaches

Canadian literature and creative writing at the University of Alberta. Rudy Wiebe has written and edited many works, including seven novels, the most recent of which are *The Temptations of Big Bear* (winner of the Governor General's Award, 1973), *The Scorched-Wood People* (1977), *The Mad Trapper* (1980), and *My Lovely Enemy* (1983), all published by McClelland and Stewart. In 1985 he edited an oral/pictorial history of 1885 (with Bob Beal): *War in the West, Voices of the 1885 Rebellion. Where Is the Voice Coming From?* (1974) and *The Angel of the Tar Sands, and Other Stories* (1982) are collections of short fiction.

For Further Reading:

F. M. Salter, *The Way of the Makers*

Leah Flater, Aritha van Herk, Rudy Wiebe, eds., *West of Fiction*

Pat Demers, ed., *The Creating Word*

DAVID WILLIAMS

David Williams was born in Souris, Manitoba where his father was a flying instructor in the Commonwealth Air Training Program. At war's end, the family moved back to northeast Saskatchewan, eventually settling on a farm near the rest of the Williams clan at Lac Vert. He studied and earned a Pastor's Diploma from Briercrest Bible Institute but never took the pulpit, believing not so much that all stories were equal but that the old stories could not make up for the embarrassment of being from Lac Vert. He went to the University of Saskatchewan in the hope that someone would teach him how writers managed to transform their worlds; he ended up playing first-string end with the Huskies and marrying Darlene Olinyk from Norquay, before emigrating to New England to begin graduate school. At Concord and Salem and Pittsfield he finally discovered Lac Vert; later he studied at Oxford and learned that the colonial mentality was his own. He holds a Ph.D. from the University of Massachusetts, having taught since 1972 at the University of Manitoba. He is currently Professor of English in Canadian, American, and Seventeenth-Century Literatures at St. Paul's College. He and his wife have two sons, Jeremy and Bryan.

As a scholar, David Williams has won Woodrow Wilson and Canada Fellowships and as a writer, Manitoba Arts Council and Canada Council Awards.

His recent publications include the novels of the *Lacjardin Trilogy* (Anansi)—*The Burning Wood* (1975), *The River Horsemen* (1981), *Eye of the Father* (1985)—and a critical study, *Faulkner's Women: The Myth and the Muse* (McGill-Queen's, 1977).

Suggestions for Further Reading:

Gotthold Ephraim Lessing, *Laocoon: An Essay Upon the Limits of Painting and Poetry*

Arthur Schopenhauer, "The Platonic Idea as the Object of Art," in *The World as Will and Idea*, Vol. I.

Friedrich Nietzsche, *Twilight of the Idols*

Carl Jung, *Answer to Job*

Otto Rank, *Art and Artist* and *Will Therapy*

Ernest Hemingway, *Death in the Afternoon*

CHRISTOPHER WISEMAN

Christopher Wiseman was born and educated in England. He served two years in the R.A.F. through no fault of his own, and, after graduating with an English degree from Cambridge, he was awarded a writing fellowship to the University of Iowa Poetry Workshop, where he stayed for three years. After a brief session of high-school teaching back in England, he was appointed as one of the two founding members of the Department of English Studies at the University of Strathclyde in Scotland, where he stayed six years. Since 1969, he and his wife and two sons have lived in Calgary, where he teaches Creative Writing and English at the University of Calgary. He has published four full-length books, several chapbooks and a pamphlet of poetry, as well as a book on the poetry of Edwin Muir. His poetry has appeared in over 50 journals, many anthologies, and many radio and TV programs in Canada, Britain and the States. He has served as President of the Writers' Guild of Alberta; he is poetry editor of *Ariel;* he is a member of the League of Canadian Poets.

Christopher Wiseman's most recent book is *An Ocean of Whispers* (Sono Nis, 1982). He has two fine-press chapbooks coming soon in England — the first, *Closings* by Priapus Press.

Suggestions for Further Reading:

Philip Larkin, *Required Writing*

Donald Justice, *Platonic Scripts*

Gary Geddes, ed., *20th Century Poetry and Poetics*

Robin Skelton, *The Practice of Poetry*

Harvey Gross, *Sound and Form in Modern Poetry*

Ted Hughes, *Poetry in the Making*

Suggestions for Further Reading

The list below emphasizes work by and about writers from the prairies. Readers are also referred to suggestions made by the authors in this collection and to such histories as *Literary History of Canada*, Frank Davey's *From There to Here*, D. G. Jones' *Butterfly on Rock*, E. K. Brown's *On Canadian Poetry*. Issues raised in this collection are addressed in a number of periodicals including *Dandelion, The Dinosaur Review, blue buffalo, The NeWest Review, Grain, CV/II, Border Crossings, Prairie Fire*.

Barclay, Patricia. "Regionalism and the Writer: A Talk with W. O. Mitchell," *Canadian Literature* No. 14 (Autumn 1962), 53-56.

Belkin, Rosalyn. "The Consciousness of a Jewish Artist: An Interview with Adele Wiseman," *Journal of Canadian Fiction* Nos. 31/32 (1981), 148-176.

Blodgett, E. D. *Configuration: Essays on the Canadian Literatures.* Downsview: ECW Press, 1982.

Canadian Literature, 1984-85, available from the Manitoba Department of Education. A series of 25 videos about the lives and work of 24 Canadian writers.

Cooley, Dennis (ed). *Draft, An Anthology of Prairie Poetry.* Winnipeg: Turnstone Press and Downsview: ECW Press, 1981.

Cooley, Dennis (ed). *RePlacing.* Downsview: ECW Press, 1980.

Davey, Frank. *Surviving the Paraphrase*. Winnipeg: Turnstone Press, 1983.

Davey, Frank (ed). *Reflections: Essays on Robert Kroetsch*. Special Issue of *Open Letter*, Fifth Series, Nos. 8-9 (Summer-Fall 1984).

Dorothy Livesay: The Woman I Am. Dir. David Tucker. Film Arts, 1981. Distributed by Kinetic Film Enterprises Ltd.

Grove, Frederick Philip. *A Stranger to My Time: Essays by and about Frederick Philip Grove*. Ed. Paul Hjartarson. Edmonton: NeWest Press, 1986.

Grove, Frederick Philip. *It Needs to Be Said*. Toronto: Macmillan, 1929.

Harrison, Dick. *Unnamed Country: The Struggle for a Canadian Prairie Fiction*. Edmonton: The University of Alberta Press, 1977.

Hiebert, Paul. "Avenues of Research Suggested by the Fletchers Castoria Box," *Canadian Literature* No. 100 (Spring 1984), 139-146.

Hiebert, Paul. "The Comic Spirit at Forty Below Zero," *Manitoba in Literature: An Issue on Literary Environment*. Ed. R. G. Collins and Kenneth McRobbie. A Special Issue of *Mosaic* Vol. 3 no. 3 (Spring 1970), 58-68.

Hilles, Doris. *Voices and Visions: Interviews with Saskatchewan Writers*. Moose Jaw: Coteau Books, 1985.

In the Feminine: Women and Words/Les Femmes et Les Mots/Conference Proceedings, 1983.

Keith, W. J. *Epic Fiction: The Art of Rudy Wiebe*. Edmonton: University of Alberta Press, 1981.

Kreisel, Henry. *Another Country: Writing by and about Henry Kreisel*. Edmonton: NeWest Press, 1985.

Kroetsch, Robert. *The Crow Journals*. Edmonton: NeWest Press, 1980.

Kroetsch, Robert. *Essays*. An issue of *Open Letter*, Fifth Series, No. 4 (Spring 1983).

Kroetsch, Robert. *Labyrinths of Voice: Conversations with Robert Kroetsch*. Shirley Neuman and Robert Wilson. Edmonton: NeWest Press, 1982.

Kroetsch, Robert, Tamara Palmer, and Beverly Rasporich (eds). *Ethnicity and Canadian Literature*. A *Canadian Ethnic Studies* Special Issue, Vol. XIV, no. 1, 1982.

Laurence, Margaret. *A Place to Stand On: Essays by and about Margaret Laurence*. Ed. George Woodcock. Edmonton: NeWest Press, 1983.

Livesay, Dorothy. "All Aboa-r-rd!" *Canadian Literature* No. 100 (Spring 1984), 200-203.

Livesay, Dorothy. "The Documentary: A Canadian Genre," in *Contexts of Canadian Criticism*. Ed. Eli Mandel. Chicago: University of Chicago Press, 1971.

Livesay, Dorothy. "A Prairie Sampler," *Manitoba in Literature: An Issue on Literary Environment*. Ed. R. G. Collins and Kenneth McRobbie. A Special Issue of *Mosaic* Vol. 3 no. 3 (Spring 1970), 85-92.

Ludwig, Jack. "You Always Go Home Again," *Manitoba in Literature: An Issue on Literary Environment*. Ed. R. G. Collins and Kenneth McRobbie. A Special Issue of *Mosaic* Vol. 3 no. 3 (Spring 1970), 107-111.

McCourt, Edward. *The Canadian West in Fiction*. Revised Edition. Toronto: Ryerson Press, 1970.

Mandel, Eli. *Another Time*. Erin: Press Porcépic, 1977.

Mandel, Eli. "Auschwitz: Poetry of Alienation," *Canadian Literature* No. 100 (Spring 1984), 213-218.

Mandel, Eli. *The Family Romance*. Winnipeg: Turnstone Press, 1986.

Margaret Laurence: *First Lady of Manawaka*. Dir. Robert Duncan. National Film Board, 1978.

Melnyk, George. *Radical Regionalism*. Edmonton: NeWest Press, 1981.

Miki, Roy. "Talking West: An Interview with Eli Mandel," *Line*, No. 1 (Spring 1983), 26-44.

Mitchell, Ken. *Sinclair Ross: A Reader's Guide*. Moose Jaw: Coteau Books, 1981.

Reaney, James. "Manitoba as a Writer's Environment," *Manitoba in Literature: An Issue on Literary Environment*. Ed. R. G. Collins and Kenneth McRobbie. A Special Issue of *Mosaic* Vol. 3 no. 3 (Spring 1970), 95-97.

Ricou, Laurence. *Twelve Prairie Poets*. Ottawa: Oberon Press, 1976.

Ricou, Laurence. *Vertical Man/Horizontal World*. Vancouver: University of British Columbia Press, 1973.

Ross, Sinclair. "Montreal and French-Canadian Culture: What They Mean to English-Canadian Novelists," *The Tamarack Review* No. 40 (Summer 1966), 46-47.

Ross, Sinclair. "On Looking Back," *Manitoba in Literature: An Issue on Literary Environment*. Ed. R. G. Collins and Kenneth McRobbie. A Special Issue of *Mosaic* Vol. 3 no. 3 (Spring 1970), 93-97.

Roy, Gabrielle. "Mon heritage du Manitoba," *Manitoba in Literature: An Issue on Literary Environment*. Ed. R. G. Collins and Kenneth McRobbie. A Special Issue of *Mosaic* Vol. 3 no. 3 (Spring 1970), 69-79.

Stephens, D. G. (ed). *Writers of the Prairies*. Vancouver: University of British Columbia Press, 1973.

Thomas, Peter. *Robert Kroetsch*. Vancouver: Douglas & McIntyre, 1980.

Vanderhaeghe, Guy. "Influences," *Canadian Literature* No. 100 (Spring 1984), 323-328.

van Herk, Aritha. "The Art of Blackmail: Secrets and Seeing," *Canadian Literature* No. 100 (Spring 1984), 329-332.

Wiebe, Rudy. *A Voice in the Land: Essays by and about Rudy Wiebe*. Ed. W. J. Keith. Edmonton: NeWest Press, 1981.

Wiebe, Rudy. "On Death and Writing," *Canadian Literature* No. 100 (Spring 1984), 354-360.

Wiseman, Adele. "A Brief Anatomy of an Honest Attempt at a Pithy Statement about the Impact of the Manitoba Environment on My Development as an Artist," *Manitoba in Literature: An Issue on Literary Environment.* Ed. R. G. Collins and Kenneth McRobbie. A Special Issue of *Mosaic* Vol. 3 no. 3 (Spring 1970), 98-106.

Wiseman, Adele. "Memoirs of a Book-Molesting Childhood," *Canadian Forum* Vol. 66 no. 758 (April 1986), 18 & 20-28.

W. O. Mitchell: A Novelist in Hiding. Dir. Robert Duncan. National Film Board, 1980.

Wood Mountain Poems. Dir. Harvey Spak. National Film Board, 1978.